USING MIXED METHODS RESEARCH SYNTHESIS FOR LITERATURE REVIEWS

SAGE Mixed Methods Research Series

Vicki L. Plano Clark and Nataliya V. Ivankova,
Series Editors

USING MIXED METHODS RESEARCH SYNTHESIS FOR LITERATURE REVIEWS

Mieke Heyvaert

KU Leuven—University of Leuven

Karin Hannes

KU Leuven—University of Leuven

Patrick Onghena

KU Leuven—University of Leuven

Los Angeles | London | New Delhi
Singapore | Washington DC | Melbourne

FOR INFORMATION:

SAGE Publications, Inc.
2455 Teller Road
Thousand Oaks, California 91320
E-mail: order@sagepub.com

SAGE Publications Ltd.
1 Oliver's Yard
55 City Road
London, EC1Y 1SP
United Kingdom

SAGE Publications India Pvt. Ltd.
B 1/I 1 Mohan Cooperative Industrial Area
Mathura Road, New Delhi 110 044
India

SAGE Publications Asia-Pacific Pte. Ltd.
3 Church Street
#10-04 Samsung Hub
Singapore 049483

Acquisitions Editor: Helen Salmon
Editorial Assistant: Yvonne McDuffee
Production Editor: Kelly DeRosa
Copy Editor: Sheree Van Vreede
Typesetter: Hurix (P) Ltd.
Proofreader: Sarah J. Duffy
Indexer: Sheila Bodell
Cover Designer: Michael Dubowe
Marketing Manager: Nicole Elliott

Copyright © 2017 by SAGE Publications, Inc.

Printed in the United States of America

Library of Congress Cataloging-in-Publication Data

Names: Heyvaert, Mieke, author. | Hannes, Karin, author. | Onghena, Patrick, author.

Title: Using mixed methods research synthesis for literature reviews/Mieke Heyvaert, University of Leuven; Karin Hannes, University of Leuven; Patrick Onghena, University of Leuven.

Description: Los Angeles: SAGE, 2016. | Series: SAGE mixed methods research series; 4 | Includes bibliographical references and index.

Identifiers: LCCN 2015038940 | ISBN 9781483358291 (pbk.: alk. paper)

Subjects: LCSH: Research—Methodology. | Research—Evaluation. | Bibliography—Methodology.

Classification: LCC Q180.55.M4 H48 2016 | DDC 001.4/2—dc23 LC record available at http://lccn.loc.gov/2015038940

This book is printed on acid-free paper.

16 17 18 19 20 10 9 8 7 6 5 4 3 2 1

CONTENTS

SAGE was founded in 1965 by Sara Miller McCune to support the dissemination of usable knowledge by publishing innovative and high-quality research and teaching content. Today, we publish over 900 journals, including those of more than 400 learned societies, more than 800 new books per year, and a growing range of library products including archives, data, case studies, reports, and video. SAGE remains majority-owned by our founder, and after Sara's lifetime will become owned by a charitable trust that secures our continued independence.

Los Angeles | London | New Delhi | Singapore | Washington DC | Melbourne

DETAILED CONTENTS

SERIES EDITORS' INTRODUCTION

The benefits of high-quality literature reviews should not be underestimated as they are equally important for informing dissertation and funded research, as well as for conducting meta-analysis studies. Despite their importance, conducting high-quality systematic literature reviews has never been an easy process. It involves identifying, collecting, synthesizing, and summarizing information that has been published on a research topic of interest. A review of the literature should not only be directly related to the research issue in question but also be comprehensive enough to be able to yield credible conclusions about what is known about the issue including the controversial evidence and gaps in knowledge. The process of systematically summarizing and analyzing published literature and the associated challenges and pitfalls have been discussed in numerous texts devoted to conducting literature reviews. However, a growing interest in mixed methods research and its ability to address complex research issues makes it a viable approach for generating systematic literature reviews by meaningfully integrating empirical evidence from quantitative measures and qualitative narratives.

This book by Mieke Heyvaert, Karin Hannes, and Patrick Onghena provides an accessible and step-by-step guide for conducting literature reviews using mixed methods research and serves as an excellent example of how mixed methods can be intersected with another methodological approach, such as systematic literature reviews. To address the complexity of doing systematic literature reviews, the authors take on a unique mixed methods perspective and show how both qualitative and quantitative information can be aggregated, combined, and integrated into an overall mixed methods research synthesis (MMRS) approach that serves as a conceptual framework for MMRS literature reviews. In using the MMRS framework, the authors effectively walk their readers through the process of conducting a literature review by discussing and illustrating each step, from developing an MMRS review protocol; to searching, critically appraising, extracting, and synthesizing data; to writing and disseminating an MMRS literature review report. Besides a wealth of useful methodological information, the book offers numerous examples, practical tips, questions for thought, exercises, and suggestions for further reading.

By having a practical focus and an applied nature, this book is an important addition to the SAGE Mixed Methods Research Series. We initiated the Series to provide researchers, reviewers, and consumers of mixed methods research with practice-focused books that address issues of current interest to the field of mixed methods in an applied and practical way. The purpose of the Series is also to engage new voices in the discourse about mixed methods research. As Series editors, we are excited to endorse *Using Mixed Methods Research Synthesis for Literature Reviews* as the fourth volume in the Series because it addresses essential aspects of applying mixed methods to conducting systematic literature reviews including the discussion of the associated challenges and strategies to overcome them. We believe this book is an important addition to the Series and will make a significant contribution to the field of mixed methods research by showing how mixed methods can be effectively intersected with the systematic literature review methodological approach to address the complexity of reviewing and synthesizing the empirical evidence on a research topic of interest.

Vicki L. Plano Clark and Nataliya V. Ivankova
Editors, *SAGE Mixed Methods Research Series*

PREFACE

Literature reviews are everywhere. They appear in master theses, doctoral dissertations, project proposals, policy documents, manuals for practitioners, and as journal publications in their own right. Before embarking on a new study, researchers want to know which studies have already been conducted on the topic of interest. Before implementing a new procedure, policy makers need to be informed about the procedure's effectiveness, feasibility, appropriateness, and meaningfulness. Before adopting and applying new knowledge and insights, practitioners want to be informed about the available scientific evidence. In any of these cases, a literature review can make a crucial contribution.

Purpose of the book. Literature reviews constitute a crucial component in most research endeavors and implementation plans, but how do you conduct such a literature review? How do you interpret the results of published literature reviews? What guidelines and quality criteria can you use to guide the literature review? The first aim of this book is to provide you with an accessible and step-by-step guide to conduct literature reviews. This book will show you the potential and the advantages of conducting a literature review, as well as the obstacles and pitfalls during the process. By doing so, we will also provide you with a unique insight into the way in which the results of published literature reviews can be understood and evaluated.

One of the first obstacles researchers, policy makers, and practitioners have to deal with when conceiving a literature review is the complexity of the scientific literature. Scientific evidence comes in many guises; it comes as lines of argument, falsified hypotheses, corroborated theories, debates and controversies, pictures, tables, graphs, and many more. Some of the evidence is of a more qualitative nature, other evidence is of a more quantitative nature, and most of the evidence contains a mixture of both. One of the distinguishing features of this book is that it takes the complexity of the scientific literature into account by adopting a *mixed methods perspective* for conducting the literature review. Therefore, the second aim of this book is to show you how both qualitative and quantitative evidence can be aggregated, combined, and integrated into one overall *mixed methods research synthesis* (MMRS). This book introduces the methods and techniques for synthesizing qualitative research, for summarizing quantitative research, and for integrating all material in a mixed methods approach to conduct the overall literature review. Furthermore, this book provides you with guidance in making choices when aggregating, combining, and integrating research from diverse methodological traditions and in communicating these choices to a broader audience.

Audiences for the book. This book is written for master's and doctoral students who want to learn about literature reviews and who want a user-friendly introduction to MMRS. Also, novice and senior researchers who plan to conduct MMRS literature reviews will find the book a helpful resource of methods and techniques for summarizing and analyzing the empirical evidence published in their scientific discipline. In addition, for policy makers and practitioners, the challenge of including best evidence within decision-making processes is overwhelming given the ever-increasing volume of studies on particular topics and areas of research and given the rising call for evidence-based policy and practice. Consequently, also policy makers and practitioners may strengthen their grasp on the research literature to a very large extent by having a better understanding of the basic methodological principles and quality issues underpinning MMRS literature reviews.

Book overview. The first chapter of this book introduces the conceptual framework for MMRS literature reviews. The eight subsequent chapters deal with the consecutive steps for conducting a literature review: preparing your MMRS literature review and developing a review protocol (Chapter 2); searching for relevant studies (Chapter 3); critically appraising the methodological quality of the studies you retrieved (Chapter 4); extracting descriptive data from the studies (Chapter 5); synthesizing the data for description, summary, evaluation, interpretation and/or integration purposes (Chapters 6, 7, and 8); and finally writing, editing, and disseminating your MMRS report (Chapter 9). The book closes with an epilogue that contains some concluding reflections and future directions for conducting MMRS literature reviews.

Book features. Because of its step-by-step didactical approach and because of its use of several pedagogical features, the book is well suited for a one-semester course on conducting literature reviews or as a supplemental textbook for graduate or postgraduate courses, seminars, and workshops on research methodology, systematic reviews, mixed methods research, or evidence-based practice. Each chapter sets the stage by providing an outline and ends with summary points, challenges, questions for thought, exercises, and suggestions for further reading that are carefully selected for more in-depth treatment, classroom discussions, and further elaboration. In addition, the text is enriched with numerous boxes containing concrete research examples and illustrations, and in each chapter, several practical tips are provided that tap into the extensive experience of the authors in conducting literature reviews. Jargon is avoided and technical terms are only introduced if necessary for a better understanding. If technical terms are needed, then they are bolded at first introduction and clearly defined. Names, references, quotes, and important terms are italicized to emphasize them or to separate them from the main flow of the text.

Acknowledgments. We would like to thank the many reviewers who provided insightful comments on our manuscript while it was in development: John Eric Baugher (University of Southern Maine), Tamara Bertrand Jones (Florida State University), Michelle E. Block (Purdue University Calumet), Ronald Chennault (DePaul University), Margaret K. Chojnacki (Barry University), Bryant Griffith (Texas A&M University, Corpus Christi), Juanita A. Johnson (Union Institute & University), Kent R. Kerley (The University of Texas at Arlington), La'Tara Osborne Lampkin (Florida State University), Şenay Purzer (Purdue University), Deborah J. Tippins (The University of Georgia), Wendy G. Troxel (Illinois State University), Yuying Tsong (California State University, Fullerton), and Jason S. Wrench (SUNY New Paltz).

We are very grateful to Vicki Plano Clark and Nataliya Ivankova, as co-editors of SAGE's Mixed Methods Research Series, for their invitation to write this book, for their encouragements throughout the writing process, and for their thoughtful editorial comments on previous drafts. We are thankful to Vicki Knight from SAGE Publications for giving us the opportunity to write this book and for her continuous guidance. We want to thank our families, friends, and colleagues at KU Leuven—University of Leuven—for their moral support and for giving us the time and space to work on this book, as well as the many international colleagues in the Cochrane Collaboration and the Campbell Collaboration for their inspiration and efforts to optimize the methodology of conducting literature reviews. Finally, we want to thank each other for the experience of working together from qualitative, quantitative, and mixed perspectives. In our joint effort to produce this book, we have increased our own understanding of how and why we need quantitative and qualitative evidence to increase our understanding of complex phenomena.

Mieke Heyvaert, Karin Hannes, and Patrick Onghena
Leuven, Belgium, April 2015

ABOUT THE AUTHORS

Mieke Heyvaert is a postdoctoral fellow at the Research Foundation—Flanders (FWO) and a member of the Faculty of Psychology and Educational Sciences, KU Leuven. In 2012, she defended a PhD project on mixed methods research synthesis. She studied the methodological possibilities and challenges of mixed methods research synthesis and conducted mixed methods research syntheses on the treatment of challenging behavior among persons with intellectual disabilities. Her postdoctoral research focuses on the meta-analysis of single-case experiments. She teaches methodology courses to graduate students with a focus on qualitative, quantitative, and mixed methods. She has authored and co-authored numerous publications on mixed methods research synthesis, meta-synthesis, and meta-analysis in both methodological and substantial international journals.

Karin Hannes is an associate professor with the Faculty of Social Sciences, KU Leuven. She has an academic background in adult education and medical-social sciences and teaches qualitative research methodology to undergraduate, master's, and doctoral students. Professor Hannes has been teaching evidence-based practice and systematic review courses for over a decade in a variety of different disciplines, including medicine, public health, education, and social welfare. She is co-convener of the Cochrane Qualitative and Implementation Research Group, co-author of the *Cochrane Handbook for Systematic Reviews of Effectiveness*, and editor of *Qualitative Evidence Synthesis: Choosing the Right Approach*. Her main research interest is in developing, applying, and refining approaches to qualitative evidence synthesis. She is mainly known for her work in the area of critical appraisal of qualitative research studies. More recently, she has been focusing on the inclusion of arts-based research in systematic reviews, building on her research interest in visual research from a critical emancipatory perspective.

Patrick Onghena is a full professor with the Faculty of Psychology and Educational Sciences, KU Leuven. He has an academic background in psychology and statistics and teaches quantitative research methods to under-graduate, master's, and doctoral students in the behavioral and educational sciences, speech and language pathology, and statistics. His research interests include mixed methods research, systematic reviews, and meta-analysis, and he has authored and co-authored numerous publications on these topics in both methodological and substantial international journals. He was associate editor of *Behavior Research Methods* and *Journal of Statistics Education*, and he was section editor of Intervention Studies/Observational Studies in *The Encyclopedia of Statistics in Behavioral Science* for which he provided many entries. Together with Wim Van den Noortgate, he elaborated the multilevel approach to meta-analysis and applied this approach in the area of single-case experimental designs. He is best known for his work on randomization tests and for co-authoring the classic handbook on this topic together with Eugene Edgington (now in its fourth edition).

⊰ 1 ⊱

INTRODUCTION TO MMRS LITERATURE REVIEWS

═══════════════════ ⤙⤚ ═══════════════════

Chapter Outline

In this chapter, we first provide a historical sketch on the development of various forms of literature reviews, including meta-analyses, meta-syntheses, and mixed methods research syntheses (MMRS), and we introduce and explain basic concepts and definitions related to these various forms of literature reviews. Second, we present an overview of the stages for conducting MMRS literature reviews. Third, we discuss ontological orientations for MMRS and how these orientations influence the MMRS process. Fourth, we provide practical guidelines for conducting MMRS. Finally, we discuss potential strengths and challenges for MMRS.

═══════════════════ ⤙⤚ ═══════════════════

HISTORICAL SKETCH, CONCEPTS, AND DEFINITIONS

The increasing amount of published scientific research articles and books has been an impetus for conducting literature reviews. When researchers, policy makers, and practitioners want to read about a topic or problem they are interested in, it is way more time-efficient to read one or a few good literature reviews than to be swamped by all primary-level studies (also called original studies) published on the topic or problem. Review authors who conduct a **literature review** seek to synthesize the content of primary-level studies and other primary-level data sources on a certain topic, problem, intervention, program, or phenomenon of interest. In Box 1.1, we explain the terminology used in this book to refer to persons who conduct a literature review and to persons who conduct a primary-level study. In the remainder of this section, we provide a historical sketch of the development of various forms of literature reviews, and we introduce and explain basic concepts and definitions related to various forms of literature reviews.

The first known records of review authors conducting literature reviews to synthesize existing knowledge and empirical evidence on a certain phenomenon of interest date back to the 18th century (Chalmers, Hedges, & Cooper, 2002). Most of these earliest literature reviews were quantitative in nature. Quantitative, statistical methods (e.g., correlation coefficients and average correlations; Pearson, 1904) were used to synthesize the empirical evidence from quantitative primary-level studies. In 1976, Gene V. Glass introduced the term **meta-analysis** to describe statistical methods for synthesizing quantitative primary-level studies (Chalmers et al., 2002). During the 20th century, meta-analyses were frequently used to synthesize quantitative primary-level evidence on the effectiveness of various treatments, interventions, and programs.

Box 1.1   Terminology Used in This Book

Throughout this book, we refer to persons who conduct a literature review as **review authors**. We use this term to refer to anybody who is undertaking a literature review for research purposes. Accordingly, also students who conduct a literature review for their master's theses or doctoral dissertations are referred to as *review authors* throughout this book even though they may not be authors of a published work. The term *review authors* is consistent with the terminology proposed and used by leading organizations promoting and disseminating literature reviews, such as the Campbell Collaboration and the Cochrane Collaboration.

We use the term **researchers** to refer to researchers who conduct primary-level studies. In a **primary-level study**, researchers typically collect qualitative and/or quantitative data directly from their research participants, for example, through interviews, observations, and/or questionnaires. These primary-level studies are *the data* included in literature reviews.

The practice of conducting quantitative effectiveness reviews was strongly influenced by the **evidence-based practice (EBP) movement**. EBP is based on the premise that high-quality research is needed to help determine what works and what types of policy and practice initiatives are likely to be most effective (Evans & Benefield, 2001). In other words, high-quality research is expected to serve as the foundation for policy and practice decisions and actions. The EBP movement encouraged review authors to conduct **systematic reviews** (Hammersley, 2001). These systematic reviews were expected to deliver high-quality cumulative knowledge that could inform policy and practice (Clegg, 2005). The Cochrane Collaboration (2015) describes systematic reviews as follows: *A systematic review attempts to identify, appraise and synthesize all the empirical evidence that meets pre-specified eligibility criteria to answer a given review question. Review authors conducting systematic reviews use explicit methods aimed at minimizing bias, in order to produce more reliable findings that can be used to inform decision making.* Systematic reviews are characterized by (a) a clearly stated set of objectives with predefined eligibility criteria for primary-level studies; (b) an explicit, reproducible methodology; (c) a systematic search that attempts to identify all primary-level studies that would meet the eligibility criteria; (d) an assessment of the validity of the findings of the included primary-level studies, for example, through the assessment of risk of bias; and (e) a systematic presentation and synthesis of the characteristics and findings of the included primary-level studies (Green et al., 2011). Advantages of these systematic literature reviews include (a) a quick assimilation of large amounts of information by researchers, policy makers, and practitioners, through consulting these systematic reviews; (b) the use of explicit and transparent methods that limit bias in identifying and rejecting studies; (c) reliable and accurate conclusions because of the systematic methods used; (d) the establishment of generalizability of findings and consistency of results due to a formal comparison of the results from the different included primary-level studies; (e) an identification of the reasons for potential heterogeneity and, consequently, the generation of new hypotheses about particular subgroups; (f) the generation of new perspectives and frameworks that transcend the retrieved primary-level studies; and (g) a potential reduction of the delay between research discoveries and implementation of effective strategies in practice (Gough, Oliver, & Thomas, 2012; Greenhalgh, 1997; Moher, Stewart, & Shekelle, 2012).

However, over time there was a growing recognition that simply quantitatively synthesizing the existing quantitative evidence on the effects of certain treatments, interventions, and programs was not sufficient for accurately informing policy and practice decisions and actions, and that it was necessary to capture the *bigger picture*. To determine which treatments, interventions, and programs were not only effective, but also feasible, appropriate, and meaningful, it was necessary to synthesize the existing empirical evidence on, for instance, user perspectives; participant behaviors, experiences, and preferences; and implementer behaviors, experiences, and preferences (Hannes, Booth, Harris, & Noyes, 2013). These questions on feasibility, appropriateness, and meaningfulness urged review authors also to synthesize the existing qualitative evidence on treatments, interventions, and programs of interest. Several qualitative **meta-synthesis** methods for summarizing qualitative primary-level studies and for generating new insights and understanding from interrelated qualitative research findings were developed, such as formal grounded theory (Eaves, 2001; Kearney, 1998, 2001), meta-ethnography (Britten et al., 2002; Noblit & Hare, 1988), thematic synthesis (Thomas & Harden, 2008), and meta-aggregative synthesis (Hannes & Lockwood, 2011).

In addition to the mono-method quantitative and qualitative literature reviews (i.e., meta-analyses and meta-syntheses), review authors developed approaches for combining empirical evidence described in various kinds of primary-level studies by using various kinds of qualitative and quantitative synthesis techniques, within a single literature review, to answer complex review questions and study complex topics and problems. When a team of review authors undertakes a literature review by applying the principles of mixed methods research (MMR), we say that they undertake a **mixed methods research synthesis** (MMRS). The data included in an MMRS are findings extracted from various qualitative, quantitative, and MMR primary articles, and various qualitative, quantitative, and mixed synthesis techniques are used to integrate the primary-level studies within the MMRS (Heyvaert, Maes, & Onghena, 2013). Other terms that are used to describe an MMRS are *mixed methods synthesis* (Harden & Thomas, 2005), *mixed research synthesis* (Sandelowski, Voils, & Barroso, 2006; Voils, Sandelowski, Barroso, & Hasselblad, 2008), and *mixed studies review* (Pluye, Gagnon, Griffiths, & Johnson-Lafleur, 2009). Following the general definition of MMR proposed by R. Burke Johnson, Anthony J. Onwuegbuzie, and Lisa A. Turner (2007), we define an MMRS as a literature review in which review authors combine qualitative, quantitative, and MMR primary-level studies and apply a mixed methods approach to synthesize and integrate those studies (e.g., using qualitative, quantitative, and MMR viewpoints, data collection techniques, data synthesis techniques, and inferential techniques), to enhance the breadth and depth of understanding complex phenomena, problems, and topics (Heyvaert et al., 2013).

A discourse that inspired the development and use of qualitative literature reviews (i.e., meta-syntheses) in addition to quantitative literature reviews (i.e., meta-analyses), and eventually the development and use of MMRS literature reviews, was the **complex interventions discourse** (Anderson et al., 2013; Petticrew et al., 2013; Squires, Valentine, & Grimshaw, 2013). To study a complex intervention or program, MMRS literature reviews offer several advantages over mono-method literature reviews.

First, most interventions and programs used in the social sciences, crime and justice sciences, educational sciences, psychology, international development, social welfare, and biomedical and health sciences are multilayered and consist of multiple components. In comparison with mono-method literature reviews, MMRS literature reviews are more appropriate to study these multiple components and layers, how these components and layers are related, and how these components and layers interact.

Second, policy makers and practitioners are often interested not only in the effectiveness of complex interventions and programs but also in their feasibility, appropriateness, and meaningfulness. The following question is related to the effectiveness of an intervention or program: *How effective is (the intervention/program) in addressing (the problem)?* The following question is related to the feasibility of an intervention or program: *What are barriers and facilitators to implementing (the intervention/program)?* The following question is related to the appropriateness of an intervention or program: *Are (the intervention's/program's) desired outcomes consistent with the target group's priorities and/or beliefs?* The following question is related to the meaningfulness of an intervention or program: *How do (the target groups) feel about participating in (the intervention/program)?* In comparison with mono-method literature reviews, MMRS literature reviews are more appropriate to study different but related review questions on effectiveness, feasibility, appropriateness, and meaningfulness of a single intervention or program in the various review strands. Questions on the effectiveness, feasibility, appropriateness, and meaningfulness of complex interventions and programs will be discussed in closer detail in Chapter 2.

Third, complex interventions and programs are not *magic bullets* that will always hit their target, and their effects often depend on context and implementation (Pawson, Greenhalgh, Harvey, & Walshe, 2005). MMRS literature reviews offer the opportunity to answer a diverse range of complementary questions on these complex interventions and programs in the various review strands, such as follows: *What is it about this intervention or program that works, for whom, in what circumstances, in what respects, and why?* (Pawson et al., 2005). It can, for instance, be interesting to study the question of *why* the program or intervention worked or did not work when applied in different contexts or circumstances, deployed by different stakeholders, or used for different purposes. We will discuss this issue in closer detail in Chapters 5 and 7.

Fourth, multiple types of empirical evidence often exist regarding a single intervention or program, which are reported in quantitative, qualitative, and MMR primary-level studies. MMRS literature reviews offer the opportunity to integrate these different types of research evidence on the same intervention or program in a single literature review.

OVERVIEW OF THE STAGES FOR
CONDUCTING MMRS LITERATURE REVIEWS

An MMRS process generally includes eight stages. In this first chapter, we provide a brief overview of the stages that will be discussed in the remainder of this book.

First, you will write a **protocol** for your MMRS. In this protocol you *a priori* document all methodological and substantive choices that you will make throughout the MMRS process. The protocol helps you to plan how you will achieve your review objectives and answer your review questions, for instance, by deciding which MMRS design, which sampling strategy, which search strategies, which inclusion and exclusion criteria, and which synthesis approaches are most appropriate for reaching your review objectives and answering your review questions. We will discuss review protocols, review objectives, review questions, and MMRS designs in Chapter 2.

Second, you will select a sampling strategy that is appropriate for your MMRS. You will decide whether you will conduct an exhaustive, selective, or purposeful search for primary-level studies to be included in your MMRS. Third, in accordance with the selected sampling strategy, you will search for primary-level studies that might be relevant to your MMRS. Fourth, you will apply the inclusion and exclusion criteria that were stipulated in the protocol to the primary-level studies that were retrieved by the search process. This fourth stage will enable you to filter out irrelevant studies, as well as to keep only the primary-level studies that are relevant for answering your review questions. We will discuss sampling strategies, search strategies, and inclusion and exclusion criteria in Chapter 3.

Fifth, you may opt to appraise critically the methodological quality of the primary-level studies you retrieved. In Chapter 4, we will provide guidance on how to appraise critically the retrieved studies. We will discuss different approaches to quality assessment of the retrieved qualitative, quantitative, and MMR primary-level studies. Also in Chapter 4, we will discuss how to document the critical appraisal process, how to assess agreement on critical appraisal scores, and how to valorize the outcome of the critical appraisal exercise.

Sixth, you will extract relevant data from the included primary-level studies. In Chapter 5, we will discuss how descriptive data can be extracted from the primary-level studies included in an MMRS literature review. The descriptive data extraction process consists of four steps: (1) deciding which data will be extracted and developing a preliminary data extraction form and coding guide, (2) piloting the extraction form and the coding guide, (3) conducting the data extraction, and (4) identifying and discussing differences in extraction between review authors. We will describe, discuss, and illustrate these four steps in Chapter 5.

Seventh, in accordance with the purpose of the MMRS, the review question(s) posed, and the data included in the MMRS, you will select and use appropriate data synthesis approaches to describe, summarize, evaluate, interpret, and/or integrate the primary-level data. We will discuss data synthesis approaches that can be used within various MMRS in Chapters 6, 7, and 8.

Eighth, you will write, edit, and disseminate your MMRS report. In Chapter 9, we will first discuss the writing process and how the intended audience for the MMRS influences this writing process. Furthermore, we will discuss ethics in the writing process and the sections to be included in the MMRS report. Finally, we will discuss publication outlets for MMRS literature reviews.

Figure 1.1   Stages for Conducting MMRS Literature Reviews

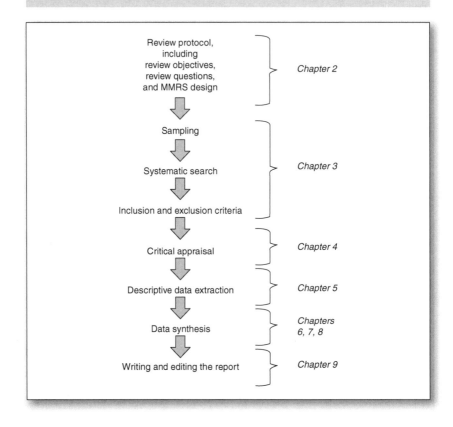

In Figure 1.1, we provide a visual overview of these eight stages for conducting MMRS literature reviews, and we indicate which stages will be discussed in which chapters of our book.

ONTOLOGICAL ORIENTATIONS FOR MMRS LITERATURE REVIEWS

Ontology is the study of *what is*, the study of *reality*. It has often been argued that researchers who conduct primary-level research should be explicit about their ontological orientation toward research. At the synthesis level too, review authors should reflect on their ontological orientation toward research and how this orientation influences their MMRS. Ontological orientations toward research are often positioned on a continuum with on the one end the realist orientations and on the other end the idealist orientations. Researchers following realist orientations consider reality to be an external, concrete structure, whereas researchers following idealist orientations consider reality to be constructed, to be a projection of human imagination (Morgan & Smircich, 1980).

Review authors with **realist orientations** toward research synthesis treat the primary reports included in their review as more or less faithfully reflecting the primary-level studies that were conducted and the findings described in those primary reports as more or less faithfully reflecting the phenomenon under study, regardless of how those primary-level studies were themselves ontologically located (Sandelowski, Voils, Leeman, & Crandell, 2012). These review authors believe that research syntheses can produce the best evidence currently available to guide and improve policy and practice. Realist orientations toward research synthesis correspond to the strategy generally promoted by the EBP movement we discussed earlier.

Review authors with **idealist orientations** toward research synthesis will often go *beyond* what is described and reflected in the primary studies they retrieved. They often seek to reveal patterns or relationships between concepts and structures that remained hidden before. These review authors often intend to challenge reigning knowledge claims and dominant discourses, including the strategies put forward by proponents of the EBP movement (Eisenhart, 1998; Sandelowski & Barroso, 2007; Sandelowski et al., 2012).

We have two important remarks related to the realist–idealist continuum. First, it is indeed a continuum, not a dichotomy. Many review authors hold ontological orientations situated somewhere in between the realist and the idealist position. An example of an intermediate ontological orientation, which leans a bit more toward the idealist position, is a team of review authors who sees reality as a social construction (Morgan & Smircich, 1980). Second, the realist–idealist continuum is not the same as the quantitative–qualitative continuum. Although the realist ontological orientation is often associated with quantitative synthesis approaches (Cohen, Manion, & Morrison, 2000), several qualitative synthesis approaches can also be associated with the realist ontological orientation. For instance, the meta-aggregative approach to qualitative evidence synthesis we will discuss in Chapter 6 is situated on the realist side of the ontological orientations continuum. However, most of the review authors situated on the idealist orientation side of the continuum are indeed qualitative review authors.

We recommend that you explicitly report on your ontological orientation toward research in the MMRS report, as this orientation will undeniably influence the decisions you make throughout the MMRS process. For instance, your ontological orientation will influence the purpose of the MMRS (Chapter 2): Do you aim to synthesize the best evidence currently available to guide and improve policy and practice? Or do you aim to question reigning knowledge claims and dominant discourses? Furthermore, your ontological orientation will, for instance, influence whether you consider it desirable to conduct a systematic, exhaustive search for empirical evidence or whether you prefer to use certain purposeful sampling strategies (Chapter 3), whether you consider it desirable to appraise the primary reports you retrieved (Chapter 4), which data synthesis approaches you consider to be appropriate for your MMRS (Chapters 6, 7, and 8), and which reporting style you consider to be appropriate for communicating the findings of your MMRS to the audience you envision (Chapter 9).

Review authors' core ontological assumptions are linked to their epistemological stance and their favored synthesis methods. **Epistemology** refers to the *theory of knowledge*; it is the study of the nature and scope of knowledge. Review authors with a realist ontological orientation toward research synthesis will most likely hold the epistemological stance that it is possible to accumulate knowledge, that empirical primary-level studies can be valid sources of knowledge, and that they can accumulate knowledge by using positivist techniques such as verification and falsification. Review authors with an idealist ontological orientation toward research synthesis will most likely hold the epistemological stance that they can obtain phenomenological insights by means of interpretive processes and by means of critically reflecting on specific processes, behaviors, and so on, in specific settings.

PRACTICAL GUIDELINES FOR
CONDUCTING MMRS LITERATURE REVIEWS

In this section we want to provide some practical guidelines for conducting MMRS literature reviews that may be perceived as common sense but are often overlooked by novice review authors. Our practical guidelines include keeping a review diary, monitoring the congruence of the choices you make throughout the MMRS process, and providing rationales for these choices. We start with discussing the advantages of keeping a review diary in Practical Tip 1.1.

Practical Tip 1.1: Keeping a Review Diary

We strongly advise you to keep a **review diary** while you are conducting your MMRS. A review diary is a digital or written record of everything that was done, considered, and reflected on during the MMRS process. The main reason for keeping a review diary is that you keep an **audit trail** during the entire MMRS process. In your review diary, you can make explicit the review choices that have been risen during the entire MMRS process (e.g., related to how the search for primary studies was conducted and how the collected data were synthesized), the reasons why you have turned down certain choices, the reasons why you have considered certain choices, and the reasons why you have made your final choices.

First of all, the review diary will urge you to write down explicitly all the choices met throughout the MMRS journey, as well as the advantages and disadvantages related to each choice alternative. It can help you to reflect on all these choices, the choice alternatives, and their consequences, as well as to engage in a dialogue on these choices with the other members of your review team.

Second, if you accurately recorded every decision made, the review diary will be a great help when you are writing up your MMRS report. For instance, in the *Methods* section of your MMRS report, you will write down *how exactly* you conducted each stage of the MMRS, and *why* you did what you did. When you took detailed notes on your actions as well as the justifications for your actions during the MMRS process, writing up the *Methods* section is relatively straightforward. Also for the *Introduction*, *Findings*, and *Discussion* sections, a detailed review diary will be of great help. Novice review authors particularly experience that writing the *Discussion* section is very hard, especially when they have to write it from scratch and when there remains only a limited amount of time to write this final section. However, if you already *during* the MMRS process kept detailed notes on the obstacles met, possible limitations of your MMRS process you considered, possible interpretations of your findings, possible implications of your MMRS, and suggestions for future research, policy, and practice based on

(Continued)

(Continued)

your study, writing the *Discussion* may not be so hard after all. Taking such notes during the MMRS process might help you to think about the content and structure of the *Discussion* before fully writing it out in the final stage, as well as might enhance the quality and clarity of this section. We will discuss the content of the various sections and subsections to be included in the MMRS report in Chapter 9, but we find it important to convince you now, at the beginning of your MMRS journey, of the importance of keeping detailed notes throughout the entire MMRS process.

Throughout the MMRS process you will make a lot of methodological and substantive decisions, relating to questions such as follows: *Which MMRS design will I use? Which sampling strategy will I use? How will I search for primary studies? Which inclusion and exclusion criteria will I apply? Which synthesis approach(es) will I use?* In Practical Tip 1.2, we discuss the importance of congruence of the decisions you make throughout the MMRS process.

Practical Tip 1.2: Importance of Congruence of Choices

Methodologically speaking, **congruence** refers to the *fit* between the choices made during the literature review process. There should be a *fit* between the different stages of your MMRS process (Figure 1.1). For instance, in your MMRS, there should be congruence between:

- Review questions—Review objectives
- MMRS design—Review questions; review objectives
- Sampling strategy—Design; review questions; review objectives
- Search strategy—Sampling strategy; design; review questions; review objectives
- Data synthesis approach—Collected data; design; review questions; review objectives

> We advise you to write down explicitly all the methodological and substantive choices you made throughout the entire MMRS process and to reflect on the consistency between the choices: *Is there a good fit between each of the choices you made? Would another choice alternative result in a better fit? For instance, would another MMRS design be a better fit for your review objectives and review questions?*

A **rationale** refers to a reason, an argument, or a justification that you can give for making certain choices. In Practical Tip 1.3, we discuss the importance of rationales for the methodological and substantive choices you make throughout the MMRS process.

Practical Tip 1.3: Importance of Rationales for Your Methodological and Substantive Choices

Throughout the MMRS process you are confronted with several choices, such as follows: *What is my review objective? How should I formulate my review question? Which design would be optimal for my MMRS?* Thinking about rationales is thinking about the pros and cons for every choice alternative. For instance, in Chapter 2, we will discuss three major MMRS designs: segregated, integrated, and contingent designs (Sandelowski et al., 2006). Thinking about the design choice for your MMRS, you can consider each of the three choice alternatives, and list for each of the alternatives the pros and cons, for instance:

	Why would this design be beneficial for my MMRS?	Why would this design be detrimental for my MMRS?
Segregated design	...	...
Integrated design	...	...
Contingent design	...	...

(Continued)

(Continued)

This thinking about rationales can be reflected in the MMRS report. Of course, it is not desirable to discuss in the MMRS report *each* choice alternative for *each* methodological and substantive choice made throughout the MMRS process. However, the choice alternatives that *were* selected should be explicitly mentioned in the MMRS report (e.g., which MMRS design was used), and a rationale for selecting this alternative should be provided (e.g., explaining why this design *worked* for your MMRS). We will discuss this in closer detail in Chapter 9.

POTENTIALS AND PITFALLS FOR MMRS LITERATURE REVIEWS

We see two major advantages of conducting MMRS literature reviews. First, in comparison with a mono-method qualitative or quantitative literature review, an MMRS can allow greater richness and broader insights, and it can allow for exploring multiple facets on a topic, problem, intervention, program, or phenomenon of interest. Accordingly, a more diverse range of complementary questions on the topic, problem, intervention, program, or phenomenon of interest can be studied within an MMRS, for instance: *What is it about this kind of intervention that works, for whom, in what circumstances, in what respects, and why?* (Pawson et al., 2005). Furthermore, complex topics, problems, interventions, programs, or phenomena can be approached from different perspectives, resulting in possibly more complete, concrete, and nuanced answers in comparison with mono-method literature reviews. This might result in more useful suggestions for policy and practice. For example, in the MMRS of James Thomas et al. (2004), the combination of quantitative controlled-trial studies describing the effects of interventions that promoted healthy eating with qualitative studies that examined the perspectives and understandings of children concerning barriers to and facilitators of fruit and vegetable intake increased the policy relevance of the literature review because it has the potential to inspire and inform the development of more effective and appropriate healthy-eating interventions (Harden & Thomas, 2005).

Second, the combination of various synthesis methods in an MMRS brings along possible advantages, such as (a) adding confidence in the literature review's conclusions when different synthesis methods, used for synthesizing various sources of primary-level evidence on a single phenomenon of interest, result in similar conclusions, and (b) revealing and developing challenging or integrating theories by comparing and combining the inferences that result from the diverse synthesis methods. Furthermore, the combination of qualitative and quantitative synthesis approaches holds the possibility to uncover and explain discrepancies between the findings of the included primary-level studies. For example, in the previously mentioned MMRS of Thomas et al. (2004), the insights gained within the qualitative strand allowed an in-depth and nuanced exploration of the statistical heterogeneity detected within the quantitative strand of the MMRS.

Although the mixing of qualitative, quantitative, and MMR empirical data and synthesis techniques in an MMRS can hold multiple opportunities, there are possible challenges concerning the implementation of an MMRS. In comparison with mono-method literature reviews, review authors conducting an MMRS have to deal with a more voluminous amount of data and more divergent data. A more voluminous amount of data included in a literature review results in an increased amount of time and resources needed to conduct each stage of the MMRS. For instance, a larger number of abstracts and full-texts will have to be screened in the data collection stage, and a potential larger number of studies will have to be critically appraised and synthesized.

Furthermore, the data included in an MMRS can be very divergent as the studies included in an MMRS can be qualitative, quantitative, and MMR primary-level studies on the phenomenon of interest. This is particularly challenging at the point where insights generated from different types of studies need to be integrated. Review authors should try to synthesize and integrate the various types of primary-level studies without ignoring the methodological identity of, and losing the intrinsic value of, all these various types of primary-level studies.

Another important challenge is that without a meaningful integration or "mix" of the qualitative and quantitative strands, a literature review can hardly be called an "MMRS." Especially when the qualitative and quantitative subteams, who are respectively involved in the qualitative and quantitative strand of an MMRS, are composed of *purely* qualitative and *purely* quantitative methodologists, skill specialization might hinder the integration of the findings (Bryman, 2007). We will elaborate on the team issue in Chapter 2.

Finally, we want to stress that the answer to the question of whether it makes sense to perform an MMRS on a certain topic depends on the topic at hand, on the kinds of empirical evidence available in the research domain, on the purpose of the synthesis, and on the posed review questions. Pawson (2008) noted that "method mix is the new methodological Holy Grail" (p. 120). Someone intending to conduct a literature review might nowadays be inclined to conduct an MMRS because conducting MMR is *hot and trendy*. However, MMRS—and MMR in general—is neither a *Holy Grail* that is the *ultimate aim* for every review author nor the *perfect choice* for every literature review. Sometimes, conducting a mono-method qualitative or quantitative literature review is way more appropriate to reach the review purposes and to answer the posed review questions. Conducting an MMRS is a time-consuming and expensive enterprise. Accordingly, the decision to conduct an MMRS should be a deliberate, rational, and well-justified decision. The review purpose and the review questions should be the key drivers for whether to choose an MMR approach. We will discuss this issue further in the next chapter.

Summary Points

- We refer to persons who conduct a literature review as review authors.
- When a team of review authors undertakes a literature review by applying the principles of mixed methods research (MMR), we say that they undertake a mixed methods research synthesis (MMRS).
- The data included in an MMRS are findings extracted from various qualitative, quantitative, and MMR primary articles, and various qualitative, quantitative, and mixed synthesis techniques are used to integrate the primary-level studies within the MMRS.
- Literature reviews were already conducted in the 18th century. Most of the earliest literature reviews were quantitative in nature. To determine which treatments, interventions, and programs were not only effective but also feasible, appropriate, and meaningful, qualitative and mixed methods approaches to literature reviews were developed.
- The complex interventions discourse inspired the development and use of MMRS literature reviews.
- The MMRS process includes eight stages: (1) writing the review protocol (including review objectives, review questions, and MMRS design); (2) sampling; (3) searching for primary-level studies; (4) applying

inclusion and exclusion criteria; (5) possibly critically appraising the methodological quality of the primary-level studies; (6) extracting relevant data from the primary-level studies; (7) interpreting, synthesizing, and integrating the data; and (8) writing and disseminating the MMRS report.

- It is important to reflect on your ontological orientation toward research and on how this orientation influences your MMRS.
- We strongly advise you to keep a review diary. This is a digital or written record of everything that was done, considered, and reflected on during the MMRS process.
- There should be congruence between the choices you make throughout the MMRS process.
- A first advantage of conducting MMRS literature reviews is that, in comparison with a mono-method qualitative or quantitative literature review, an MMRS can allow greater richness and broader insights, and it can allow for exploring multiple facets on a topic, problem, intervention, program, or phenomenon of interest.
- A second advantage is that the combination of various synthesis methods in an MMRS may allow us to (a) add confidence in the literature review's conclusions when different synthesis methods, used for synthesizing various sources of primary-level evidence on a single phenomenon of interest, result in similar conclusions; (b) reveal and develop challenging or integrating theories by comparing and combining the inferences that result from the diverse synthesis methods; and (c) uncover and explain discrepancies between the findings of the included primary-level studies.
- A first challenge of conducting an MMRS literature review is that, in comparison with a mono-method literature review, you have to deal with a more voluminous amount of data and more divergent data.
- A second challenge is that without a meaningful integration or "mix" of the qualitative and quantitative strands, a literature review can hardly be called an "MMRS."
- The review purpose and the review questions should be the key drivers for choosing an MMRS approach.

Questions for Thought

- Think about your ontological orientation toward research synthesis. Do you situate yourself more on the realist end of the ontological orientations continuum, and do you believe that research syntheses can produce the best evidence currently available to guide and improve policy and practice? Or do you situate yourself more on the idealist end of the ontological orientations continuum, and do you intend to reveal patterns or relationships between concepts and structures that remained hidden before, and/or to undermine reigning knowledge claims and dominant discourses by means of your research synthesis? Or do you situate yourself somewhere in between the realist and the idealist position?

- Think about the topic, problem, intervention, program, or phenomenon you want to focus your literature review on. Consider whether a quantitative literature review, a qualitative literature review, or an MMRS would be the most appropriate approach for your literature review. You can do this by listing your preliminary review objectives and review questions and by listing for each of the three approaches (i.e., quantitative literature review, qualitative literature review, and MMRS) whether it is likely to allow you to reach your review objectives and to answer your review questions.

Exercises

- Start keeping a review diary and record everything that you did, considered, and reflected on during your MMRS process in this diary (Practical Tip 1.1). Decide whether you want to keep a digital or written review diary.
- Make the first entries in the review diary. These first entries can for instance relate to the *Questions for Thought* we posed earlier. In addition, you can reflect on any topic mentioned in this first chapter in your review diary.
- Create an overview table in your review diary, including five columns.
  - o In the first column of this table, you list the major MMRS stages that were depicted in Figure 1.1: (1) writing the review protocol (including review objectives, review questions, and MMRS design); (2) sampling; (3) searching for primary-level studies; (4) applying

inclusion and exclusion criteria; (5) possibly critically appraising the methodological quality of the primary-level studies; (6) extracting relevant data from the primary-level studies; (7) interpreting, synthesizing, and integrating the data; and (8) writing and disseminating the MMRS report.

o In the second column, you will later on mention the specific choices made within each of these stages. For instance, for the sampling stage (which will be discussed in Chapter 3), you can note down in the second column whether you will conduct an exhaustive, selective, or purposeful search for primary-level studies to be included in your MMRS.

o In the third column, you will leave a place to add rationales for the choices described in the second column. A rationale refers to a reason, an argument, or a justification that you can give for making certain choices (Practical Tip 1.3).

o In the fourth column, you will leave a place to reflect on the congruence of your choices for the different stages of your MMRS (Practical Tip 1.2). For instance, for the sampling stage, you can note down in the fourth column whether your choice to conduct an exhaustive, selective, or purposeful search for primary-level studies is congruent with your review objectives and review questions.

o In the fifth column, you will leave a place to reflect on the congruence of each of your choices with your ontological orientation toward research synthesis. For instance, for the sampling stage, you can note down in the fifth column whether your choice to conduct an exhaustive, selective, or purposeful search for primary-level studies is congruent with the ontological orientation toward research synthesis you described in your review diary.

Suggestions for Further Reading

Heyvaert, M., Maes, B., & Onghena, P. (2013). Mixed methods research synthesis: Definition, framework, and potential. *Quality & Quantity*, *47*, 659–676. doi:10.1007/s11135-011-9538-6

Sandelowski, M., Voils, C. I., Leeman, J., & Crandell, J. L. (2012). Mapping the mixed methods-mixed research synthesis terrain. *Journal of Mixed Methods Research*, *6*, 317–331. doi:10.1177/1558689811427913

References

Anderson, L. M., Oliver, S. R., Michie, S., Rehfuess, E., Noyes, J., & Shemilt, I. (2013). Investigating complexity in systematic reviews of interventions by using a spectrum of methods. *Journal of Clinical Epidemiology, 66*, 1223–1229. doi:10.1016/j.jclinepi.2013.06.014

Britten, N., Campbell, R., Pope, C., Donovan, J., Morgan, M., & Pill, R. (2002). Using meta ethnography to synthesise qualitative research: A worked example. *Journal of Health Services Research & Policy, 7*, 209–215. doi:10.1258/135581902320 432732

Bryman, A. (2007). Barriers to integrating quantitative and qualitative research. *Journal of Mixed Methods Research, 1*, 8–22. doi:10.1177/2345678906290531

Chalmers, I., Hedges, L. V., & Cooper, H. (2002). A brief history of research synthesis. *Evaluation & the Health Professions, 25*, 12–37. doi:10.1177/0163278702025 001003

Clegg, S. (2005). Evidence-based practice in educational research: A critical realist critique of systematic review. *British Journal of Sociology of Education, 26*, 415–428. doi:10.1080/01425690500128932

Cochrane Collaboration. (2015). *About Cochrane systematic reviews and protocols.* Retrieved from http://www.thecochranelibrary.com/view/0/AboutCochrane SystematicReviews.html

Cohen, L., Manion, L., & Morrison, K. (2000). *Research methods in education* (5th ed.). London, England: Routledge Falmer.

Eaves, Y. D. (2001). A synthesis technique for grounded theory data analysis. *Journal of Advanced Nursing, 35*, 654–663. doi:10.1046/j.1365-2648.2001.01897

Eisenhart, M. (1998). On the subject of interpretive reviews. *Review of Educational Research, 68*, 391–399. doi:10.3102/00346543068004391

Evans, J., & Benefield, P. (2001). Systematic reviews of educational research: Does the medical model fit? *British Educational Research Journal, 27*, 527–541. doi:10.1080/01411920120095717

Gough, D., Oliver, S., & Thomas, J. (2012). *An introduction to systematic reviews.* London, England: Sage.

Green, S., Higgins, J. P. T., Alderson, P., Clarke, M., Mulrow, C. D., & Oxman, A. D. (2011). Chapter 1: Introduction. In J. P. T. Higgins & S. Green (Eds.), *Cochrane handbook for systematic reviews of interventions Version 5.1.0* (updated March 2011). Retrieved from http://www.cochrane-handbook.org

Greenhalgh, T. (1997). Papers that summarise other papers (systematic reviews and meta-analyses). *British Medical Journal, 315*(7109), 672–675. doi:10.1136/bmj.315.7109.672

Hammersley, M. (2001). On "systematic" reviews of research literatures: A "narrative" response to Evans & Benefield. *British Educational Research Journal, 27*, 543–554. doi:10.1080/0141 1920120095726

Hannes, K., Booth, A., Harris, J., & Noyes, J. (2013). Celebrating methodological challenges and changes: Reflecting on the emergence and importance of the role of qualitative evidence in Cochrane reviews. *Systematic Reviews*, *2*, 84.

Hannes, K., & Lockwood, C. (2011). Pragmatism as the philosophical foundation for the Joanna Briggs meta-aggregative approach to qualitative evidence synthesis. *Journal of Advanced Nursing*, *67*, 1632–1642. doi:10.1111/j.1365-2648.2011.05636

Harden, A., & Thomas, J. (2005). Methodological issues in combining diverse study types in systematic reviews. *International Journal of Social Research Methodology*, *8*, 257–271. doi:10.1080/13645570500155078

Heyvaert, M., Maes, B., & Onghena, P. (2013). Mixed methods research synthesis: Definition, framework, and potential. *Quality & Quantity*, *47*, 659–676. doi:10.1007/s11135-011-9538-6

Johnson, R. B., Onwuegbuzie, A. J., & Turner, L. A. (2007). Toward a definition of mixed method research. *Journal of Mixed Methods Research*, *1*, 112–133. doi:10.1177/1558689806298224

Kearney, M. H. (1998). Truthful self nurturing: A grounded formal theory of women's addiction recovery. *Qualitative Health Research*, *8*, 495–512. doi:10.1177/104973239800800405

Kearney, M. H. (2001). Enduring love: A grounded formal theory of women's experience of domestic violence. *Research in Nursing & Health*, *24*, 270–282. doi:10.1002/nur.1029

Moher, D., Stewart, L., & Shekelle, P. (2012). Establishing a new journal for systematic review products. *Systematic Reviews*, *1*, 1–3. doi:10.1186/2046-4053-1-1

Morgan, G., & Smircich, L. (1980). The case for qualitative research. *Academy of Management Review*, *5*, 491–500. doi:10.5465/AMR.1980.4288947

Noblit, G. W., & Hare, R. D. (1988). *Meta-ethnography: Synthesising qualitative studies*. London, England: Sage.

Pawson, R. (2008). Method mix, technical hex, and theory fix. In M. M. Bergman (Ed.), *Advances in mixed methods research: Theories and applications* (pp. 120–137). Thousand Oaks, CA: Sage.

Pawson, R., Greenhalgh, T., Harvey, G., & Walshe, K. (2005). Realist review—A new method of systematic review designed for complex policy interventions. *Journal of Health Services Research & Policy*, *10*, 21–34. doi:10.1258/1355819054308530

Pearson, K. (1904). Report on certain enteric fever inoculation statistics. *British Medical Journal*, *3*, 1243–1246.

Petticrew, M., Rehfuess, E., Noyes, J., Higgins, J., Mayhew, A., Pantoja, T., . . . Sowden, A. (2013). Synthesizing evidence on complex interventions: How meta-analytical, qualitative, and mixed-method approaches can contribute. *Journal of Clinical Epidemiology*, *66*, 1230–1243. doi:10.1016/j.jclinepi.2013.06.005

Pluye, P., Gagnon, M. P., Griffiths, F., & Johnson-Lafleur, J. (2009). A scoring system for appraising mixed methods research, and concomitantly appraising qualitative, quantitative, and mixed methods primary studies in mixed studies reviews.

International Journal of Nursing Studies, *46*, 529–546. doi:10.1016/j.ijnurstu. 2009.01.009

Sandelowski, M., & Barroso, J. (2007). *Handbook for synthesizing qualitative research*. New York, NY: Springer.

Sandelowski, M., Voils, C. I., & Barroso, J. (2006). Defining and designing mixed research synthesis studies. *Research in the Schools*, *13*, 29–40. doi:10.1016/j. bbi.2008.05.010

Sandelowski, M., Voils, C. I., Leeman, J., & Crandell, J. L. (2012). Mapping the mixed methods-mixed research synthesis terrain. *Journal of Mixed Methods Research*, *6*, 317–331. doi:10.1177/1558689811427913

Squires, J. E., Valentine, J. C., & Grimshaw, J. M. (2013). Systematic reviews of complex interventions: Framing the review question. *Journal of Clinical Epidemiology*, *66*, 1215–1222. doi:10.1016/j.jclinepi.2013.05.013

Thomas, J., & Harden, A. (2008). Methods for the thematic synthesis of qualitative research in systematic reviews. *BMC Medical Research Methodology*, *8*, 45. doi:10.1186/1471-2288-8-45

Thomas, J., Harden, A., Oakley, A., Oliver, S., Sutcliffe, K., Rees, R., . . . Kavanagh, J. (2004). Integrating qualitative research with trials in systematic reviews. *British Medical Journal*, *328*, 1010–1012. doi:10.1136/bmj.328.7446.1010

Voils, C. I., Sandelowski, M., Barroso, J., & Hasselblad, V. (2008). Making sense of qualitative and quantitative findings in mixed research synthesis studies. *Field Methods*, *20*, 3–25. doi:10.1177/1525822X07307463

2

PREPARING FOR AN MMRS LITERATURE REVIEW

---- ᔥᔈᔥ ----

Chapter Outline

The successful accomplishment of an MMRS project highly depends on having the right people, with the right sort of expertise, on your team. Success is further facilitated by the development of an *a priori* protocol, outlining the decisions the review authors make in terms of methodological approach and rationale for the combination of evidence from quantitative, qualitative, and mixed primary studies. In this chapter, we consecutively offer the reader guidance on how to best establish a balanced review team and on how to develop and write a review protocol. It includes information on how to scope the literature to define the boundaries of your review, how to engage with different domains of scientific inquiry to develop appropriate questions, what sort of MMRS designs are available, and how to take into account some of the ethical dimensions of an MMRS.

---- ᔥᔈᔥ ----

BUILDING A REVIEW TEAM

If you want to conduct an MMRS, it is helpful to start by thinking about the sort of people you need to involve in your review team. After all, MMRS often result from a team effort. First, actions such as searching, screening for relevance, and extracting data from original studies all benefit from being done by more than one person independently, to assure the quality of the work.

For example, studies missed by one review author might have been picked up by another and discussions on whether a particular study qualifies for inclusion could increase a review author's sensitivity toward a particular content.

Second, it is unlikely that the whole set of relevant knowledge and skills to conduct an MMRS can be claimed by one review author. Methodologically trained review authors who do embark on such a journey tend to prioritize breadth of methodological experience over depth of understanding of the methodological options available for conducting the review. They may end up with a review that is methodologically robust, but they will fail to engage with important aspects of the content area because of their inability to interpret and integrate the findings on a more conceptual level. A review team lacking methodological expertise, therefore, may not be able to deliver a trustworthy review at the end of the process. A good review team succeeds in balancing such methodological and topical expertise.

Methodological Expertise

It is crucially important to create optimal methodological conditions, allowing MMRS teams to transcend the distinct methodological and epistemological differences encountered. The quality of the MMRS will not depend on the expertise delivered by each member of the team but on the collective capacity generated across the individuals. This will allow all team members to learn from the abilities and experience of other experts involved. The exact methodological compilation of an MMRS review team is often driven by the nature of the review questions and the methods base available to answer them. Review teams that decide to include a cost–benefit analysis, a multilevel meta-analysis of single-case experimental designs, a Bayesian synthesis approach, or a realist synthesis approach might need additional input from statisticians, economists, or qualitative researchers mastering the evidence synthesis approach opted for. Ideally, MMRS review teams will include at least one person specialized in each of the methods applied in the review.

Topical Expertise

Topical expertise can be brought in by engaging scholars or researchers specializing in a certain content area. However, expertise does not necessarily have to come from academics. Many review projects benefit from having experience-based experts on their team, referring to, for example, lay people, representatives of a particular population, or the public more generally. Whether an MMRS is perceived as useful is also influenced by the degree to which the review responds to queries that are deemed important by the potential end-users, such as policy makers, practitioners, clients, members of the target group addressed, and so on. In the last decade, the number of review authors including one or more public stakeholders on their team has increased. These stakeholders can be involved at multiple points in the review process, most obviously in formulating the review question and providing a lay summary of the scientific insights generated. However, they can also assist review authors in interpreting the review findings: Why do we end up with heterogeneous results? What sort of underlying processes may be at play in an intervention? Which configuration of information pieces will increase the comprehensiveness of the theories we develop? A successful roll-out deployment of an MMRS not only requires a team featuring a combination of quantitative and qualitative research expertise, but also requires a variety of different types of content experts. Such a team would generate the capacity to "support and challenge one another in each aspect of the [review] so as to produce the highest quality research" (Creswell et al., 2011, p. 12). Split opinions about, for example, the inclusion of a particular review question, specific aim, or quality criterion may lead to a further refinement of the collective understanding in the team on how to proceed with the MMRS. It also engages the team into thinking about the larger objectives of the review project and the reasons why a mixed method approach was opted for. Bringing different stakeholders together stimulates discussion and generally leads to challenging each other's assumptions (Oliver, Dickson, & Newman, 2012).

Complex review projects such as MMRS should best be managed by a **team leader** with experience in both the coaching of a review team and the reviewing of a complex body of scientific literature. In an ideal situation, the person leading the review is knowledgeable on both the content of the review as well as the different methodological traditions that are brought together in the MMRS project. A successful leader of a review team may not be "the greatest expert in any one approach, but rather the person who is able to bridge the differences and create synergy" between the members of the review team (Creswell et al., 2011, p. 13). The real benefit of a team approach in conducting MMRS is obtained when team members engage in open discussions of expectations, needs, and personal gains. It is important for a team leader to develop a core set of values about how the MMRS team should operate. This may include an outline of what authors are expected to contribute, in which phase of the project, how the team members will interact with each other, and how potential conflicts or different points of view will be dealt with. The leader should also be able to determine whose expertise is relevant in which particular phase of the review. Methodological skills related to conducting and evaluating a comprehensive search strategy, for example, should be readily available to the team in the early stages of the review, while knowledge brokers translating the insights from the review in plain language to engage with end-users might be a good asset to the review team in the end phase of the review project.

PREPARING FOR THE PROTOCOL PHASE

Writing a protocol for a review requires a substantial amount of time, effort, and expertise. However, a well-developed protocol facilitates a smooth review process. Review teams embarking on an MMRS should spend some time (a) developing an argument for their choice to combine quantitative and qualitative research evidence and, (b) where necessary, conducting a scoping review to explore the potential for an MMRS.

Developing an Argument for Your MMRS

Given the high demand in terms of time and resources, the decision to study a particular phenomenon from an MMRS perspective should thoroughly be justified by a team. A commonly used argument to promote an MMRS approach is that one strand of evidence is missing on a meta-level. For example, a review of effectiveness on the impact of a doula on personal well-being of young mothers has been conducted. However, a qualitative synthesis of studies exploring experiences of young mothers with the involvement of doulas has not been conducted yet. It could be the other way around as well. Consequently, review authors may want to conduct a supplemental review that responds to the gaps in the review literature and to the limitations identified in the previously published review of quantitative or qualitative evidence. Although this is a valid reason for conducting a review, it is not a strong argument for selecting an MMRS approach. It feeds into the idea that qualitative and quantitative findings retrieved from primary studies should be treated separately on a meta-level (Sandelowski, Voils, & Barosso, 2006). In addition, this argument contributes to the widespread misunderstanding that MMRS are the ultimate choice for every review project. The core question for review authors to answer prior to conducting a review is whether an MMRS approach is appropriate for the phenomenon under review. For example, questions related to understanding the meaning of a particular phenomenon, such as how people make sense of living with a disability or as a member of a minority group, or why youngsters with a drug addiction problem behave or feel the way they do, can perfectly be explored in a stand-alone qualitative evidence synthesis. Likewise, review authors evaluating the effect of a simple intervention, for example, the effect of a manual versus an electronic toothbrush to reduce tooth decay, may not find it worthwhile to explore qualitative literature for other reasons than to identify potential subgroups they need to consider in the comparing of both interventions. In these cases, MMRS is most likely not the most appropriate approach to synthesizing evidence. Moreover, there are some serious trade-offs of MMRS projects that need to be considered, for example, in terms of complexity of the review process as well as time and manpower investments. MMRS should only be considered when a review's purpose and type of questions warrant a combination of quantitative and qualitative strands of evidence and when the benefits of conducting an MMRS rule out the disadvantages, for example, in terms of breadth and depth of understanding of the phenomenon under review.

The rationale to combine for the purpose of breadth and depth is different from combining evidence from a traditional **methodological triangulation** perspective. Methodological triangulation strategies have originally been developed to evaluate whether similar results are being found using different methods, in order to establish a degree of validity. A triangulation exercise allows review authors to build on the strengths of one particular method to compensate for the weaknesses of another. The intention of the authors to use triangulation is therefore methodologically inspired, rather than content driven. A stronger argument for mixed method types of reviews would be that the combination of quantitative and qualitative evidence enables review authors to view problems from multiple perspectives, in other words, to address fundamentally different questions while looking at the same phenomenon. In this case, merging insights from quantitative and qualitative research evidence enhances and enriches the meaning of a singular perspective and allows review authors to develop a more complete understanding of a problem

(Greene, Caracelli, & Graham, 1989). A first example is that qualitative evidence may be used to provide illustrations of context for effect measures reported in a quantitative part of a review. A second example is that research accounts on lived experiences can be presented in conjunction with outcome measures or to follow up on some of the unexpected results that require a more in-depth exploration. A third example is that heterogeneity in an effectiveness review may prompt the search for explanations in qualitative studies, or vice versa. A fourth example is that potential relations between concepts outlined in theoretical or logic models developed in a qualitative evidence synthesis could further be explored in a quantitative type of review.

Scoping the Literature

If you are certain that an MMRS approach is the best choice for your project, you may benefit from an initial scoping review. **Scoping reviews** are defined by the Canadian Institutes of Health Research (n.d.) as "exploratory projects that systematically map the literature available on a topic, identifying the key concepts, theories, sources of evidence, and gaps in the research." Scoping reviews are often preliminary to full syntheses and undertaken when feasibility is a concern of the review authors. Concerns can be related to a potential diverse literature in terms of method, theoretical orientation or discipline, or to the suspicion that not enough literature exists. Scoping reviews entail a systematic selection, collection, and summarization of existing knowledge, like systematic reviews. However, the area that is tackled is generally broad and not particularly related to a well-defined question as is the case in MMRS. Although most scoping exercises are perceived as preparatory work and therefore a substantial part of any MMRS, some more extensive scoping reviews can be considered stand-alone projects with an exploratory focus, which in rare cases are also preceded by their own review protocol (Coemans, Wang, Leysen, & Hannes, 2015). Bear in mind that such reviews require a lot of time and resources. In a worst-case scenario, exploratory scoping reviews may compromise the time available for your MMRS project.

In this chapter, we mainly focus on the preparatory type of scoping review. Scoping typically involves searching for existing studies to grasp the full range of potentially relevant sources that inform the current state of the art on their topic of interest. It helps review authors to determine the value of undertaking a full systematic review by undertaking a preliminary mapping of the literature to identify whether a full systematic review is feasible (does any literature exist?) or relevant (have systematic reviews already been conducted?). As such, it provides an estimate of the potential costs of conducting a full systematic review (Arksey & O'Malley, 2005). Scoping reviews further assist review authors in defining the boundaries of their MMRS project. They generally inform the background section and development of review questions by contributing important information on the sorts of questions that have inspired authors. They also provide relevant information about populations, interventions, and outcomes to consider as well as about issues related to perceptions, experiences, options, and preferences of the target group under review (Armstrong, Hall, Doyle, & Waters, 2011). This information may feed into decisions about potential subgroups to be considered and potential inclusion or exclusion criteria to be defined for the MMRS.

The development of a protocol for an MMRS generally requires this "understanding of existing literature, including gaps and uncertainties, clarification of definitions related to the review question, and an understanding of the way in which these are conceptualized within existing literature" (Armstrong et al., 2011, p. 147). For example, in developing a protocol for an MMRS addressing the topic of team learning processes in employees, review authors may want to inventory what is known from existing literature about the (perceived) effectiveness, cost-effectiveness, and experiences of employees with team learning processes in Western European countries. Likewise, the review authors may seek to identify appropriate interventions or outcome measures to evaluate. Potential scoping questions could also be as follows: "What interventions promote team learning in employees, and what are the possible effects of these team learning processes on the economic output of the employees, their motivation, or their well-being?"

In some cases, scoping reviews may also help to refine the concepts used in an MMRS. For example, the plethora of definitions and theoretical frameworks available on topics such as team learning can be identified through a scoping review and will allow review authors to improve conceptualization of "teams" and "team learning." Such a comprehensive understanding of important concepts used also helps to set boundaries for a review (Hannes, Raes, Vangenechten, Heyvaert, & Dochy, 2013).

Review authors considering a scoping review may benefit from using Hilary Arksey and Lisa O'Malley's (2005) methodological framework, including five key phases and an optional phase of scoping the variety of literature on a particular topic. To a great extent, their outline follows the logic of the stepwise approach to systematically reviewing the literature visually outlined in Figure 1.1 from the first chapter of this book. Table 2.1 includes a description of each scoping phase of Arksey and O'Malley's (2005) framework.

Scoping reviews generally use broader review questions than systematic reviews, inclusion and exclusion criteria are more often developed post hoc, and there is no structural approach to assessing the quality of the studies included in the scoping exercise, a strategy that is often recommended for systematic reviews (Armstrong et al., 2011). They do not necessarily move

Table 2.1   Overview of the Arksey and O'Malley (2005) Methodological Framework for Conducting a Scoping Review

Arksey and O'Malley Framework Stage	Description
1: Identifying the research question	Identifying the research question provides the roadmap for subsequent stages. Relevant aspects of the question must be clearly defined as they have ramifications for search strategies. Research questions are broad in nature as they seek to provide breadth of coverage.
2: Identifying relevant studies	This stage involves identifying the relevant studies and developing a decision plan for where to search, which terms to use, which sources are to be searched, time span, and language. Comprehensiveness and breadth is important in the search. Sources include electronic databases, reference lists, hand searching of key journals, and organizations and conferences. Breadth is important; however, practicalities of the search are as well. Time, budget and personnel resources are potential limiting factors and decisions need to be made upfront about how these will impact the search.
3: Study selection	Study selection involves *post hoc* inclusion and exclusion criteria. These criteria are based on the specifics of the research question and on new familiarity with the subject matter through reading the studies.
4: Charting the data	A data-charting form is developed and used to extract data from each study. A 'narrative review' or 'descriptive analytical' method is used to extract contextual or process oriented information from each study.

Arksey and O'Malley Framework Stage	Description
5: Collating, summarizing, and reporting results	An analytic framework or thematic construction is used to provide an overview of the breadth of the literature but not a synthesis. A numerical analysis of the extent and nature of studies using tables and charts is presented. A thematic analysis is then presented. Clarity and consistency are required when reporting results.
6: Consultation (optional)	Provides opportunities for consumer and stakeholder involvement to suggest additional references and provide insights beyond those in the literature.

Source: Reprinted with permission from Levac, D., Colquhoun, H., & O'Brien, K. K. (2010). Scoping studies: Advancing the methodology. *Implementation Science, 5,* 69. doi:10.1186/1748-5908-5-69.

beyond a descriptive mapping of the literature with an analytical, interpretive perspective. Scoping reviews provide a summary of data rather than a synthesis in which data are aggregated or integrated. Scoping can be done by one or multiple members of the review team. Although there are no clear rules about who should be involved in scoping the literature or how the team should be balanced, you will benefit from a joined debate on the sort of parameters needed to map the characteristics of the studies retrieved (Practical Tip 2.1).

Practical Tip 2.1: Extracting Relevant Data

A useful strategy to deal with the outcome of a scoping exercise is to summarize the information you extract into a "data charting form" using the database program Excel or a table format in Word. Arksey and O'Malley (2005) propose to include the following basic information on the studies you explore within your scoping review: (a) the study population, (b) the type of intervention, (c) the outcome measures or type of evaluation (experiences, perceptions) employed, and (d) the study design. They further suggest to extract

(Continued)

(Continued)

additional information related to the author(s) of the study, the year of publication, the study location, the intervention type, the comparator (if any), the duration of the intervention, the study population (for example, provider as well as target group), the aims of the study, the methodology, the outcome or evaluation measures (in terms of effects, perceptions or experiences, cost–benefit, etc.), and important results or findings. You may want to add the final conclusion of the authors as an additional category. This process is very similar to the data extraction process undertaken by an MMRS (for more information, see Chapter 5).

Arksey and O'Malley's (2005) framework has been applied, discussed, and further enhanced by Danielle Levac, Heather Colquhoun, and Kelly K. O'Brien (2010). Their recommendations may increase the consistency with which you will undertake and report on your scoping study. Levac and colleagues developed the following suggestions for potential users of the framework in the context of a review: (a) clarify and link the purpose and review question in stage 1; (b) balance feasibility with breadth and comprehensiveness of the scoping process in stage 2; (c) use an iterative team approach to select studies and extract data in stage 3; (d) incorporate a numerical summary and qualitative thematic analysis in stage 4; (e) identify the implications of the study findings for policy, practice, or research in stage 5; and (f) adopt the "consultation phase" promoted by Arksey and O'Malley as stage 6 in the scoping study methodology as an absolute required component. More recent applications of the framework in the context of a literature review further emphasize the benefits of engaging a large, interprofessional team (Daudt, van Mossel, & Scott, 2013).

Scoping reviews generally aim to identify a broad range of insights related to the topic of review, regardless of study design. They aim to increase familiarity with the research literature and can inform review authors on more specific, contextual issues of relevance. Scoping the literature can help review authors to understand how characteristics of a particular target group influence the outcome of a program and whether the program and/or antici-pated research outcomes are relevant to the target group. They may reveal information on the extent to which social interactions among, for example, professionals, volunteers, clients, and participants interfere with the outcome of an intervention or program (Harris, 2011), or provide information on diverse population characteristics that may contribute to decision making about potential relevant subgroups and secondary review questions. Qualitative data generated from such a scoping review can also inform the selection of interventions and outcomes that are meaningful to participants (Armstrong et al., 2011). These types of studies are particularly useful to consult when evaluating complex interventions or life circumstances.

DEVELOPING A PROTOCOL

Protocol development is an important early step in the MMRS process, enabling the review authors to document *a priori* the (methodological or other) choices that are made and to anticipate potential problems in the con-ceptualization of the review components. Protocols also prevent ad hoc decision making during and after the review process that may influence the findings and facilitate the detection of selective reporting when compared with the completed MMRS. Special attention should be given to the writing process in the protocol phase as it is likely that several group members will contribute pieces from their own particular area of expertise and in their own writing style. The use of an MMRS approach has implications for each part of the protocol development phase. Consequently, the mixed methods strategy should be embedded throughout the protocol, starting with a thorough consideration of how to build important components of the mixed method approach into the aims and review questions, design specifications, and analytical approach to synthesis. The first step for the review team, however, is to decide on an appropriate design for their MMRS.

Choosing an Appropriate Design

A variety of different typologies have been developed for MMRS designs, drawing on the important work of, among others, John W. Creswell (2003); John W. Creswell and Vicki L. Plano Clark (2007); Jennifer C. Greene, Valerie

J. Caracelli, and Wendy F. Graham (1989); R. Burke Johnson and Anthony J. Onwuegbuzie (2004); Nancy L. Leech and Anthony J. Onwuegbuzie (2009); Donna M. Mertens (2005); David L. Morgan (1998); Janice M. Morse (1991); Abbas Tashakkori and Charles Teddlie (1998, 2010); and Charles Teddlie and Abbas Tashakkori (2009). Many of them developed mixed methods research designs for primary research studies. Most of the work of these pioneers has been adopted by researchers developing typologies for MMRS. The typology from Mieke Heyvaert, Bea Maes, and Patrick Onghena (2013) and the typology from Pierre Pluye and Quan Nha Hong (2014), for example, adopted one or more of the three dimensions outlined by Nancy L. Leech and Anthony J. Onwuegbuzie (2009) to assist review authors in choosing their design. First, review authors should decide on the weight of the qualitative part versus the quantitative part in their mixed method study: Should one strand of evidence be given dominant weight in the MMRS, or should both strands of evidence be given equal weight? Second, review authors should decide on the temporal orientation of their review project. In some review projects, the quantitative and the qualitative strands of evidence will be reviewed concurrently, whereas in other projects, one strand will be synthesized prior to the other. The latter is generally referred to as a sequential type of review. Third, it is important to think about the level of mixing of the quantitative and qualitative strands of evidence. Will the review team be mixing evidence in one phase of the review process or in several phases? For example, the conclusions from both strands of evidence could be integrated at the end point of the review process, in the discussion section. Another option would be to mix research evidence in different phases of the review. In the phase of question formulation, qualitative evidence on user perspectives can be used to inform an effectiveness question and prevent it from being exclusively author driven. This user perspective could then again be used to frame the interpretation and discuss implications for practice and policy.

The above-mentioned typologies generally provide good guidance to review authors. However, an important limitation of such typologies is that they may leave potential review authors with the impression that combining or configurating elements from the proposed dimensions automatically leads to an optimal design choice for each review project. They may work well for MMRS projects where the questions are outlined in advance. However, in cases where questions and review opportunities tend to emerge during the review process, a more dynamic approach to synthesis that supports an iterative logic might be more appropriate (Hannes, 2015). Margarete Sandelowski, Corrine I. Voils, and

Julie Barroso (2006) acknowledge this variation in positions review authors may take in their project. They discuss three major MMRS designs, which we will adopt for the further outline of this book.

The first type of MMRS design Sandelowski and colleagues (2006) discuss is a **segregated MMRS design**. It is based on the assumptions that (a) qualitative and quantitative studies are wholly different entities and, therefore, should be treated separately; (b) qualitative and quantitative studies can readily be distinguished from each other; (c) the differences between qualitative and quantitative studies warrant separate analyses and syntheses of their findings; (d) syntheses of qualitative findings require methods developed just for synthesizing qualitative findings; and (e) syntheses of quantitative findings require methods developed just for synthesizing quantitative findings (Sandelowski et al., 2006). In its most basic form, it is an MMRS literature review presented in two separate articles, one focusing on the quantitative data, and the other one focusing on the qualitative data, which are published alongside each other, for instance, in the same journal issue, as a two-part series (e.g., Heyvaert, Saenen, Maes, & Onghena, 2014, 2015). The background section of the first article may include an introduction to the two-part series. The relevance or added value of introducing an additional synthesis may be addressed in the discussion section. Likewise, the discussion section of the second article may include an overall synthesis across both strands of evidence. A segregated review logic is also applied when two different teams work in parallel but independently focus on synthesizing insights of one particular strand of evidence.

The second type of MMRS design Sandelowski et al. (2006) propose is an **integrated MMRS design**. It is based on the assumptions that (a) any differences between qualitative and quantitative studies that do exist do not warrant separate analyses and syntheses of their findings; (b) studies designated as qualitative or quantitative are not necessarily distinguishable from each other; (c) both qualitative and quantitative studies in a common research domain can address the same research purposes and questions; and (d) syntheses of both qualitative and quantitative findings can be produced from methods developed for qualitative and quantitative findings (Sandelowski et al., 2006). Qualitative findings retrieved from original articles included in a synthesis are being transformed into quantitative data (*quantitizing*; Sandelowski, Voils, & Knafl, 2009) or the quantitative findings are transformed into qualitative data (*qualitizing*) to facilitate their integration. For example, percentages addressed

in questionnaires may be translated into textual data (for example, the majority
of the participants, some participants, only limited participants agreed on *x*) to
facilitate the creation of a narrative storyline or qualitative data, or the verbal
counts in a qualitative study may be converted into numbers (for example,
x times finding/category/theme A), although the latter is not appropriate for
highly interpretive types of qualitative research that feature a rich description
of a complex phenomenon.

The third MMRS design Sandelowski et al. (2006) present is a **contingent
MMRS design**. It is more complex to grasp conceptually since it may borrow
elements from segregated or integrated designs. Its defining feature, however, is
the cycle of research synthesis studies conducted to answer questions raised by
previous phases in an MMRS or a stand-alone synthesis produced previously. It
does not buy into the logic that studies or methods should necessarily be
grouped and categorized as qualitative and quantitative. Instead, it promotes a
cycle of systematically reviewing evidence until a comprehensive research synthesis can be presented that addresses review authors' objectives rather than a
set of predefined review questions. It is generally more appealing to review
authors using an iterative logic to reviewing research evidence. Figure 2.1

Figure 2.1   Stepwise Approach to Conducting an MMRS

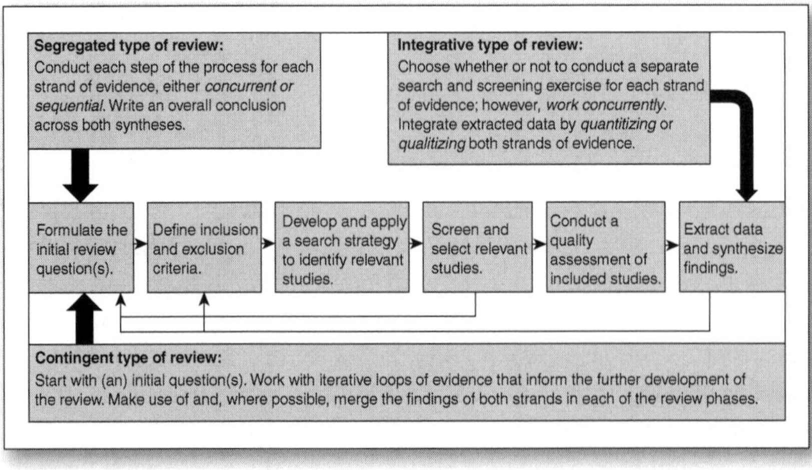

Source: Figure 9.1 on p. 91 of Hannes, K. (2015). Building a case for mixed method
reviews. In D. Richards D. & I. Hallberg (Eds.), *Complex interventions in health: An overview of research methods*. Oxon, England: Routledge.

outlines how these three types of reviews may relate to the standard review procedure outlined in Chapter 1 (process from formulating a review question to extracting and synthesizing data) and to the temporal orientation (concurrent versus sequential) and level of mixing dimensions (separate treatment of qualitative and quantitative data or more integrated approach to synthesis) presented earlier.

The selection of the design is influenced by many factors, including, for example, the nature of the MMRS team, the resources available, the nature of the research to be included, and the nature of the review author(s). The first two criteria are rather pragmatic but crucially important for a successful review process. Some review designs require a higher level of expertise because the synthesis procedure is more complex. This is particularly the case for integrative types of reviews. Also, a more interpretive type of qualitative synthesis requires more knowledge of qualitative research procedures than a purely descriptive type of project. Likewise, Bayesian procedures or multilevel analyses may require a more specialized statistical background. In terms of resources, the number of articles retrieved via a scoping review provides an estimate of how much time it is going to cost to screen, extract, and synthesize the data. The nature of the research refers to the goal review authors put forward for a synthesis. If the aim is to generate theory, then the style of synthesis will most likely be interpretive rather than descriptive or aggregative. What you can do on the meta-level also depends on the sort of numerical and textual data that are available in the original research articles. If the reports are thin, the potential for interpretive or advanced statistical research in your MMRS is limited. Think about your own nature as a review author as well. How much ambiguity would you allow in a review procedure? What are you comfortable with, and how much structure do you generally need? And finally, how does this relate to your own epistemological position as a review author?

Once the type of design is chosen, the review team can start writing the different sections of its protocol. Review protocols for an MMRS should outline (a) the background of the review, (b) the review objectives and questions, (c) the methods used for searching and synthesizing data, and (d) a reference section. Depending on the disciplinary field, review authors may draw from the handbooks and methods briefs produced by major review organizations such as the Cochrane Collaboration (health care), the Campbell Collaboration (education, social welfare, criminology, and international development), the What Works Clearinghouse (education), the Joanna Briggs Institute (health care), or the Evidence for Policy and Practice Institute (public health and social work). Each of these organizations supports review authors in protocol development and offers templates for protocols on its website. The methods part also includes a specification of which original research papers should be selected for the MMRS. In addition, most protocols include acknowledgments, a paragraph outlining the contribution of each author, and a declaration of sources of support. It is also important to declare potential conflicts of interest. This may relate to financial support but also to competing interests on a personal, political, or academic level. Most protocols include a set of annexes, for example, a document illustrating how the search strategy was developed. Some review authors include a screening instrument to assess the relevance of a retrieved study for the MMRS in annex, a data extraction form, or the frameworks considered for the quality assessment of potentially relevant studies. A protocol should include details of the review authors, a short biography, and a working title for the review. The title should reflect the intention to conduct an MMRS. The core sections of an MMRS protocol will be outlined next.

Writing the Background Section of the MMRS

Most protocols start with a background section that provides context on the review question to be addressed and that describes the phenomenon of interest. This section is important and should be clearly worded to make the MMRS accessible to those interested in the findings of the review. Background sections are first of all used to justify the decision to mix quantitative and qualitative strands of evidence. Second, they allow the review authors to introduce the topical area of the review and generally outline what the content area for the review is, which topic will be addressed, what is already known on the topic, and why it is important to conduct the review. Most protocols include a description or definition of the main topic of interest. In case of an evaluation of a program or intervention, review authors may want to outline how a program works according to theoretical literature consulted. They may want to present what is already known on the relationship between different concepts introduced. A lot of the reviews published in the past decade have been criticized for being "a-theoretical." It is now more common for review authors to present either a theory or a logic model in the background section of their protocol. Theories generally provide guidance and direction for the review under consideration. They help review authors to choose between different options of approaching a particular problem, which may or may not contradict or challenge each other. Theories generally provide an insight into potential pathways that could be taken to try to understand a particular problem. The search for relevant theories may or may not be part of the general scoping review outlined earlier. An example of the use of a theory is presented as Practical Tip 2.2.

Practical Tip 2.2: A Theory in Your MMRS

A nice example of the use of theory in a systematic review was featured in the draft review protocol of Subash Thapa, which is currently being published by Subash Thapa, Karin Hannes, Margaret Cargo, Anne Buvé, and Catharina Matheï (2015). The review author team builds on the insights from Lisanne Brown, Kate Macintyre, and Lea Trujillo (2003). In their review, Brown and colleagues analyzed 21 different interventions that have explicitly attempted to decrease HIV stigma. They grouped the interventions into four different categories, namely, information-based approaches, coping skills acquisition, counseling approaches, and contact with affected groups. Information-based approaches are used in nearly all the interventions and in advertisements, information packs, or presentations in a class or lecture. Coping skills were applied at the individual or small-group level involving role-play, group desensitization, master imagery, and so on. Similarly, counseling approaches included one-to-one counseling or group counseling. Last, contact with the affected group included interaction with people living with HIV and so on. Thapa et al. (2015) include the different pathways identified by Brown et al. (2003) and link them to their primary outcome measure: HIV testing uptake.

(Continued)

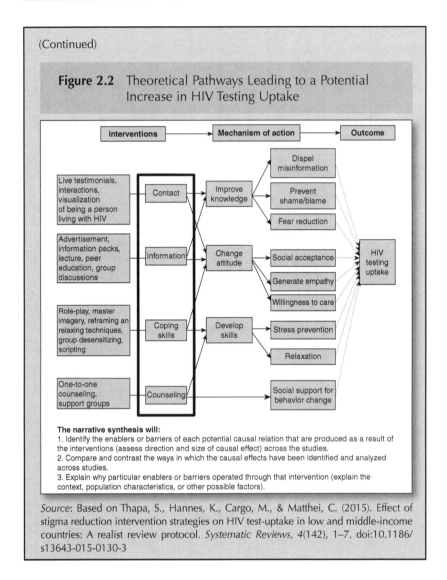

(Continued)

Figure 2.2   Theoretical Pathways Leading to a Potential Increase in HIV Testing Uptake

The narrative synthesis will:
1. Identify the enablers or barriers of each potential causal relation that are produced as a result of the interventions (assess direction and size of causal effect) across the studies.
2. Compare and contrast the ways in which the causal effects have been identified and analyzed across studies.
3. Explain why particular enablers or barriers operated through that intervention (explain the context, population characteristics, or other possible factors).

Source: Based on Thapa, S., Hannes, K., Cargo, M., & Matthei, C. (2015). Effect of stigma reduction intervention strategies on HIV test-uptake in low and middle-income countries: A realist review protocol. *Systematic Reviews, 4*(142), 1–7. doi:10.1186/s13643-015-0130-3

Logic models, on the other hand, are meant to narrow the scope of your review. In addition, they will help the reader understand how, for example, a program under review has been designed to achieve its intended outcomes and what the connections are between the determinants of the outcomes you consider. Logic models will aid you in conceptualizing your review focus, illustrating hypothesized causal links, identifying effect mediators or moderators, specifying intermediate outcomes and potential harms, and justifying *a priori* subgroup analyses when differential effects are anticipated (Anderson et al., 2011). Review authors should bear in mind, though, that logic models are not static. They can partially be developed before a review begins and further refined during the course of reviewing the literature. Most MMRS involve some configuring of findings (qualitative synthesis) and some aggregation of findings (statistical pooling) (Oliver et al., 2012) that will further inform the conceptual framework of your review. An example of the use of a logic model is presented in Practical Tip 2.3.

Practical Tip 2.3: A Logic Model in Your MMRS

An example of a review outlining a logic model is the context-specific review from Susan Goerlich Zief, Sherri Lauver, and Rebecca A. Maynard (2006) outlining how after-school programs for low-income elementary school children are expected to work in the North American region and how parental, behavioral, and social-emotional aspects might impact the long-term academic outcome measures proposed by the review authors.

Figure 2.3 Logic Model for Understanding the Theory of Change for Low-Income Elementary Youth in an After-School Program

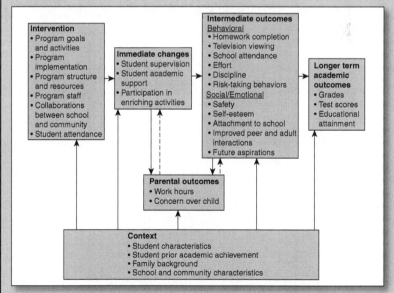

Source: Reprinted with permission from Zief, S. G., Lauver, S., & Maynard, R. A. (2006). Impacts of after-school programs on student outcomes. *Campbell Systematic Reviews, 3*. doi:10.4073/csr.2006.3.

The background section is also likely the place where review authors will embed information on their rationale for conducting an MMRS. They may refer to the limitations of previously conducted single method reviews in studying a complex phenomenon or to the importance of studying a phenomenon from different perspectives. Although this is an acceptable strategy, it does not truly inform the reader about what the knowledge gaps are, how the MMRS will contribute to advancing the scientific knowledge base, how it will help to improve practice, or how it might impact at the policy level. Protocols should therefore clearly outline what the critical barriers to progress in the field of interest are and how the review authors intend to respond to them. Most review authors will somehow link their ideas with the sort of inquiries they are interested in. For example, questions of effectiveness will enable review authors to answer the question "what works," whereas inquiries into the acceptability of interventions will inform the reader on "why, for whom, and under which circumstances" a program will work, or why some people benefit more from a program than others. The relevance review authors assign to their MMRS project will help to determine the specific objectives of the review.

Objectives and Review Questions

Objectives. Review authors should first of all state an overall goal for their MMRS addressing the overarching review problem or question. The goal should reflect the original intention to conduct the review and inform the specific aims of the review. If this preparatory work is done properly, it should naturally lead to a set of well-defined review questions. The methodological approach needed to accomplish the aims and provide an answer to the questions should easily be identifiable and firmly tied to the original goals of the review. A good starting point to develop such an outline is to consult previously published protocols available in journals such as *Systematic Reviews* or the libraries of relevant review organizations (see Practical Tip 2.4).

Review questions. Question formulation is an integral part of developing a robust protocol for an MMRS. Review questions generally specify the population or target group of interest, the phenomenon of interest, and the types of outcomes, perceptions, or experiences the review authors are interested in. Well-defined review questions assist review authors in deciding on the prespecified eligibility criteria for a review (Higgins & Green, 2011) and serve as a guiding principle for the whole review process. Review author teams established to

Practical Tip 2.4: Building on Previously Published Review Protocols

You may want to draw inspiration from previously published protocols to be found in both the Cochrane and the Campbell Library[1] as well as in the open access journal *Systematic Reviews*. For example, the MMRS protocol from Michael Hurley, Kelly Dickson, Nicola Walsh, Hanan Hauari, Robert Grant, Jo Cumming, and Sandy Oliver (2013) on exercise interventions and patient beliefs for people with chronic hip and knee pain nicely outlines the major goal and specific aims of the review. The review authors further outline how they intend to conduct their review, proposing separate quantitative and qualitative types of evidence synthesis with an overarching synthesis at the end of the review project. The protocol specifies both quantitative and qualitative review questions and contains an extensive background section introducing several theoretical models underpinning the review authors' rationale for conducting an MMRS. This protocol may serve as an example for you:

Main objective: To improve our understanding of the complex inter-relationship among pain, psychosocial effects, physical function, and exercise.

Specific aims and objectives: To review systematically the evidence on the impact of physical exercise on patients' pain and physical and psychosocial functioning, including (a) identifying the most effective formats for delivering exercise advice; (b) explaining why some exercise interventions may be more effective than others; and (c) recommending exercise formats and content by constructing a toolbox that describes the most effective exercise interventions for healthcare providers and patients to use. The objectives will be achieved by conducting (a) a synthesis of quantitative data on the benefits and harm of exercise interventions for improving pain and physical and psychosocial functioning; (b) a synthesis of qualitative data on participants' experiences, opinions, and preferences of physical exercise; and (c) a cross-studies

---

[1]Relevant URLs to online libraries: http://www.thecochranelibrary.com/view/0/index.html and http://www.campbellcollaboration.org/lib/

(Continued)

(Continued)

synthesis of the quantitative and qualitative data to assess the extent to which existing evaluated interventions address the needs and concerns of people living with osteoarthritis.

Review questions: (a) What are the effects of exercise-based rehabilitation programs on physical and psychosocial functioning for patients with chronic knee and/or hip pain? (b) What are patients' experiences, opinions, and preferences of exercise-based rehabilitation programs and the advice they receive about exercise? (c) What implications can be drawn, from the qualitative synthesis of people's views, to inform the appropriateness and acceptability of exercise-based rehabilitation programs for people living with osteoarthritis?

conduct an MMRS generally engage themselves in different types of inquiries. The outline of the inquiries potentially relevant to review authors presented next is based on the work of Alan Pearson, Rick Wiechula, Anthea Court, and Craig Lockwood (2005). These authors identified four major types of evidence: evidence of effectiveness, feasibility, appropriateness, and meaningfulness. The first three mainly relate to evaluations of programs or interventions, whereas the fourth may also refer to how people give meaning to a certain condition, situation, or event. Evidence of feasibility and evidence of appropriateness both refer to aspects of applicability. Each type of evidence emphasizes a different line of research inquiry and, consequently, a different set of review questions to consider. In what follows, we define these lines of inquiry.

Inquiries into **effectiveness** mainly evaluate "the extent to which a particular program or intervention, when used appropriately, achieves an intended effect" (Pearson et al., 2005, p. 210). Review authors evaluating effectiveness often compare different interventions to develop an understanding of which interventions are most beneficial. A benefit can be defined as the extent to which an intervention might be helpful, advantageous, or good for a particular target group. Likewise, review authors may want to consider an evaluation of potential harmful effects of an intervention and develop review questions related to potential disadvantages of an intervention for subpopulations within the target group, or the target group in general. Originally strongly influenced

by the evidence-based practice movement, inquiries into effectiveness have
been dominating the systematic review community for the past few decades.
Over time, the number of systematic reviews including evidence generated
through different types of inquiry has been growing due to a growing recognition that the role of user perspectives and practitioner observation in delivering
a holistic approach to feasible, meaningful, and cost-appropriate services was
important in supporting decision-making processes (Hannes, Booth, Harris, &
Noyes, 2013). Consequently, review authors have become more sensitive to
including evidence related to the applicability of programs or interventions,
their meaningfulness, and the affordability of the programs and interventions
in their reviews.

Inquiries into the **applicability** of programs mainly address the conditions
or circumstances that need to be fulfilled for an intervention or program to
work in the way it was intended or, in other words, the feasibility and appropriateness of a program for the target group. **Feasibility** is the "extent to which
an intervention is practical and applicable" (Pearson et al., 2005, p. 210). It
refers to whether a program or an intervention is "physically, culturally, and
financially practical or possible within a given context" (Pearson et al., 2005,
p. 210). For example, review authors may want to identify obstacles in applying the intervention, program characteristics that positively (or negatively)
impact on a successful roll-out of a program, or strengths and weaknesses of
the program itself. Inquiries into **appropriateness** evaluate "the extent to
which a program fits with or is apt to fit in a situation" (Pearson et al., 2005,
p. 210) from the perspective of both the target group and the providers.
Sensitivity for aspects of feasibility and appropriateness will lead review
authors into exploring how a program matches the expectations of the target
group or how certain conditions and circumstances in the ecological context
where the program takes place may impact the outcome of a review. For
example, review authors may want to evaluate the effectiveness of prevention
campaigns in decreasing the infection rate in the school environment. Such
campaigns may target young children's hand-washing behavior. The school
may have developed prevention materials such as videos and posters to
increase awareness. However, if the soap that should be used is not readily
available, the height of the washing tables is inappropriate for toddlers, or the
cloths available to dry the children's hands are experienced as unpleasant, the
program may not reach its targets even if there is nothing wrong with the
intrinsic quality of the program itself. Review authors developing a protocol

for an MMRS need to consider the different layers of evidence that will allow them to provide accurate answers to different types of questions.

Inquiries into **meaningfulness** in the context of program evaluation refer to "the extent to which a program or activity is positively experienced" by the target group (Pearson et al., 2005, p. 210). It relates to "the personal opinions, values, thoughts, beliefs, and interpretations" of members of the target group (Pearson et al., 2005, p. 210). Insights from qualitative studies addressing meaning can be used to inform the development of a logic model, the type of moderators potentially influencing the effect of a program, or the type of subgroups to be considered in a quantitatively oriented review part because these may reveal important variations in experiences reported by the target group under consideration. As mentioned, questions related to understanding the meaning of a particular phenomenon do not always link into aspects of interventions or programs. Like effectiveness questions, questions about meaning are valuable in their own right. They may also relate to how people make sense of a particular condition, their living circumstances, and the roles and positions they fulfil in society, on a school or family level. MMRS may also aim to generate meaningful insights into why people behave or feel the way they do without necessarily linking this inquiry to a micro- or meso-scale program evaluation. There is a natural distinction between "meaning" studied from a qualitative perspective and "effectiveness" measured in quantitative parts of an MMRS that reconciles a topic under review to an exclusive quantitative or qualitative research paradigm. Some aspects related to meaning cannot and should not be measured through scales, although many basic researchers are tempted to approach inquiries into meaning via such tools. It gives them the analytic advantage of working with numerical and presumably more "objective" data. How informative is a score 3 on a scale from 1 to 5 if it indicates that students appreciate a teacher because of his or her potential to engage students but fails to explain his or her theories comprehensively? Likewise, what is the value and policy relevance of a perceived effect if it is never accurately measured? On a meta-level, we need to remain sensitive to the potential loss of insights we initiate by, for example, translating quantitative into qualitative data to enable a synthesis, or the other way around. Table 2.2 offers a framework for discussing the lines of inquiry discussed earlier. Although not useful for all types of MMRS, it offers assistance to those working in the area of program evaluation. It may need to be adapted or extended with review questions that explore, for example, particular

Table 2.2 Typology of Review Questions for Inquiries Into Effectiveness, Feasibility, Appropriateness, and Meaningfulness Related to Program Evaluation

Inquiry	Effectiveness	Applicability		Meaningfulness
		Feasibility	Appropriateness	
Quantitative	• What is the effectiveness of (intervention/program) (compared to…) on (target group)? • How effective is (intervention/program) in addressing (problem)? • Is there a positive/negative impact of (intervention/program) on (target group)? • Does (intervention/program) positively or negatively influence ([characteristics of] target group)? • Does (intervention/program) work better for some than others? • How well does (intervention/program) solve (problem)? • Which variables act as moderators that impact the effectiveness of (intervention/program)?	• How well does (intervention/ program) satisfy the goals outlined in the protocol? • What is the (intervention's/ program's) impact on the local environment?	• Do the desired outcomes address the needs of (target group)? • Does (intervention/ program) deliver the desired outcomes?	• How do people feel about (participating in) (intervention/ program) on a scale from x to x?

(Continued)

Table 2.2 (Continued)

| Inquiry | Effectiveness | Applicability | | Meaningfulness |
		Feasibility	Appropriateness	
Qualitative	• How do people perceive the effectiveness of (intervention/program) (compared to…)? • In what ways, if any, has (intervention/program) changed the way things are done since it began? • In what way, if any, has (intervention/program) influenced the target group's practice? • What does (target group) think the primary goal of (intervention/program) is?	• What are the strengths/weaknesses of (intervention/program)? • What are the opportunities/threats related to (intervention/program)? • What are barriers/facilitators to (implementing) the (intervention/program)?	• Are the desired outcomes consistent with (target group) priorities and/or beliefs? • What is (target group's) perception/experience of negative consequences of (intervention/program)? • What particular events, beliefs, attitudes, or policies may impact on the outcome of (intervention/program)?	• What does it mean to have (condition)? • What does it mean to be (characteristic of individual or target group)? • How do (target group) feel about (participating in) (intervention/program)? • What was personally gained from participating in (intervention/program)? • What is the problem of (target group)? • What do people prefer?

Source: Hannes, K., Thomas, J., Noyes, J. (2014). *Integrating quantitative and qualitative research evidence: Mixed-method synthesis approaches for complex reviews.* Cochrane Colloquium. Hyderabad, India, 22–26 September 2014.

discourses, concepts, theories, correlations, and relations that have been outlined in the broad variety of primary research studies available in the literature.

A lot of review authors will pick and choose review questions related to the type of inquiry they will engage in, based on the goals specified in the review protocol, and advance a combined set of review questions in their review protocol. In the context of deciding on review questions, it is worthwhile to consider a more integrated type of review question that directly addresses the mixing of the quantitative and qualitative strands of evidence, for example: Does the theme of social support help to explain why some students become bullied in schools (Tashakkori & Creswell, 2007) or why particular programs are more effective to prevent bullying? Such a question focuses not only on the content area of the review but also on the intent to mix quantitative and qualitative findings, as well as on the overall aim to provide a more comprehensive and nuanced understanding of the phenomenon of bullying.

Some review authors will define their questions prior to the review process. Other authors conducting a review that consists of several phases, building on the findings of previously summarized information, may want to add questions whenever they emerge in the process. For example, some questions may only become relevant once the preliminary findings of one particular strand of evidence are known, for example, when heterogeneity in effects measured in the quantitative part warrant a follow-up using qualitative evidence to understand better what is going on. The mechanisms that push review authors into exploring different pathways in their overall review projects are not always known in advance. They require a more flexible attitude from review authors.

The types of inquiries discussed in Table 2.2 are not exhaustive. Some review authors engage in an exploration of particular theoretical concepts, looking into the different meanings people assign to, for example, community-building initiatives, arts-based methods (Coemans, Wang, & Hannes, 2015), or pedagogical content knowledge (Depaepe, Verschaffel, & Kelchtermans, 2013). These authors use a conceptual lens of inquiry in their review in an attempt to create order in an otherwise chaotic field of disciplinary jargon. Some may be interested in cost–benefit issues related to a particular intervention and use an economic lens of inquiry for their review, assessing the affordability of interventions or programs (see Practical Tip 2.5 for a more extensive discussion on the topic).

Practical Tip 2.5: Inquiries Related to "Affordability" Issues

The list of dimensions of inquiry presented earlier is far from comprehensive. Depending on what your funder requires you to do or the area you work in, your questions may, for instance, relate to the affordability of an intervention or program. You may want to evaluate the cost-effectiveness of a particular program. The purpose of adding an economic component to your review will be to inform the allocation of resources, finances, and manpower. Consequently, the type of question that will guide this part of your review will present itself to the reader as "how cost-effective are the programs compared in the review?" If you are interested in adding an economical dimension to your MMRS project, please consider the type of questions the Joanna Briggs Institute (2008) proposes: (a) Cost minimization: What is the least costly program where multiple programs have demonstrated similar benefits? (b) Cost effectiveness: What are the unknown or potentially different resource implications for programs that achieve similar outcomes? (c) Cost utility: What is the benefit of a particular program in terms of quantity and quality of life? (d) Cost benefits: What do we gain or lose from applying a particular program in terms of monetary ratio?

Rhiannon Whitaker and colleagues (2014) published an example of an MMRS protocol addressing the issue of unintended teen pregnancies that includes an economic dimension of inquiry. Cost–benefit analyses are added to the series of study designs considered for inclusion in the review. Cost-effectiveness is listed as an outcome measure of interest. The approach to synthesizing economic evidence includes five different components: (a) a narrative review of economic evaluations of interventions specifically designed to address the issue in question; (b) a stratification of any economic studies found by the public health lever mechanism used, including, for example, policy documents, public information, and reports on school-based group or targeted interventions; (c) an economic, evaluative perspective of analysis, for example, cost analysis, cost–benefit analysis, cost-effectiveness analysis, or cost-utility analysis; (d) a documentation of the way that these studies have attempted to overcome the particular methodological challenges of this type of complex, preventative, behavior change-based intervention; and (e) where possible, a meta-analysis of the economic evidence (Whitaker et al., 2014, p. 7).

A useful strategy to help direct review questions is to imagine or project what the review team wishes to occur as the result of the MMRS (Paterson, Thorne, Canam, & Jillings, 2001). Relevant examples include the development of a comprehensive framework outlining the effects, potential moderators, and mediators of a program, or a critique of how authors have methodologically approached the evidence base on a particular topic. This may then inform the direction of the review questions, the theoretical orientation toward the review phenomenon, the lens of inquiry, and the methodological approach that needs to be considered.

Methods

In the methods section, review authors generally outline their strategies for searching and screening evidence, critically appraising retrieved literature, data extraction, and synthesis. Review teams benefit from specifying clearly which type of studies should be included in the MMRS and which should not be included, based on the characteristics of the design, the population, the phenomenon of interest, and the sort of outcomes or evaluation measures the team wants to use.

Criteria for considering studies. In the protocol phase, review authors generally specify which studies they will consider for inclusion in their MMRS. These criteria relate to the type of studies and population considered for inclusion, as well as to what the characteristics are of their phenomenon of interest. Where relevant, review authors can specify which particular outcomes or evaluation measures they are interested in. Where possible, the decision to include or exclude particular studies should preferably be based on formal scientific or theoretical justifications rather than on unsubstantiated pragmatic reasoning. Most review authors develop a screening form outlining specific inclusion and exclusion criteria that may assist co-authors in deciding on the relevance of a particular study for the MMRS.

Type of study designs. In defining the inclusion criteria for study types, most review authors use the principle of "fitness for purpose" as the lead criterion. The choice for inclusion will mainly be guided by the type of review questions formulated. Fitness for purpose does not equal "anything goes." MMRS review teams should carefully consider the methodological expertise that is available within their team, particularly when they have no direct access to experts with the right set of skills. Most review authors specify a selection of designs they are willing to consider, limited to, for example, controlled trials, group designs, or single-case experimental designs. Sometimes, the justification to exclude particular studies is inspired by the lack of instruments or techniques to deal with them in the context of a review. A commonly used argument for the exclusion of purely descriptive, historical, or philosophical papers in the qualitative strand of an MMRS is that there are no tools available to properly assess their quality. In this particular case, review authors may want to exclude all studies that do not have a clear methods and results section. Other review authors may argue that opinion pieces and editorials should be included because they bring a different layer of critique or insight to a particular phenomenon and therefore contribute to, for example, theory development or refinement. Review authors should keep in mind that there is an increasing amount of mixed method primary studies being published. They should include an argument on how they will handle discrete parts of such studies in their synthesis or whether they will actively trace qualitatively oriented sibling studies containing process and implementation related elements from experimental studies published. Alternatively, authors may choose to include a general statement in their protocol, outlining that they will consider all sorts of study designs, including economic studies where relevant.

Type of participants. In most cases, the population of interest or the target group is exactly the same for both the quantitative and the qualitative strand in the MMRS. In this case, review authors may just want to define the boundaries of who is considered "in" the population of interest and who falls out. For example, review authors planning to evaluate the barriers to attending self-help groups in addicts and the impact of these groups on abstinence rates should specify the age group they will be looking at since the programs for youngsters might differ from those developed for adults. Review authors studying the effectiveness and experience of inclusive education in pupils could benefit from specifying whether the target group should be limited to those with mental disorders or whether the discussion on inclusive education should be extended to the group of pupils with physical disabilities. In some cases, the target groups may vary for different strands in the MMRS. By building on the previous example, we might be interested in studying the effectiveness of inclusive education on pupils with a learning disorder in the quantitative evidence synthesis part and include the perspectives of the teachers and the school directors in the qualitative evidence synthesis part. This can be specified in advance.

Phenomenon of interest. Choosing which topic to review is one of the more important decisions review authors have to make because it directly informs the review questions and consequently the design choices that need to be made. For some review authors, their topic of interest equals an intervention or program, or a series of interventions that may be relevant to consider solving a particular problem. In this case, review authors should always describe their intervention of interest in detail, particularly if it is multifaceted. The more precise the description is, the easier it will be to determine appropriate inclusion criteria for the review. Where relevant, review authors should highlight which comparators are considered for the evaluation of the impact of an intervention or program of interest for the quantitative strand of their review. Bear in mind, though, that most MMRS seek to answer broad review questions and that limiting the type of comparators may not be appropriate or even desirable in an MMRS that includes an explorative component. Review authors may equally be interested in exploring perceptions and experiences of their target group or issues of power and politics. In these cases, review authors benefit from a reflection concerning the ecological context of relevance to their review. For a health-care type of MMRS, this may, for example, relate to "cultural factors such as geographical location, specific racial or gender based interests, detail about the setting such as acute care, primary health care, or the community as they relate to the experiences or meanings individuals or groups reported in the studies" (Joanna Briggs Institute, 2008, p. 24).

Type of outcome/evaluation measures. The description of outcome or evaluation measures varies for quantitative and qualitative components of an MMRS. The measures specified for the quantitative part often relate to measures of effectiveness, whereas qualitative evaluation measures might be specified as experiences, perceptions, opinions, or viewpoints. The latter are subjective in nature and may refer to the interaction of the target group with the program, as is the case of reviews evaluating programs that include an inquiry related to the acceptability of the program, or what it means to be a participant. There are always more outcomes affected by any topic under review than those reported on by the review authors in their protocol. This is the logical consequence of trying to justify the outcomes specified by the information provided in the background section of your protocol. Outcome measures are often divided into primary and secondary outcomes. **Primary outcomes** are those directly relevant to the target group, resulting from their "exposure" to the phenomenon of interest. **Secondary outcomes** may refer to the impact of the program on others or to an impact that is not directly emphasized by a program. All measures listed should be appropriate to the specific aims of the review, although the weight given to certain evaluation measures may vary (see Practical Tip 2.6).

Search strategy. Information retrieval is an essential component of every MMRS. Without a transparent reporting of how and where studies were sought

---

Practical Tip 2.6: Practical Example of Defining Outcome Measures

Marc van Nuland, Karin Hannes, Bert Aertgeerts, and Jozef Goedhuys (2005), in their protocol for a review on the impact of educational interventions for improving the communication skills of general practice trainees in the clinical consultation, decided to group their outcome measures by distinguishing between primary, or patient-related, outcomes and secondary outcomes more closely related to the trainee or to the consultation process or content.

The primary outcomes were defined as (a) consumer satisfaction with care, including satisfaction with the received care and satisfaction with the care environment; (b) consumer assessment of the quality of the clinical consultation, including consumer involvement or participation in discussion or decision making, consumer satisfaction with communication (for example, with the information provided or the ways in which decisions are made), and consumer understanding of the information, options, and choices provided; (c) patients' healthcare behavior, including adherence to management plans and therapy; and (d) health outcome measures, including healthrelated quality of life, physiological measures of disease control including blood pressure and blood sugar control, and psychological health of patient.

The secondary outcomes related to (a) trainee use of communication skills in clinical consultations with real patients in day-to-day practice; (b) trainee competence with communication skills, such as during Objective Structured Clinical Examination

(OSCE) with standardized patients; (c) trainee knowledge of communication skills, such as knowledge about the skills necessary for different clinical consultations; and (d) subjective trainee outcomes, including satisfaction with the clinical consultation and self-confidence.

and found, it will be difficult for readers to judge whether the literature retrieved is representative for the phenomenon under review. In addition, it will be challenging to evaluate the potential impact of review authors on the selection of the included studies. Consequently, review authors spend considerable time planning their search strategy prior to conducting their review. A protocol usually contains information about the design of the literature search, which information sources will be searched, how the search procedure will be rolled out in the selected information sources, and how the review authors will manage the references found during the search process. The inclusion criteria related to population, phenomenon of interest, design, and type of outcome or evaluation measure directly inform how the search is designed and what key terms will be used. Most review authors further specify the boundaries of their search, for example, by communicating limits related to the language in which the research reports are written or the time frame in which they were published.

A particular challenge for authors of MMRS is to decide whether the search strategies they develop should be distinct for either strand of the review. For example, review authors could decide on an exhaustive search to retrieve quantitative studies and a purposeful sampling technique for the qualitative evidence strand. In this case, the review authors should make two separate statements on searching procedures in their protocol. Another approach to searching could be the development of a broad search strategy encompassing many different study designs. This would imply separating the quantitative from the qualitative research findings in the screening phase of the review. Chapter 3 will outline the many complexities in the area of information retrieval for MMRS.

Quality assessment. Quality assessment of primary studies is now generally perceived as a valuable asset in the development of a literature review. A plethora of instruments to assess the quality of a variety of different study designs is currently available in the scientific literature. Review authors conducting an MMRS should make four important decisions. First of all, they have to decide whether they will conduct a quality assessment of the quantitative, qualitative, and mixed method studies retrieved. Second, they need to decide on the use of a generic type of criteria list, outlining basic quality measures that cut across different designs, or a design-specific list of criteria that addresses methodological features relevant to the research tradition opted for in the study. Third, review authors need to decide which particular checklist or criteria they will use and justify their choice. This is important because the choice of an instrument or the set of criteria selected may impact on the overall outcome of a literature review (Hannes & Aertgeerts, 2014). Fourth, they need to decide how they are going to deal with the outcome of the critical appraisal exercise. What is considered an acceptable degree of quality? What is the potential impact of potentially flawed papers on the overall synthesis? Do they intend to use quality as a criterion for the exclusion of papers, and if not, how will the studies judged as "weak" be flagged in the overall synthesis? Further guidance on how to deal with these issues will be provided in Chapter 4.

Data extraction and synthesis. In this phase of the protocol, review authors should document the process of recording relevant data from the primary research studies considered for inclusion. Data extraction refers to the collection of descriptive information from the studies, often related to characteristics of the target group, the phenomenon of interest, the outcome and evaluation measures, and relevant contextual issues. A standard extraction form is usually developed and added to the protocol to facilitate consistency of data extraction between different review authors involved in this phase. Review authors further extract numerical and textual data from the studies that allows them to synthesize the information further on a meta-level. For qualitative parts of an evidence synthesis, the very act of extracting findings from an article is generally considered the first step in a meta-synthesis, followed by a more abstract categorization of these findings on a descriptive and conceptual level. The categorization may lead review authors into developing of a line or argument, a theoretical framework, or a set of suggestions to policy or practice. The numerical data extracted further facilitate the statistical pooling of individual study results, generally referred to as meta-analysis. Review authors of MMRS need to decide how and at which point the different streams of evidence will inform their review. Where relevant, the authors need to develop a plan that outlines the different phases in their review as well as which particular approaches to synthesis will be considered in each phase. More information on the options for synthesis will be provided in Chapters 6–8.

ETHICS INVOLVED IN CONDUCTING MMRS LITERATURE REVIEWS

Many of the review questions we generate are somehow related to our personal interests and areas of expertise. Although reviews generally contribute to a better understanding of the sort of issues that are relevant to consider in developing our review question, logic model, or inclusion and exclusion criteria, they do not always spark the sort of ethical awareness about who should benefit from the review findings and how people might benefit from the review project conducted. The general idea that a review should directly be relevant and usable most likely has its roots in the idea that review authors should address the concerns of their target group and the end users of the review rather than serve their individual, often academic, interests. This is one of the main reasons why it is important to involve different types of stakeholders in your review team. Several authors have pleaded for a more transformative type of review in the recognition that an input from the target group in shaping review questions and in defining the boundaries of the review will address potential issues of inequality and injustice in society (e.g., Mertens, 2012; Sweetman, Badiee, & Creswell, 2010). As indicated by Mertens (2007), methodological inferences based on the underlying assumptions of the transformative paradigm reveal the potential strength of combining qualitative and quantitative strands of evidence. A qualitative dimension to a review is needed to gather community perspectives at each stage of the review process, whereas a quantitative dimension provides an opportunity to demonstrate pooled outcome measures that are somehow credible for the larger group of stakeholders targeted. Ideally, the participation of stakeholders in a review process also provides a mechanism for addressing the challenges involved in studying complex realities in culturally complex settings. In a best-case scenario, this provides a basis for social change.

Ethical awareness campaigns targeting review authors have focused on the important aspect of equity, referring to the idea that disadvantaged people might be put at further disadvantage due to a lack of sensitivity of review authors for the needs of these groups. They may neglect disadvantaged groups in the subgroups they propose, the sort of characteristics they ascribe to an intervention, and the application of the program they opt for in terms of acceptability for different target groups. Review authors can respond to this challenge by building several layers into the review protocol that can be considered proof for the project team's sensitivity to equity. In judging the relevance of particular studies for inclusion, review authors should remain sensitive to those who provide insights that are relevant and important for potential disadvantaged categories of people. Where appropriate, review authors can include a descriptive matrix outlining why, how, when, and under what circumstances particular aspects of their program or intervention with different target groups are likely to be successful, in addition to, or as an alternative for, a logic model underpinning their review. Where relevant, this may include a description of contextual factors or profiles that impact on the final outcomes or insights generated from the MMRS project. The following questions proposed by Janet Harris (2011), based on the advice of the Cochrane Health Equity Field, can help to define the population under review: (a) Is the population defined to include indicator(s) of disadvantage or status that are relevant to the review topic? (b) Is the population defined to include representatives from all groups who are eligible for the intervention?

Practical Tip 2.7: Progressing Equity in Literature Reviews

You might want to consider the PROGRESS acronym developed by Vivian Welch and colleagues (2013) to guide you in this process. It can assist you in defining your groups of interest and in identifying relevant subgroups or moderators in the context of developing your logic model. The mnemonic refers to place of residence (P), race/ ethnicity (R), occupation (O), gender (G), religion (R), education (E), socioeconomic status (S), and social capital (S). In addition to these eight components, the PLUS variant of the mnemonic includes some additional dimensions that could be important to look at, such as age, disability, sexual orientation, or in the context of health-care reviews, comorbidity (Welch et al., 2013). Bear in mind, though, that authors of original studies do not have the routine to report on the characteristics suggested by the PROGRESS acronym, which limits the opportunities for review authors to address equity issues on a meta-level.

The PROGRESS acronym was used in the review by Josephine Kavanagh and colleagues (2009) on school-based cognitive behavioral interventions as a theoretical lens focusing on differences between members of the target group that are perceived as unjust. The aim of their review was to increase what is known about promoting good mental health and mental health inequalities. It focused on the role of interventions based on the techniques of cognitive behavioral therapy (CBT) for preventing and reducing suicidality, depression, and anxiety in young people. A further aim of the review was to "use the systematic review as a case study to applying an 'equity lens' to a review topic" (Kavanagh et al., 2009, p. 15). The review authors presented two review questions: (a) Are secondary school-based mental health promotion interventions based on CBT techniques effective in preventing or alleviating depression, anxiety, and suicidality among young people? (b) To what extent do they reduce or increase inequalities in depression, anxiety, and suicidality experienced by some groups of young people? They conclude that only a few studies have provided useful data that might be used to examine the impact of CBT-based interventions on inequalities in mental health. None of the included original studies presented data relevant to evaluating the differential impact of interventions according to differences related to the PROGRESS acronym. None of the subgroup analyses in the original studies were on the basis of sociodemographic characteristics of the target group. As a consequence, the review authors pleaded for better reporting on these PROGRESS characteristics in the original studies. Noteworthy, they also pleaded for the involvement of young people in the design of the program to increase its appropriateness to young people. This suggests that the authors expected a benefit from including a qualitative evidence strand to the review to explore aspects of acceptability.

Ethical issues also arise once review authors arrive in the phase of trying to synthesize their findings. It is advisable to strive toward a social-cultural sensitivity approach in the interpretation of the findings.

ADVANTAGES AND PITFALLS
OF THE PREPARATORY PHASE

Overall, we highly recommend the development of an *a priori* protocol. Major advantages include the opportunity for review authors to consider the options available in each phase of the review and to strengthen the arguments on why a particular choice is made and how this choice further influences other decisions to be made. It provides clarity and transparency and facilitates further communication among members of the review team. Protocols are perceived and promoted as a useful tool to guide review teams to set the boundaries for a review and to facilitate an in-depth reflection about options available in each phase of a review process. Several databases provide access to published protocols. Examples include the Cochrane Library (http://www.cochranelibrary.com/), the Campbell Library (http://www.campbellcollaboration.org/lib/), and the Prospero protocol register (http://www.crd.york.ac.uk/PROSPERO/). Please check the major review organizations in your particular discipline and consult their databases for additional examples that may be relevant to you.

Review authors should bear in mind that MMRS can be very demanding in terms of building collective capacity and generating the necessary resources and manpower required to carry out the multiple steps that are involved in the review process. We suggest that review teams writing a proposal for an MMRS project think carefully about what they can deliver in terms of output and balance this carefully with the amount of funding requested. The scientific, policy, or practical importance (and, ideally, the symbiotic relation among the three) of the work should be considerable to motivate the rather extensive budget that may be necessary to complete the task successfully.

If you only have a limited timeframe available, you are advised to invest in the search for experts with the right topical expertise. These people may be able to provide a shortcut to scoping the literature. In discussing the best approach to reviewing the literature and deciding on the types of inquiries useful to explore a phenomenon, certain gaps in the expertise available may prompt you into recruiting additional experts. This will most likely prevent methodological discomfort from arising, but it may complicate the discussions about design options. It requires more time to learn and appreciate each other's jargon. Indeed, a strict compartmentalization of the roles and responsibilities of the review authors involved in the team based on methodological specialty may hinder rather than facilitate the integration of findings (Bryman, 2007).

In addition, predefined protocols may provide you with a sense of "security." They may risk contributing to the widespread illusion that there is a single methodological answer to combining quantitative and qualitative strands of evidence for every type of inquiry or every review phenomenon, or one optimal reality of conducting an MMRS. We already know that reviews can be fixed in nature (with methods predetermined at the start of the process and a clear intention to mix) or emergent (with methods decided on during the review process and embedded in a more iterative logic to reviewing that may or may not involve mixing). The limitation of developing an *a priori* protocol for the latter type of MMRS may lie in its inability to anticipate all the important decision points. These may shift, and some will only become fully relevant once the review project has started (Coemans et al., 2015). But even if the MMRS appears to have a fixed nature, the content of a protocol can most likely not be rigidly applied. Review authors should be open to (re)evaluate, adapt, and motivate their configurations of search and synthesis methods, techniques, and approaches based on opportunities that arise and new methodological insights that become available. It is appropriate to mention any deviations from the original protocol produced in your final MMRS.

Summary Points

- Review authors should have a clear rationale for conducting an MMRS.
- The successful accomplishment of an MMRS might be advanced by the establishment of a balanced team of methodological and topical experts.

- A scoping review should be considered to increase familiarity with the research literature on the topic of interest and inform the background and criteria for inclusion sections of the protocol.
- The lead review questions of an MMRS should inform the choice of the MMRS design, not the other way around.
- There are three major designs review authors could use as a framework: segregated, integrated, and contingent MMRS designs. The type of MMRS design selected should match the position of the review authors and should be clarified and justified in the protocol phase.
- Review authors should build several layers into the review protocol that show proof of their sensitivity to equity issues related to their target group.
- By using the standard template for a protocol introduced in this chapter, the review authors contribute to the transparent and uniform reporting of search procedures, inclusion criteria, critical appraisal of primary studies, data extraction, and synthesis in MMRS.
- Protocols for MMRS should not be considered rigid formats. MMRS projects require the flexibility to respond to review questions or issues that may emerge during the review process.

Questions for Thought

- Define your topic of interest. Why do you think a mixed method approach to synthesis would be beneficial for studying your phenomenon, and what arguments would you use?
- What do you consider the strengths and weaknesses of each of the MMRS designs introduced, and which one would you pick for your review?
- Think about the target group for your MMRS. Which disadvantaged populations should be included in your review, and what aspects of the PROGRESS equity mnemonic would be relevant to your MMRS project?
- Can you think of types of inquiries other than those presented in this chapter (Table 2.2) that are relevant to your field of interest and have not been discussed? Which ones? How would you operationalize them in terms of review questions?

Exercises

- Define your topic of interest, and outline what a quantitative and a qualitative synthesis could contribute to your understanding of the topic.
- Develop a series of review questions related to your topic of interest, and link them to the type of inquiries discussed in this chapter. For questions that do not fit the typology, develop an extra line of inquiry, put them in a "practical tip" box, and send it to the authors for future updates of the book.
- Prepare a template for your protocol, outlining the major sections. Check out some published review protocols within your area of interest to assist you in completing the task. Protocols are available in the Cochrane and Campbell libraries, as well as in the open access journal *Systematic Reviews*.
- Produce an outline of the ethical decisions that need to be made within your review team, prior to starting the review process.

Suggestions for Further Reading

Campbell Collaboration. (n.d.). *Guidelines for preparation of review protocols*. Retrieved from http://www.campbellcollaboration.org/artman2/uploads/1/C2_Protocols_guidelines_v1.pdf

Green, S., & Higgins, J. P. T. (2011). Chapter 2: Preparing a Cochrane review. In J. P. T. Higgins & S. Green (Eds.), *Cochrane handbook for systematic reviews of interventions Version 5.1.0* (updated March 2011). Retrieved from http://www.cochrane-handbook.org

Harris, J. (2011). Chapter 2: Using qualitative research to develop robust effectiveness questions and protocols for Cochrane systematic reviews. In J. Noyes, A. Booth, K. Hannes, A. Harden, J. Harris, S. Lewin, & C. Lockwood (Eds.), *Supplementary guidance for inclusion of qualitative research in Cochrane systematic reviews of interventions Version 1* (updated August 2011). Retrieved from http://cqrmg.cochrane.org/supplemental-handbook-guidance

Joanna Briggs Institute. (2011). *Joanna Briggs Institute reviewers' manual: 2011 edition*. The University of Adelaide, South Australia. Retrieved from http://joannabriggs.org/assets/docs/sumari/ReviewersManual-2011.pdf

Pluye, P., Hong, Q. N., & Vedel, I. (2013). *Toolkit for mixed studies reviews*. Retrieved from http://toolkit4mixedstudiesreviews.pbworks.com

Suri, H. (2008). Ethical considerations in synthesizing research. Whose representations? *Qualitative Research Journal, 8*, 63–73. doi:10.3316/QRJ0801062

References

Anderson, L. M., Petticrew, M., Rehfuess, E., Armstrong, R., Ueffing, E., Baker, P., . . . Tugwell, P. (2011). Using logic models to capture complexity in systematic reviews. *Research Synthesis Methods, 2*, 33–42. doi:10.1002/jrsm.32

Arksey, H., & O'Malley, L. (2005). Scoping studies: Towards a methodological framework. *International Journal of Social Research Methodology, 8*, 19–32. doi: 10.1080/1364557032000119616

Armstrong, R., Hall, B. J., Doyle, J., & Waters, E. (2011). "Scoping the scope" of a Cochrane review. *Journal of Public Health, 33*, 147–150. doi:10.1093/pubmed/fdr015

Brown, L., Macintyre, K., & Trujillo, L. (2003). Interventions to reduce HIV/AIDS stigma: What have we learned? *AIDS Education and Prevention, 15*, 49–69. doi:10.1521/aeap.15.1.49.23844

Bryman, A. (2007). Barriers to integrating quantitative and qualitative research. *Journal of Mixed Methods Research, 1*, 8–22. doi:10.1177/2345678906290531

Canadian Institutes of Health Research. (n.d.). *Knowledge translation*. Retrieved from http://www.cihr-irsc.gc.ca/e/29418.html

Coemans, S., Wang, Q., & Hannes, K. (2015). *The ultimate irony of developing an a priori, systematic review protocol for studying the literature on arts-based research methods in the area of community-based research.* Abstract for paper proposal for the 3th Conference on Arts-Based Research and Artistic Research, January 28–30, 2015, Porto, Portugal.

Coemans, S., Wang, Q., Leysen, J., & Hannes, K. (2015). The use of arts-based methods in community-based research with vulnerable populations: Protocol for a scoping review. *International Journal of Educational Research, 71*, 33–39.

Creswell, J. W. (2003). *Research design: Qualitative, quantitative, and mixed methods approaches* (2nd ed.). Thousand Oaks, CA: Sage.

Creswell, J. W., Klassen, A. C., Plano Clark, V. L., & Smith, K. C., for the Office of Behavioral and Social Sciences Research. (2011). *Best practices for mixed methods research in the health sciences.* National Institutes of Health. Retrieved from http://obssr.od.nih.gov/mixed_methods_research

Creswell, J. W., & Plano Clark, V. L. (2007). *Designing and conducting mixed methods research.* Thousand Oaks, CA: Sage.

Daudt, H. M., van Mossel, C., & Scott, S. J. (2013). Enhancing the scoping study methodology: A large, inter-professional team's experience with Arksey and O'Malley's framework. *BMC Medical Research Methodology, 13*, 48. doi:10.1186/1471-2288-13-48

Depaepe, F., Verschaffel, L., & Kelchtermans, G. (2013). Pedagogical content knowledge: A systematic review of the way in which the concept has pervaded mathematics educational research. *Teaching and Teacher Education, 34*, 12–25. doi:10.1016/j.tate.2013.03.001

Greene, J. C., Caracelli, V. J., & Graham, W. F. (1989). Toward a conceptual framework for mixed-method evaluation designs. *Educational Evaluation and Policy Analysis, 11*, 255–274. doi:10.3102/01623737011003255

Hannes, K. (2015). Building a case for mixed method reviews. In D. Richards & I. Hallberg (Eds.), *Complex interventions in health: An overview of research methods.* Oxon, England: Routledge.

Hannes, K., & Aertgeerts, B. (2014). Review projects should reveal the reviewers' rationale to opt for particular quality assessment criteria. *Academic Medicine, 89*, 370–370.

Hannes, K., Booth, A., Harris, J., & Noyes, J. (2013). Celebrating methodological challenges and changes: Reflecting on the emergence and importance of the role of qualitative evidence in Cochrane reviews. *Systematic Reviews, 2*, 84. doi: 10.1186/2046-4053-2-84

Hannes, K., Raes, E., Vangenechten, K., Heyvaert, M., & Dochy, F. (2013). Experiences from employees with team learning in a vocational learning or work setting: A systematic review of qualitative evidence. *Educational Research Review, 10*, 116–132. doi:10.1016/j.edurev.2013.10.002

Harris, J. (2011). Chapter 2: Using qualitative research to develop robust effectiveness questions and protocols for Cochrane systematic reviews. In J. Noyes, A. Booth, K. Hannes, A. Harden, J. Harris, S. Lewin, & C. Lockwood (Eds.), *Supplementary guidance for inclusion of qualitative research in Cochrane systematic reviews of interventions. Version 1* (updated August 2011). Retrieved from http://cqrmg .cochrane.org/supplemental-handbook-guidance

Heyvaert, M., Maes, B., & Onghena, P. (2013). Mixed methods research synthesis: Definition, framework, and potential. *Quality & Quantity, 47*, 659–676. doi:10.1007/s11135-011-9538-6

Heyvaert, M., Saenen, L., Maes, B., & Onghena, P. (2014). Systematic review of restraint interventions for challenging behaviour among persons with intellectual disabilities: Focus on effectiveness in single-case experiments. *Journal of Applied Research in Intellectual Disabilities, 27*, 493–590. doi:10.1111/jar.12094

Heyvaert, M., Saenen, L., Maes, B., & Onghena, P. (2015). Systematic review of restraint interventions for challenging behaviour among persons with intellectual disabilities: Focus on experiences. *Journal of Applied Research in Intellectual Disabilities, 28*, 61–80. doi:10.1111/jar.12095

Higgins, J. P. T., & Green, S. (2011). *Cochrane handbook for systematic reviews of interventions Version 5.1.0* (updated March 2011). Retrieved from http:// www .cochrane-handbook.org

Hurley, M., Dickson, K., Walsh, N., Hauari, H., Grant, R., Cumming, J., & Oliver, S. (2013). Exercise interventions and patient beliefs for people with chronic hip and knee pain: A mixed methods review. *Cochrane Database of Systematic Reviews, 12*. doi:10.1002/14651858.CD010842

Joanna Briggs Institute. (2008). *Reviewers' manual.* Adelaide, Australia: Author.

Johnson, R. B., & Onwuegbuzie, A. J. (2004). Mixed methods research: A research paradigm whose time has come. *Educational Researcher, 33*, 14–26. doi: 10.3102/0013189X033007014

Kavanagh, J., Oliver, S., Caird, J., Tucker, H., Greaves, A., Harden, A., . . . Thomas, J. (2009). *Inequalities and the mental health of young people: A systematic review of secondary school-based cognitive behavioural interventions.* London, England: EPPI-Centre.

Leech, N. L., & Onwuegbuzie, A. J. (2009). A typology of mixed methods research designs. *Quality & Quantity, 43*, 265–275. doi:10.1007/s11135-007-9105-3

Levac, D., Colquhoun, H., & O'Brien, K. K. (2010). Scoping studies: Advancing the methodology. *Implementation Science, 5*, 69. doi:10.1186/1748-5908-5-69

Mertens, D. M. (2005). *Research and evaluation in education and psychology: Integrating diversity with quantitative, qualitative, and mixed methods* (2nd ed.). Thousand Oaks, CA: Sage.

Mertens, D. M. (2007). Transformative paradigm, mixed methods and social justice. *Journal of Mixed Methods Research, 1*, 212–215. doi:10.1177/1558689807302811

Mertens, D. M. (2012). Transformative mixed methods addressing inequities. *American Behavioral Scientist, 56*, 802–813. doi:10.1177/0002764211433797

Morgan, D. L. (1998). Practical strategies for combining qualitative and quantitative methods: Applications to health research. *Qualitative Health Research, 8*, 362–376. doi:10.1177/104973239800800307

Morse, J. M. (1991). Approaches to qualitative-quantitative methodological triangulation. *Nursing Research, 40*, 120–123.

Oliver, S., Dickson, K., & Newman, M. (2012). Getting started with a review. In D. Gough, S. Oliver, & J. Thomas (Eds.), *An introduction to systematic reviews* (pp. 66–83). London, England: Sage.

Paterson, B. L., Thorne, S. E., Canam, C., & Jillings, C. (2001). *Meta-study of qualitative health research: A practical guide to meta-analysis and meta-synthesis.* Thousand Oaks, CA: Sage.

Pearson, A., Wiechula, R., Court, A., & Lockwood, C. (2005). The JBI model of evidence-based healthcare. *International Journal of Evidence-Based Healthcare, 2*, 207–215. doi:10.1111/j.1479-6988.2005.00026.x

Pluye, P., & Hong, Q. N. (2014). Combining the power of stories and numbers: Mixed methods research and mixed studies reviews. *Annual Review in Public Health, 35*, 29–45.

Sandelowski, M., Voils, C. I., & Barroso, J. (2006). Defining and designing mixed research synthesis studies. *Research in the Schools, 13*, 29–40.

Sandelowski, M., Voils, C. I., & Knafl, G. (2009). On quantitizing. *Journal of Mixed Methods Research, 3*, 208–222. doi:10.1177/1558689809334210

Sweetman, D., Badiee, M., & Creswell, J. W. (2010). Use of the transformative framework in mixed methods studies. *Qualitative Inquiry, 16*, 441–454. doi: 10.1177/1077800410364610

Tashakkori, A., & Creswell, J. W. (2007). The new era of mixed methods. *Journal of Mixed Methods Research, 1*, 3–7. doi:10.1177/2345678906293042

Tashakkori, A., & Teddlie, C. (1998). *Mixed methodology: Combining qualitative and quantitative approaches.* Thousand Oaks, CA: Sage.

Tashakkori, A., & Teddlie, C. (Eds.). (2010). *Handbook of mixed methods in social and behavioral research* (2nd ed.). Thousand Oaks, CA: Sage.

Teddlie, C., & Tashakkori, A. (2009). *The foundations of mixed method research: Integrating quantitative and qualitative techniques in the social and behavioral sciences.* Thousand Oaks, CA: Sage.

Thapa, S., Hannes, K., Cargo, M., Buvé, A., & Matthei, C. (2015). Effect of stigma reduction intervention strategies on HIV test-uptake in low and middle-income countries: A realist review protocol. *Systematic Reviews, 4*(142), 1–7. doi:10.1186/s13643-015-0130-3

van Nuland, M., Hannes, K., Aertgeerts, B., & Goedhuys, J. (2005). Educational interventions for improving the communication skills of general practice trainees in the clinical consultation (Protocol). *Cochrane Database of Systematic Reviews, 4.* doi:10.1002/14651858.CD005559

Welch, V. A., Petticrew, M., O'Neill, J., Waters, E., Armstrong, R., Bhutta, Z. A., . . . Tugwell, P. (2013). Health equity: Evidence synthesis and knowledge translation methods. *Systematic Reviews, 2.* doi:10.1186/2046-4053-2-43

Whitaker, R. H., Hendry, M., Booth, A., Carter, B., Charles, J., Craine, N., . . . Williams, N. (2014). Intervention Now To Eliminate Repeat Unintended Pregnancy in Teenagers (INTERUPT): A systematic review of intervention effectiveness and cost-effectiveness, qualitative and realist synthesis of implementation factors and user engagement. *BMJ Open, 4.* doi:10.1136/bmjopen-2013-004733

Zief, S. G., Lauver, S., & Maynard, R. A. (2006). Impacts of after-school programs on student outcomes. *Campbell Systematic Reviews, 3.* doi:10.4073/csr.2006.3

⊰ 3 ⊱

SEARCHING FOR
RELEVANT STUDIES

══════════════════ ⭗ ══════════════════

Chapter Outline

After formulating the review question(s) and developing the review protocol, you can start your search for relevant studies to be included in the MMRS. In this chapter, we will first discuss the search process. We will describe several sampling strategies for MMRS literature reviews and various strategies for searching primary-level studies to be included in an MMRS literature review. Second, we will discuss how you can develop and apply inclusion and exclusion criteria. Third, we will discuss how the search process and results can be documented and reported.

══════════════════ ⭗ ══════════════════

SEARCH PROCESS

After formulating the review question(s) and writing the review protocol (see Chapter 2), the next step in the MMRS process is to search for studies to be included in the literature review, in accordance with the strategy that is described in the review protocol. The aim of the search process is to generate a list of primary-level studies that may be relevant for answering the MMRS review question(s). It is important to conduct this search process in a transparent way. The notion of **transparency** relates to the replicability of the search process. For the search process to be replicable, you have to be transparent about the sampling strategy you used, which resources you searched and all the details of the conducted searches (e.g., which electronic databases were searched and how these databases were searched), the number of publications you retrieved for each resource, the inclusion and exclusion criteria you used, and the number of studies you included and excluded, along with the reasons for exclusion, in every screening stage. Second, you have to be transparent about the rationale or the motivations behind your decisions, and what the implications are of your decisions (e.g., which types of bias were introduced, as we will discuss further in this chapter) in the MMRS report.

Using Separate Searches for the Separate Strands of the MMRS

Depending on the topic and goal of the MMRS and the selected MMRS design (see Chapter 2), you have to decide whether the search strategies you develop should be different for the separate strands of evidence of the MMRS. One option is that the MMRS involves one overall data collection phase covering all strands. In that case, a broad search strategy encompasses many different study designs and is aimed at retrieving primary-level quantitative, qualitative, and possibly mixed methods studies.

The other option is that the MMRS involves separate searches for the separate strands. An argument in favor of the latter approach could be that the goals of the qualitative and quantitative strand of the MMRS are so different that they warrant different search strategies. We discuss three possible examples of MMRS involving separate searches for the separate strands.

A first example is an MMRS with different sampling strategies for the separate strands. For instance, an exhaustive search strategy could be selected to retrieve quantitative evidence and a purposeful sampling strategy for retrieving qualitative evidence (see the next section for a discussion of sampling strategies). In this case, the search and screening stages would be conducted separately for the qualitative and quantitative strands of the MMRS.

A second example of an MMRS with separate searches for the separate strands is an MMRS involving different methodological filters for the separate strands. Methodological filters can be used when you only want to retrieve studies with certain designs or studies that use certain methodologies to be included in the MMRS (this will be discussed further in this chapter). For the qualitative strand of such an MMRS, other methodological filters would of course be used than for the quantitative strand of the MMRS.

A third example of an MMRS with separate searches for the separate strands is an MMRS with different resources that are searched in the separate strands. Possible resources that can be searched to find studies relevant to be included in an MMRS are, for instance, bibliographic databases, gray literature databases (i.e., databases containing literature that is not formally published in sources such as books or journal articles; please note that it is "gray" in American English spelling and "grey" in British English spelling; Lefebvre, Manheimer, & Glanville, 2011), relevant journals, reference lists, and citation indexes, as well as contacting experts and authors of primary articles. It is possible that some types of studies, for instance, certain qualitative studies, are not easily retrievable through consulting these regular resources, and that alternative search options have to be consulted (examples will be provided further in this chapter). On the other hand, it is also possible that the quantitative strand would lead to the consultation of other search resources, such as randomized controlled trials registers (e.g., for an MMRS in the health sciences).

In the remainder of this chapter, we will discuss the various elements involved in the process of searching for primary studies. These elements apply to MMRS with an overall data collection phase covering all strands, as well as to MMRS with separate searches for the separate strands.

Sampling Strategy: Exhaustive, Selective, or Purposeful

The sampling units of an MMRS literature review are primary-level studies, and the data included in the MMRS are the data reported in these primary studies. With respect to the way in which the primary-level studies can be sampled for an MMRS literature review, three types of sampling strategies can be distinguished: exhaustive, selective, and purposeful sampling (Booth, 2006). The selective sampling strategy can be considered a variant of the exhaustive sampling strategy. Purposeful sampling strategies follow a different logic than the exhaustive and selective sampling strategies. The sampling strategy should be selected in accordance with the topic and purpose of the MMRS. In the following sections, we describe why you could select an exhaustive, a selective, or a purposeful sampling strategy for your MMRS.

Exhaustive sampling strategy. When collecting studies to be included in your MMRS literature review, you will search for primary quantitative, qualitative, and mixed methods studies that can provide an answer to your review question(s). An **exhaustive** or **comprehensive sampling strategy** is a strategy aiming at identifying *all* relevant studies on the topic or phenomenon of interest. The rationale behind selecting an exhaustive sampling strategy is that you want to limit the risk of biases such as publication bias and location bias (this will be discussed further in this chapter). Several resources can be interrogated during the exhaustive search process, such as bibliographic databases, gray literature databases, relevant journals, reference lists, citation indexes, and experts and authors of primary articles.

Figure 3.1 presents a possible outline of an exhaustive search process for an MMRS. Most review authors start searching for primary studies by consulting bibliographic and gray literature databases. Bibliographic databases contain records of journal articles. **Gray literature** or fugitive literature is literature "produced on all levels of government, academics, business and industry in electronic and print formats not controlled by commercial publishers (i.e., where publishing is not the primary activity of the producing body)" (Farace, Frantzen, Schöpfel, Stock, & Boekhorst, 2006, p. 74), and it can be retrieved by consulting gray literature databases (examples of gray literature databases will be provided further in this chapter). You can use reference management software to save the search results and remove duplicates from the search. After having removed the duplicates, you can determine how many unique primary-level publications you retrieved. A first screening can be done based on the titles and abstracts of all retrieved publications. Publications that are clearly irrelevant to answer the posed review question are excluded. For the publications that might be relevant to answer the review question, full texts should be retrieved and screened. In addition to searching bibliographic databases and gray literature databases, you can, for instance, search relevant journals, search reference lists, search citation indexes, and contact experts and authors of original articles for additional studies that might be relevant to answer your review question. Then the final screening can be conducted. For the final screening, you use a formal in/exclusion form to determine which studies you will ultimately include in the MMRS. In the remainder of this chapter, we will provide more information and practical guidance on every step of the search process.

Several scholars and organizations plead for exhaustive sampling strategies. They argue that comprehensive strategies are essential to draw together all available knowledge on a topic area and that comprehensive strategies enhance the overall quality of literature reviews (Grant & Booth, 2009). However, other scholars question the cost–benefit balance of exhaustive searches: How efficient are exhaustive searches in use of time and funds?

Figure 3.1 Possible Outline of an Exhaustive Search Process

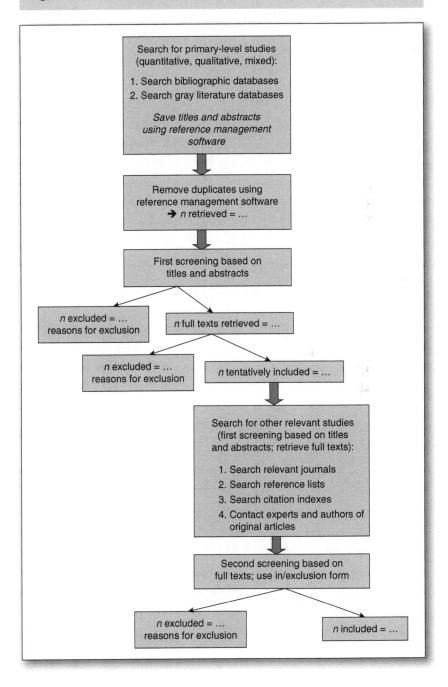

They raise the following questions: What is the most appropriate action after the point of diminishing returns is reached? Should you proceed with the search process, or can the process be terminated earlier? The latter group of scholars might prefer to use selective or purposeful sampling strategies over exhaustive sampling strategies.

Selective sampling strategy. An alternative to the exhaustive search strategy is the **selective sampling strategy**. You can choose this strategy when you want to consult only a limited number of resources or to identify all relevant studies but only within specified limits (Booth, 2006). Figure 3.1 contains six different resources for searching studies that can be included in an MMRS: bibliographic databases, gray literature databases, journals, reference lists, citation indexes, and contacting experts and authors for unpublished data. However, not all MMRS are this comprehensive and use these six resources. How many (and which specific) resources you decide to search and the limits to the search (e.g., time frame for the search and language of the research reports) might depend on substantive and sometimes on pragmatic issues.

An example of a substantive reason for applying a selective sampling strategy is when you are conducting an MMRS on a certain intervention, but that intervention only started to be used at a certain moment in time (e.g., 1995). Accordingly, you are only interested in studies published from 1995 onward and can decide to limit the time frame for the search based on this theoretical argument. Another example of a substantive reason for applying a selective sampling strategy is when you are conducting an MMRS that aims to be generalized only to a selective context. In that case, you can narrow the search in terms of geographical context and setting to ensure that the evidence could be readily applied to the context of interest and that the provided lines of actions or theories are sensitive to the local setting (e.g., Hannes & Harden, 2011).

Furthermore, the search can also be narrowed based on pragmatic reasons. For instance, due to time management reasons or because of the urgency of a project, review authors sometimes decide to only search bibliographic databases and relevant journals. Such literature reviews in which only a limited number of resources are searched are called **rapid reviews**. A rapid MMRS literature review can, for instance, be conducted for government decision makers or institutions that request evidence to be delivered in shortened timeframes (Ganann, Ciliska, & Thomas, 2010).

Figure 3.2 presents a possible outline of a selective search process for an MMRS. In this example, the MMRS review authors only searched bibliographic databases. They used reference management software to save the search results and removed duplicates from the search. After having removed the duplicates, they determined how many unique primary-level publications they retrieved. A first screening was done based on the titles and abstracts of the retrieved publications. Publications that were clearly irrelevant to answer the review question were excluded. For the publications that might be relevant to answer the review question, full texts were retrieved and screened using a formal in/exclusion form.

Figure 3.2 Possible Outline of a Selective Search Process

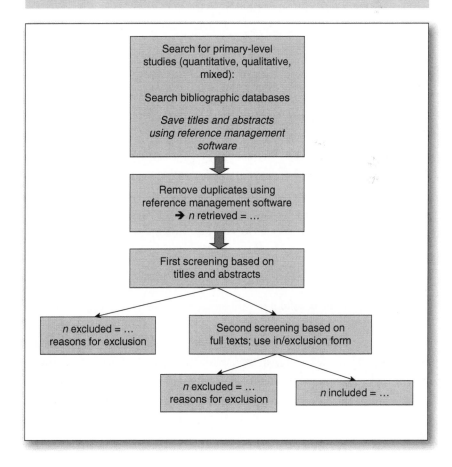

Selective sampling strategies are sometimes considered an unwelcome concession to the need for evidence-based decisions within a policy maker's time frame: When there is not enough time to conduct an exhaustive search, MMRS review authors can conduct a selective search (Grant & Booth, 2009). We want to stress that review authors using selective sampling strategies should aim to be rigorous and explicit in the search methods used, and although they perhaps make concessions to the breadth or depth of the search process, they should explicitly report the likely effect of these concessions (Butler, Deaton, Hodgkinson, Holmes, & Marshall, 2005). The most important disadvantage of using a selective sampling strategy is the risk of introducing biases such as publication bias and location bias (this will be discussed further in this chapter). Accordingly, in case you use a selective sampling strategy, we advise you to document the search methodology carefully and highlight which limitations and potential biases were introduced to the MMRS (Grant & Booth, 2009).

Purposeful sampling strategy. A third sampling strategy for MMRS literature reviews is the **purposeful sampling strategy**. In contrast to the exhaustive strategy that aims to collect *all* relevant studies, and the selective strategy that aims to identify *all* relevant studies within specified limits, the purposeful strategy aims to find information-rich studies that will provide an answer to the posed review question(s). In case you select a purposeful sampling strategy for your MMRS, you have to consider which specific purposeful sampling strategy (or combination of strategies) optimally fits your MMRS's topic and purpose. In Table 3.1, we provide an overview of the most often used purposeful sampling strategies for MMRS. This table is based on the work of Harsh Suri (2011), who examined the adaptability of Michael Patton's (1990) framework for primary-level purposeful sampling strategies to the literature review level.

Figure 3.3 presents a possible outline of a purposeful search process for an MMRS. All decisions relating to the purposeful search process should correspond to the purpose of the MMRS, the topic of the MMRS, and the (preliminary) review questions. Based on the purpose, topic, and posed review questions, you should consider which resources can best be searched for achieving your MMRS's purpose, for instance, whether databases, journals, and/or experts should be consulted, and which specific databases, journals, and/or experts should be consulted. When consulting these resources, you can select key papers: papers that are highly relevant to answering the posed review questions. By starting from these key papers, you can search for additional papers that are relevant to the MMRS, for instance, by (a) scrutinizing

Table 3.1 Purposeful Sampling Strategies for Research Syntheses (based on Suri, 2011)

Purposeful sampling strategy	Description
Deviant/ extreme sampling	**Aim:** To select *illuminative* primary studies + Learn from highly unusual manifestations of the phenomenon of interest (e.g., outstanding successes, notable failures) – Not for generalizability purposes **Example:** An MMRS to investigate how a program is likely to work under particular circumstances by examining primary studies on very successful as well as unsuccessful implementations of the program
Maximum variation/ heterogeneous sampling	**Aim:** To identify key dimensions and select studies that vary from each other as much as possible + To document diverse variations; to identify essential features (i.e., common patterns that appear across variations) and variable features of a phenomenon as experienced by diverse stakeholders among various contexts to facilitate informed global decision making **Example:** An MMRS that aims to construct a holistic understanding of the phenomenon *collaborative learning curricula* by synthesizing primary studies on this phenomenon that differ in their study designs on several dimensions
Homogeneous sampling	**Aim:** To select studies that are relatively homogeneous in their study design and conceptual scope; describe a homogenous subgroup of studies in depth + Reduces variation; simplifies analysis and facilitates meaningful comparisons over studies; not *mixing apples and oranges* **Example:** A group of secondary math teachers intending to introduce collaborative learning activities into their classroom might benefit more from together conducting an MMRS on collaborative learning research in secondary math rather than an MMRS on collaborative learning research across all grade levels and different disciplines
Typical study sampling	**Aim:** To illustrate or highlight what is typical (normal, average) to readers unfamiliar with the phenomenon or setting; to attempt to gain consensus about which studies are typical and which

(Continued)

Table 3.1   (Continued)

Purposeful sampling strategy	Description
	criteria are being used to define *typicality* (e.g., describe typical methodologies and study designs employed to examine the phenomenon) **Example:** Review authors could select typical primary studies employed in a research field of interest with the cooperation of key researchers in the field to describe typical methodologies and study designs employed to examine the phenomenon of interest, in order to study how common themes recurring in the published literature might be related to the relative strengths and weaknesses of the typical methodologies or theories underpinning the typical studies
Critical study sampling	**Aim:** To select studies based on the premise: *"If it happens there, it will happen anywhere"* or *"If it does not happen there, it won't happen anywhere"* + For logical generalization purposes **Example:** An MMRS on a program that produces desirable outcomes, but is being rejected by many practitioners as they believe that its implementation requires substantial resources. An MMRS of primary studies that describe in detail successful implementation of the innovation with minimal resources might be useful to alleviate the practitioners' resistance toward the innovation.
Snowball/chain sampling	**Aim:** To identify relevant studies by starting with a few relevant publications (i.e., *key informant publications*) and then tracing other relevant publications by searching the reference lists of the key publications (discussed further in this chapter) and looking at who cited these key publications (discussed further in this chapter) + To locate a specific population of primary studies – Might result in a rather homogeneous pool of included publications; the *key informant publications* might have a strong impact on the final sample; the final sample might not be representative for the target population of primary studies (e.g., the final sample actually represents only a small subgroup of the target population of primary studies)

Purposeful sampling strategy	Description
	Example: A student conducting an MMRS can start reading the relevant publications that were passed on by the supervisor. Afterward, the student can locate other relevant studies on the topic of interest by searching the reference lists of these publications. Finally, the student can search for additional relevant studies by looking at who cited the already retrieved relevant publications.
Criterion sampling	**Aim:** To include all studies that meet a predetermined criterion of importance, for instances relating to methodological rigor + Exclude methodologically weak studies to avoid that the MMRS's findings are based on questionable evidence − Very strict criteria for methodological rigor can result in inclusion of such a small number of studies that the transferability of synthesis' findings becomes questionable **Example:** An MMRS that only includes the primary studies on the topic of interest that achieved a high- to very high-quality score, and excludes primary studies with low and questionable methodological rigor according to the quality scale used
Theory-based/ theoretical/ operational construct sampling	***Theory-based/Theoretical sampling*: Aim:** To include studies that represent important theoretical constructs about the phenomenon ***Operational construct sampling*: Aim:** To include studies that represent real-world (i.e., operational) examples of the concept(s) of interest **Example:** An MMRS for which operational definitions of the key constructs about the phenomenon of interest have been set forth. The boundaries of these operational definitions are further articulated by explicitly stating in/exclusion criteria in relation to selecting primary studies.
Confirming and disconfirming studies	***Confirming studies:* Aim:** To find additional examples that fit already emergent patterns; these studies validate, confirm, and elaborate the findings, and add richness, depth, and credibility **Example:** MMRS review authors may seek confirming primary studies to validate the perceptions of a particular group of marginalized stakeholders

(Continued)

Table 3.1 (Continued)

Purposeful sampling strategy	Description
	Disconfirming studies: **Aim:** To seek exceptions to deepen initial analysis and test variation; these studies are sources of rival interpretations and place boundaries around confirmed findings **Example:** MMRS review authors may seek disconfirming studies to shake complacent acceptance of popular generalizations in a research field
Sampling politically important studies	**Aim:** To select (or sometimes avoid) politically sensitive studies to attract attention to and increase the impact of the MMRS **Example:** In a synthesis of key criticisms of educational research published in the 1990s, Alis Oancea (2005) illustrated her key observations through a detailed analysis of three politically important documents that were frequently cited in the newspapers, so that the synthesis gained the attention of different stakeholders and the synthesis's findings got often used
Convenience sampling	**Aim:** To include studies that can easily be accessed + Saves time, money, and effort − Poorest rationale; lowest credibility; yields an information-poor sample **Example:** An MMRS in which only studies and reports that are easy to access, that can be read free of charge, and that are written in the mother tongue of the review authors are included
Combination/ mixed purposeful sampling	**Aim:** To combine several purposeful sampling strategies to answer multiple interests and needs (based on purposes of the MMRS); review authors using a combination of sampling strategies should report on how those strategies complement each other + Triangulation; flexibility in meeting the needs of multiple stakeholders **Example:** Review authors may use snowball sampling to retrieve relevant primary studies to be included in the MMRS, but additionally may use typical study sampling to provide their readers with an immediacy of typical studies that contributed toward informing the more abstract findings of the MMRS

Source: Adapted from Suri, H. (2011). Purposeful sampling in qualitative research synthesis. *Qualitative Research Journal, 11*, 63–75. doi:10.3316/QRJ1102063.
Notes: + Advantage of this sampling strategy; − Disadvantage of this sampling strategy.

the reference lists of the key papers, (b) consulting citation indexes to see which papers cited the key papers, and (c) searching for additional published and unpublished work from the authors of the key papers. Based on the set of key papers, complemented by the papers that were additionally found through (a), (b), and (c), you can compile the final set of relevant studies that will be included in the MMRS.

In contrast to Figures 3.1 (exhaustive search process) and 3.2 (selective search process), where a linear search process is depicted, the process depicted in Figure 3.3 for the purposeful search process is more dynamic and iterative, involving processes of *reconsidering* and *going back*. The bold dashed lines in Figure 3.3 refer to these processes of *reconsidering* and *going back*. It implies that the preliminary review questions that were posed at the beginning of the search process are not necessarily the final review questions that will be answered by the MMRS. The posed review questions might be reformulated or adapted based on the resources that were consulted, the key papers that were selected, and the final set of studies that was compiled (see Figure 3.3).

Figure 3.3 Possible Outline of a Purposeful Search Process

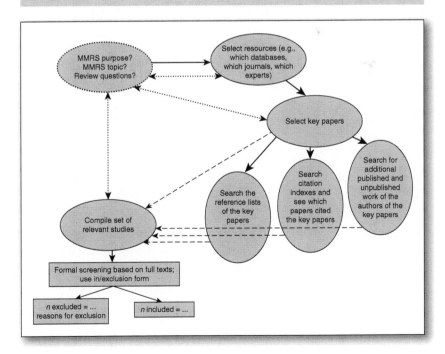

This contrasts with exhaustive and selective search processes, where the MMRS review questions are not reformulated or adapted based on the search process.

The most important question you have to ask yourself in order to determine which sampling strategy you have to select for your MMRS relates to the purpose of the MMRS (see Chapter 2). You should select a sampling strategy that is conceptually aligned with the purpose of your MMRS: a sampling strategy that credibly and sufficiently addresses the purpose of your MMRS (Kemper, Stringfield, & Teddlie, 2003). For instance, whereas the exhaustive sampling strategy aims to collect all relevant studies in order to allow broad empirical generalizations, the purposeful sampling strategy aims to find information-rich studies that will yield insights and in-depth understanding of the phenomenon of interest.

For exhaustive, selective, and purposeful searches, the decision associated with enacting closure to the search process is guided by the purpose of the MMRS. For instance, the purpose of an exhaustive sampling strategy is **comprehensiveness**. Accordingly, when conducting an exhaustive search for an MMRS, the data collection stops when all the resources that were decided on in advance (see *review protocol* discussed in Chapter 2) are searched. For purposeful searches, the data saturation logic or the data sufficiency logic can be used for guiding decisions related to enacting closure when searching for relevant primary-level studies to be included in the MMRS (Suri, 2011). The **data saturation logic** refers to the logic that the data collection stops when a saturation point is reached. As the search process goes on, the inclusion of more studies does not necessarily lead to additional insights related to the topic of interest, and it does not necessarily lead to a more accurate answer to the review question(s). The **data sufficiency logic** is a bit more contested by the literature review community. The data sufficiency logic says that *true data saturation* is only very rarely reached in literature review projects. The data sufficiency logic argues that the review authors themselves should decide and justify what constitutes sufficient evidence for achieving the purpose of their literature review (Suri, 2011). For instance, criteria that can be used for data sufficiency decisions are as follows: (a) Were sufficient data collected to answer the review question? (b) Were sufficient data collected to permit comparisons among selected dimensions and constructs? (c) Do the included reports reflect the work of several distinct and independent investigators? (Paterson, Thorne, Canam, & Jillings, 2001, p. 37).

Planning the Search and Managing the Resources

We advise you to plan carefully and document the search process, whether you decide to conduct an exhaustive, a selective, or a purposeful search for your MMRS. In Practical Tip 3.1, we provide helpful suggestions for planning the search process.

Before you start the search process, you have to consider how you will store and save the search results. When searching bibliographic and gray literature databases, the use of **reference management software** can be both work and time efficient. Examples of free reference management software are EndNote Basic, Zotero, and Mendeley. Examples of commercial reference management software are EndNote, Reference Manager, RefWorks, and Review Manager. The software can help to save the references, titles, and abstracts from the retrieved publications. By using them, you can electronically collect, organize, and manage the references.

Reference management software allows you to export directly the retrieved references, titles, and abstracts from bibliographic and gray literature databases, as well as to merge all the records retrieved. Working in a team on an MMRS, you can use the software to share references of retrieved publications. A final advantage is that the software provides the opportunity to identify and remove duplicates easily from a search. Because of the high overlap between bibliographic databases (overlap estimates range between 8%

Practical Tip 3.1: Planning the Search

You can consult a librarian or an information specialist affiliated to your institution to develop an optimal search strategy for your MMRS. These persons are trained in the efficient retrieval of information, have a wide knowledge of information resources and of how to locate information services, and will be able to help with document acquisition and record management (Harris, 2005; University of York, 2014). If you want to develop and conduct the search all by yourself, you need to make sure that you are sufficiently familiar with the resources you will consult, so that you can plan to search those resources that are most appropriate to your MMRS (Dundar & Fleeman, 2014).

and 60%), software programs are invaluable in the production of a large-scale MMRS (Lorenzetti & Ghali, 2013). However, some duplicates might be missed by the software because of minor differences in how a reference is indexed in different databases (Dundar & Fleeman, 2014). So, after using the software to remove duplicates, you may have to remove some remaining duplicates manually. After removing duplicates, you can see the number of unique publications that were retrieved (see Figures 3.1–3.3).

Minimizing Bias in the Search Results

Biases in search results refer to the unplanned and unintentional exclusion of primary-level evidence, which might distort the findings of literature reviews. Review authors conducting an exhaustive MMRS are particularly focused on the question of how different types of bias might affect their conclusions. There are several potential types of bias you can consider when designing and conducting an MMRS. Biases may influence which studies will be retrieved and included, thereby compromising the validity of the MMRS. In the remainder of this section, we will discuss potential types of bias and strategies that you can use to minimize bias in your search results.

A first potential source of bias is **publication bias**. It refers to the tendency for authors to submit, and for journals to accept, manuscripts for publication based on the direction, magnitude, or significance of the study findings (Hopewell, Loudon, Clarke, Oxman, & Dickersin, 2009). Basically, the issue under consideration is whether the retrieved studies are representative of all studies conducted on the topic (Dundar & Fleeman, 2014). For MMRS literature reviews of intervention or evaluation studies, published studies are more likely to report on positive effects of the studied intervention and statistically significant results than nonpublished studies. Statistically significant negative studies or null results studies are more likely not to be submitted and published. As such, publication bias can lead to an overestimation of treatment effects. Qualitative studies that do not show clear, striking, or easily described findings also have a smaller chance of getting published (Petticrew et al., 2008). The main implication is that an MMRS may be biased if it only relies on published papers. To minimize the problem of publication bias, you can conduct a search for published as well as unpublished papers. More precisely, to minimize the problem of publication bias we advise you to not only search bibliographic databases for published papers but also search gray literature databases, journals, conference proceedings, reference lists, and citation indexes, and/or to contact experts and authors for unpublished data.

A second potential source of bias is **location bias**. It implies that studies are sometimes published in journals that are not indexed in bibliographic databases and therefore may not be identified by the search (Dundar & Fleeman, 2014). To minimize this source of bias, you can use a search strategy that includes more than bibliographic databases alone. For instance, you can additionally search relevant gray literature databases and hand-search relevant journals.

A third source of bias is **multiple publication bias**. It implies that interesting, controversial, or intriguing results are likely to be repeatedly reported in several publications (Egger & Smith, 1998). This type of bias can occur even after removing exact duplicates from the search using reference management software. Using the software can only help to determine how many unique *publications* were retrieved by the search. The issue of multiple publication bias refers to unique *studies*. Because each study may have been reported in several articles and reports, the search process may identify several publications relating to the same study (Higgins & Deeks, 2011). The *study* itself, and not the publication, is the unit of interest for an MMRS. Multiple publications on a single study should be linked together, and each study should only be included once in the MMRS. You can verify that multiple abstracts, articles, or reports refer to the same study by looking at the authors, the location and setting of the study, the details of the study design, and the number of participants included in the study. Box 3.1 includes an example of how you can report on multiple publication bias.

Searching Bibliographic Databases

The most commonly searched resources for conducting MMRS literature reviews are bibliographic databases, containing records of journal articles. The records minimally include the title and author(s) of the article, the source, and the publication date. In addition, an abstract is often included, along with keywords. First, you will have to decide which databases you will consult. Second, you will have to find out how to navigate the different databases efficiently.

Box 3.1   Multiple Publication Bias

The *study* itself, and not the publication, is the unit of interest for an MMRS. Sometimes the same idea or the same empirical data set is described in several publications. It is important to include each idea or empirical data set only once in the final data set.

Here is an example of how you can report on multiple publication bias in an MMRS report (based on Heyvaert, Hannes, Maes, & Onghena, 2013):

Aim of Heyvaert et al. (2013)'s search: *We searched for publications reporting on critical appraisal frameworks (CAFs) that evaluate the methodological quality of original mixed methods articles.*

How Heyvaert et al. (2013) reported on the issue of multiple publication: *We retrieved 18 unique publications answering to our inclusion criteria. However, we additionally excluded five articles from this review, because they described the same CAF as presented in one of the already included studies. The references to those five articles are preceded by double asterisks (**) in the annotated bibliography. As a result, our final database included 13 unique CAFs. The articles containing these frameworks are preceded by an asterisk (*) in the annotated bibliography. Results from the search are presented in a flowchart.* (Heyvaert et al., 2013, p. 305)

Source: Based on Heyvaert, M., Hannes, K., Maes, B., & Onghena, P. (2013). Critical appraisal of mixed methods studies. *Journal of Mixed Methods Research, 7*, 302–327. doi:10.1177/1558689813479449

Which bibliographic databases will you consult? Which bibliographic databases you will search depends on the topic of the MMRS and on the research discipline. Some databases are multidisciplinary, whereas others are specifically designed for a particular discipline. Box 3.2 provides an overview of some multidisciplinary and discipline-specific bibliographic databases. Even within the same research domain, different databases index different journals. Accordingly, it is highly recommended to search several (relevant) bibliographic databases, particularly when conducting an exhaustive search.

Box 3.2   Examples of Multidisciplinary and Discipline-Specific Bibliographic Databases (based on Hammerstrøm, Wade, & Jørgensen, 2010)

Multidisciplinary bibliographic databases

Academic Search Premier; FRANCIS; Google Scholar; JSTOR; Scopus; Web of Science

Discipline-specific bibliographic databases

Biology and pharmacology: BIOSIS; Biological Abstracts; BIOSIS Previews; Derwent Drug File; International Pharmaceutical Abstracts

Communication and language: Communication Abstracts; Linguistics and Language Behavior Abstracts (LLBA)

Economics: Econlit; National Bureau of Economic Research; Research Papers in Economics (RePEc)

Education: British Education Index; Education Abstracts; Education Full Text: Wilson; Education Resources Information Center (ERIC); Education & Information Technology Digital Library (Ed/ITLib); Educational Research Abstracts online (ERA)

Health and nursing: Allied and Complementary Medicine Database (AMED); British Nursing Index (BNI); CIRRIE Database of International Rehabilitation Research; Cochrane Central Register of Controlled Trials (CENTRAL); Cumulative Index to Nursing and Allied Health (CINAHL); Database of Promoting Health Effectiveness Reviews (DoPHER); EMBASE; EMCare; EPPI Centre databases; Global Health; Health Economic Evaluations Database (HEED); Joanna Briggs Institute EBP Database; Medline/PubMed; OTseeker; Physiotherapy Evidence Database (PEDro); POPLINE; REHABDATA (NARIC)

Law sciences: Criminal Justice Abstracts; Criminology: A SAGE Full-Text Collection

Social and community health and welfare: AgeLine; Childdata; CommunityWISE; Social Care Online; Social Services Abstracts

Social sciences, psychology, and psychiatry: Applied Social Science Index and Abstracts (ASSIA); Campbell Library; International Bibliography of Social Science (IBSS); PsycInfo; Social Policy and Practice; Social Sciences Index; Sociological Abstracts

Source: Based on Hammerstrøm, K., Wade, A., & Jørgensen, A. M. K. (2010). *Searching for studies: A guide to information retrieval for Campbell Systematic Reviews: Supplement 1.* doi:10.4073/csrs.2010.1

How can you efficiently interrogate bibliographic databases? To search bibliographic databases, you can use index terms, free-text words, or a combination of both. Because empirical research shows that using one strategy results in missing relevant records (Shaw et al., 2004), we advise you to combine the index terms and free-text words search strategies, especially when conducting an exhaustive search.

Index terms. Index terms (also called *controlled vocabulary* or *thesaurus terms* or *subject headings*) are terms assigned to publications by authors and compilers of bibliographic databases. The authors and compilers identify topics central to the publication, rather than just words that appear within the (title or abstract of the) publication (Jesson, Matheson, & Lacey, 2011). When using index terms, you have to consult the list of subject headings for all the bibliographic databases you are interested in. An advantage of the thesaurus strategy is that it generally yields results with a higher precision compared with the free-text words strategy (Shaw et al., 2004). However, there are several drawbacks: (a) Authors may not describe their methods or objectives well; (b) indexers are not always experts in the subject areas or methodological aspects of the articles that they are indexing; and (c) the available indexing terms might not correspond to the terms the searcher wishes to use (Lefebvre et al., 2011). As a result, some relevant papers might not be retrieved. Another difficulty is that the thesaurus terms used in each bibliographic database vary according to the specific indexing system. Accordingly, you have to customize the index terms search for each bibliographic database you want to consult. Due to the existing variation in indexing practices, we advise you to search more than one bibliographic database, particularly if you use an exhaustive search strategy for your MMRS.

Free-text words. When you search using free-text words, you look for words located within the title, abstract, or full text of a publication. In the remainder of this section, we describe how bibliographic databases can be interrogated using free-text words.

The key search terms or **keywords** are a first issue to consider in designing the strategy for searching bibliographic databases. These keywords refer to the most important elements of the topic of interest and the review question(s). For instance, you can use keywords for the phenomenon or intervention you are studying, for the population of interest, and for the outcome or evaluation measure you are interested in. In Practical Tip 3.2, we provide helpful suggestions for selecting keywords.

Second, you can consider how **Boolean operators** might be relevant for your MMRS search strategy. The AND operator can be used to combine diverse concepts. AND can, for instance, be used between two concepts when you want *both* concepts to be in the title/topic in order for the article to be retrieved. The OR operator is often used for synonyms and similar concepts. You can use OR when *one* of the concepts in the title/topic is already sufficient in order for the article to be retrieved. Practical Tip 3.3 shows an example of how to use the Boolean operators AND and OR.

A third issue to consider is **truncation**. When you use truncation in an MMRS search strategy, some letters in the words are replaced by symbols (as wildcards). For instance, if you search for *"intellectual disabilit*"* in Web of Science, you will get the search results not only for "intellectual disability" but also for "intellectual disabilities." Truncation can also be used to include both U.K. and U.S. spellings of certain terms (e.g., *"challenging behavi*r"*). Accordingly, search strings can be shortened by using truncation.

Practical Tip 3.2: Using Free-Text Words to Search Bibliographic Databases

You can look at a few articles that were already identified as relevant for your MMRS from the scoping review exercise (see Chapter 2) to develop a free-text word search strategy. You can study the title, abstract, keywords, and/or full text of a publication, and note down which keywords were used. This can help you to decide which keywords to include in your free-text words search.

Practical Tip 3.3: How to Use the Boolean Operators AND and OR

If you search for *"intellectual disabilities"* AND *"social stories"* in the title/topic, only articles with both "intellectual disabilities" and "social stories" in the title/topic will be retrieved.

If you search for *"problem behavior"* OR *"challenging behavior,"* all articles with "problem behavior" in the title/topic, as well as all articles with "challenging behavior" in the title/topic, will be retrieved by the search.

Fourth, you can use **double quotes** *(" ")* to search for a specific string of words. Using double quotes can help you to filter out irrelevant articles. For example, if you search for *"social stories"* (using double quotes), then an article with a title/topic containing the words "social" and "stories" not directly following one another will not be retrieved by this search.

Search limits are a fifth issue to consider. Depending on the topic and purpose of the MMRS, as well as on practical considerations, you might, for instance, want to limit the search on the publication language, publication type, or publication period. When reporting on the MMRS, the search limits and the rationale for these limits should be provided. For instance, with regard to the publication period, the start and end dates with justification for the time period chosen should be mentioned (Booth, 2006). Most importantly, the types of bias introduced to the MMRS by setting these limitations should be discussed.

In Practical Tip 3.4, we discuss how you can develop, save, and test your search strategy.

Practical Tip 3.4: Scoping Searches and Saving Searches

When designing your strategy for searching bibliographic databases, you can test several variations of your search string (i.e., **scoping searches**). You can try out different keywords, Boolean operators, truncation, double quotes, and search limits. Based on the scoping searches, you may decide that you have to limit or broaden your search string. Most of the bibliographic databases allow you to register for an account. You can use the account to save and re-run your searches. This can be interesting when developing your MMRS search strategy because it allows you to re-do your search quickly to see whether new items have been added.

Each bibliographic database has its own unique organization (e.g., subject headings, indexing, and search limits). When the scoping process is completed and the final search strategy is decided on, it is important that you use equivalent search strings and search limitations for each bibliographic database. We recommend you keep detailed records of the bibliographic databases you searched, and the search strings and search limitations you used, along with their rationales. After each search, you can record the number of retrieved publications.

In most MMRS literature reviews, bibliographic databases are the back-bone of the data collection strategy. Out of all the search methods, they tend to cast the widest net, and their restrictions are well known and can be compensated for by the use of other complementary search strategies (Cooper, Hedges, & Valentine, 2009). The main restrictions of searching bibliographic databases are as follows: (a) They particularly include references to published research and underrepresent unpublished research (see *publication bias*); (b) there can be a considerable time lag between the moment when a study is completed and the moment when the reference appears in a bibliographic database (although the recent use of *online first publications* partially alleviates the disadvantage associated with this restriction); and (c) there are restrictions related to topical and disciplinary boundaries of a database (Cooper et al., 2009).

Methodological Filters

An important consideration related to the MMRS search process is whether you will use methodological filters. Depending on the MMRS topic and goal, it might or might not be meaningful to use methodological filters. **Methodological filters** can be used when you only want to retrieve studies with certain designs or studies that use certain methodologies to be included in the MMRS. In that case, methodological filters can be used to narrow the focus of the search. It implies that you include in your search strategy search terms that are related to the specific qualitative, quantitative, or mixed methods designs and methodologies you are interested in. However, you do not need to add methodological filters if your in/exclusion criteria are all substantive and you are not considering a study's methodology or design as criteria for in/exclusion.

For MMRS literature reviews where the use of methodological filters might be appropriate, we note a few considerations. A drawback of using methodological filters is that this procedure can result in missing (groups of) relevant studies due to, for instance, inconsistencies in the naming of qualitative, quantitative, and mixed methods designs and methodologies. Also, most substantive articles are only referred to by substantive keywords, not necessarily by the designs and methods used in the study. Accordingly, searching only titles and keywords of publications will probably not be sufficient when conducting a design-specific bibliographic databases search. It will be necessary to search abstracts and full texts as well. When using controlled vocabulary to search bibliographic databases, you can be confronted with the problem that not all databases adequately index terms related to qualitative, quantitative, and mixed methods research designs, and that there is a lack of consistency between the thesauri of various bibliographic databases for indexing research designs (Saini & Shlonsky, 2012).

Addressing the Issue of Gray Literature

When conducting an MMRS literature review, searching solely bibliographic databases—even if several bibliographic databases are searched—is considered inadequate by the greater part of the academic community (Hammerstrøm et al., 2010). It is generally advised to consult multiple resources to retrieve potentially relevant studies and to search for published as well as unpublished studies. For instance, in addition to bibliographic databases, gray (or "grey" per British English spelling) literature databases can be included in the search process. Examples of gray literature are conference proceedings, dissertations, government reports, policy documents, and unpublished research reports. Nowadays several gray literature databases exist containing references to and full texts of gray literature reports. Because most gray literature reports are not included in bibliographic databases, it is important to search gray literature databases when conducting an MMRS literature review. Some examples of gray literature databases are displayed in Box 3.3. Most gray literature databases can be searched using the same specific search strategy you developed for searching bibliographic databases (e.g., using keywords, Boolean operators, truncation, double quotes, and search limits).

Hand-Searching Journals

In addition to searching bibliographic and gray literature databases, you can also hand-search relevant journals. Reasons for adding this step to the search strategy are as follows: (a) Not all journals are indexed by database producers, (b) not all indexed journal articles are retrievable from databases, and (c) some databases only index selectively and may not index supplements or special issues (University of York, 2014). Physical hand searches

---

Box 3.3   Examples of Gray Literature Databases

British Library Electronic Theses Online Service (EThOS)

CORDIS Library

Educational Technology and E-Learning (EdITLib)

Grey Literature Database of the Canadian Evaluation Society

Healthcare Management Information Consortium (HMIC) database

Index of Conference Proceedings

Index to Theses in Great Britain and Ireland

National Technical Information Service (NTIS) database

Networked Digital Library of Theses and Dissertations (NDLTD)

NHS Evidence Search

OpenGrey (System for Information on Grey Literature in Europe)

ProQuest Dissertations & Theses

PsycEXTRA

Social Science Research Network (SSRN) eLibrary

System for Information on Grey Literature in Europe (SIGLE)

Theses Canada

(i.e., *hard-copy searches*) can be conducted in libraries. However, nowadays most of the *hand searches* are performed electronically: You can scan journals' electronic tables of contents.

A challenge relating to hand-searching journals is the process of selecting the journals that will be scrutinized. Nowadays, many scientific journals exist, scattered over various disciplines, fields, topic areas, and publishers. The number of journals in which relevant studies might appear is generally far greater than the number of journals that a single scholar examines routinely

(Cooper et al., 2009). The cost–benefit balance should be considered when selecting the number of journals that will be scrutinized.

In case you conduct a design-specific search for an MMRS (i.e., searching for specific qualitative, quantitative, or mixed methods designs to be included in the MMRS) and you want to carry out a hand search of journals, it can be a challenge that the studies relating to specific designs are published in various methodological as well as substantive journals. Accordingly, the number of journals to be hand-searched can be rather large. Because the studies can be published across a multitude of journals spanning several substantive disciplines, composing the list of journals to be hand-searched is often not an easy endeavor.

Searching Reference Lists

In addition to searching bibliographic and gray literature databases and hand-searching relevant journals, relevant studies can be found by **backward tracking**. This strategy entails screening all the reference lists of the included publications based on the previous search steps. The reference lists are scanned for relevant studies that were not picked up through the previous search steps.

There are several limitations of this search method: (a) Reference lists in primary studies are rarely exhaustive overviews of all relevant research, (b) the lists tend to include references to other work available through the same outlet or published in the same journal, (c) the sets of references tend to be more homogeneous than the overall group of relevant studies, and (d) published research is overrepresented in reference lists because published research is generally easier to find than unpublished research (Cooper et al., 2009). An additional drawback is of course that recently completed and published studies will most likely not be retrieved by means of this search method. Accordingly, we advise against an MMRS search strategy that solely consists of searching reference lists, as might be the case in certain snowball or chain sampling strategies (see Table 3.1). However, we encourage you to include searching reference lists as an additional search step, as a complementary way to search other resources.

Consulting Citation Indexes

The inverse strategy of *backward tracking* by searching reference lists is **forward tracking** or **citation tracking**. Using this strategy implies that you search for additional relevant publications that cited the publications retrieved by the previous search steps (e.g., searching bibliographic and gray literature databases, hand-searching relevant journals, and searching reference lists). As such, you can search forward in time from the publication of a relevant article to identify additional relevant future articles that refer to that previous relevant article.

Most of the drawbacks relating to searching reference lists also apply to consulting citation indexes: (a) The method tends to result in retrieving references to other work available through the same outlet or published in the same journal, (b) the sets of retrieved references tend to be more homogeneous than the overall group of relevant studies, and (c) the method tends to result in an overrepresentation of published research and accordingly might induce a publication bias (Cooper et al., 2009). Parallel to our conclusion relating to searching reference lists, we advise against an MMRS search strategy that solely consists of consulting citation indexes, although we encourage this search method to be included as a complementary way to search other resources.

Contacting Authors and Experts

In the final stage of the search, authors or experts can be emailed in order to ask whether they can point toward other studies that were not yet included in the MMRS. For instance, you can contact authors of relevant primary studies to ask whether additional published or unpublished studies are available that meet your inclusion criteria.

Libraries, Internet Searches, and Additional Search Options

Depending on the research discipline and MMRS topic, it might be relevant to consult other resources than the ones discussed earlier. When relevant to your MMRS topic, you can, for instance, search newspaper archives, randomized controlled trials registers (e.g., for an MMRS in the health domain), government databases, Organisation for Economic Co-operation and Development (OECD) libraries and databases, and court databases (e.g., http://www.pacer.gov/). Experts on the topic might give you advice on which additional resources you can search to retrieve studies relevant to your MMRS.

Another search option is a free Internet search (e.g., Google, Altavista, Bing, and Yahoo!Search). An Internet search can identify websites of relevant organizations, companies, and academic centers that can then be scanned for relevant research studies (University of York, 2014). A possible drawback related to free Internet searches concerns the lack of quality control. In contrast with studies published in journals that include a peer review process, Internet websites can be constructed by anyone who has website constructing skills and there is no control of the quality of the material that is published on a website (Cooper et al., 2009). Accordingly, parallel to our conclusion relating to searching reference lists and consulting citation indexes, we advise against an MMRS search strategy that solely consists of free Internet searches.

An important final group of resources that can be consulted are libraries. Although it might nowadays seem like everything is available on the Internet, some publications and reports are only available in printed form. For instance, although master theses and doctoral dissertations might be included in some gray literature databases (as we discussed previously in this chapter), certainly not all universities and institutions will index and make available the master theses and doctoral dissertations resulting from the work of their students online. Furthermore, as we discussed in the section *Hand-Searching Journals*, physical hand searches of journals that are not indexed online should also be conducted in libraries. Searching libraries in an efficient way can be facilitated by consulting library databases and by involving research librarians in the search process (for an example, see Harris, 2005).

INCLUSION AND EXCLUSION CRITERIA

After having conducted the search for primary studies, you have to judge which studies will be included in the MMRS (i.e., because they will allow you to answer the review questions) and which ones will be excluded. We make a distinction between an initial and a final screening stage. Afterward, we will discuss how you can assess agreement on study inclusion.

Initial Screening Stage

After saving the titles and abstracts from the retrieved publications and removing the duplicates from the search results, you can conduct an initial screening. This stage entails screening the titles and abstracts from the retrieved publications in order to judge which publications will definitely not be included in the MMRS and which publications might be included. The aim of this first screening stage is to exclude publications that are obviously irrelevant to the MMRS. This initial screening can include a limited number of questions, such as follows: Does this study address the phenomenon or intervention of interest? Does this study address the population of interest? Does this study address the outcome or evaluation measure you are interested in? We advise you to document and save the reasons for excluding publications from the MMRS. To increase the validity of the MMRS, it is recommended that at least two independent review authors are involved in the initial screening stage using the listed questions. In Practical Tip 3.5, we provide helpful suggestions relating to the initial screening stage.

Final Screening Stage

Next, the final screening can be conducted by applying the inclusion and exclusion criteria (i.e., **eligibility criteria**) to the publications' full texts to check their relevance to answer the posed review question(s). Only studies that meet all the inclusion criteria and do not meet any of the listed exclusion criteria will be included in the MMRS. Based on the topic of the MMRS and the key elements of the review question(s), the eligibility criteria were specified *a priori* in the review protocol (see Chapter 2). The eligibility criteria can refer to the phenomenon or intervention under study, the population of interest, the outcome or evaluation measures of interest, the geographical location, the setting, the time span, the language, the research methodology, and any other

Practical Tip 3.5: Initial Screening

If you are in doubt on whether you should include or exclude a publication based on reading the title and abstract, it is safest to keep it included. After conducting the initial screening, you can retrieve the full texts of the publications that passed the initial screening stage. Based on the full texts, you can conduct the final screening to make a determination.

criterion relevant to the MMRS. Whereas inclusion criteria tend to be broad and inclusive so that the results will be generalizable (although still reflecting the focused nature of the review question), exclusion criteria tend to be few and limit the sample of studies to increase the homogeneity and maintain the focus of the MMRS (see Montori, Swiontkowski, & Cook, 2003). Parallel to the initial screening stage, it is recommended that at least two independent review authors screen all the remaining publications in the final screening stage using a formal screening form. In Practical Tip 3.6, we discuss how you can develop a formal screening form for the final screening stage.

Assessing Agreement on Study Inclusion

To increase the validity of an MMRS, it is recommended that at least two independent review authors are involved in the initial and final screening stage. After independently doing the screening exercise, the two review authors can compare their results and in/exclusion decisions. When the two

---

Practical Tip 3.6: Developing the Screening Form for the Final Screening

It is highly recommended to use a formal screening form in the final screening stage (i.e., the screening of full texts). If a study does not satisfy one (or more) of the inclusion criteria, it should be excluded from the MMRS. Accordingly, when developing the screening form, it is recommended to list the inclusion criteria in order of importance on the form, so that the first *no* response can be used as the primary reason for exclusion of a study, and the remaining criteria need not be assessed (Higgins & Deeks, 2011). In a parallel manner, the exclusion criteria can be added in order of importance to the form, so that the first *yes* response can be used as the primary reason for exclusion of a study.

For example, Mieke Heyvaert, Bea Maes, Wim Van den Noortgate, Sofie Kuppens, and Patrick Onghena (2012) searched for single-case and small-*n* studies on the effects of interventions for reducing challenging behavior in persons with intellectual disabilities. The following form was used in the final screening phase:

	Study 1		Study 2			Study 3	...
	Participant A	Participant B	Participant A	Participant B	Participant C	Participant A	
Publication period: The study was published between January 2000 and April 2011	Y / N	Y / N	Y / N	Y / N	Y / N	Y / N	
Study type: The study is a single-case or small-n study (see definition of Onghena, 2005)	Y / N	Y / N	Y / N	Y / N	Y / N	Y / N	
Participant: The participant has an intellectual disability	Y / N	Y / N	Y / N	Y / N	Y / N	Y / N	
Intervention: A contextual, behavioral, and/or pharmacological intervention is used	Y / N	Y / N	Y / N	Y / N	Y / N	Y / N	
Study aim: The aim of the experiment is to reduce the challenging behavior of this participant	Y / N	Y / N	Y / N	Y / N	Y / N	Y / N	
Raw data—A: The level of challenging behavior for this participant is presented in graphical format	Y / N	Y / N	Y / N	Y / N	Y / N	Y / N	
Raw data—B: The level of challenging behavior for this participant is plotted under at least one baseline and at least one treatment condition	Y / N	Y / N	Y / N	Y / N	Y / N	Y / N	
Raw data—C: Both the baseline and the treatment condition for this participant contain at least two data points	Y / N	Y / N	Y / N	Y / N	Y / N	Y / N	
Decision: Include or Exclude?							

(Continued)

> (Continued)
>
> We recommend first to pilot the screening form that will be used for the final screening exercise. The pilot test of the screening form can be used to refine and clarify the eligibility criteria, as well as to ensure that the criteria can be applied consistently by more than one person (Higgins & Deeks, 2011). Several review authors can be involved in piloting the form. They can independently look at a small set of retrieved publications (e.g., 10 to 20 publications) and use the screening form to decide which publications will be included and which will be excluded from the MMRS. During this piloting exercise, they can additionally note any ambiguities or suggestions for improving the form. Afterward, they can compare in/exclusion decisions. If there are any inconsistencies in the in/exclusion decisions and/or ambiguities in the form, the screening form should be revised. After piloting (and possibly revising) the screening form, it can be used for the final screening stage.

review authors are undecided about whether to include or exclude a study, they can consult a third review author or the review panel. At the end of the screening exercise, they will have decided which studies are excluded from the MMRS (and have noted the reasons for excluding studies) and which ones are included.

To quantify the (dis)agreements between the two review authors, statistical measures that indicate agreement beyond chance, like **Cohen's kappa statistic** (κ), can be used (Higgins & Deeks, 2011; Montori et al., 2003). In Practical Tip 3.7, we show how Cohen's kappa can be calculated. Values of Cohen's kappa between 0.40 and 0.59 are considered to reflect fair agreement, values between 0.60 and 0.74 to reflect good agreement, and values of 0.75 or more to reflect excellent agreement (Higgins & Deeks, 2011; Orwin, 1994).

Another measure that is sometimes used for assessing agreement between independent assessors is the **agreement percentage**: The number of agreements is divided by the number of agreements plus disagreements. An agreement percentage of 80% or more is considered to reflect good agreement (Mokkink et al., 2010).

Practical Tip 3.7: Calculating Cohen's Kappa Statistic (Based on Higgins & Deeks, 2011)

Suppose that N primary studies are distributed according to numbers a to i as in Table 3.2, with the total number of included, excluded, and unsure studies for review author 1 denoted as I_1, E_1, and U_1, respectively, and with the total number of included, excluded, and unsure studies for review author 2 denoted as I_2, E_2, and U_2, respectively.

Then

$$\kappa = \frac{P_o - P_E}{1 - P_E}$$

where

$$P_o = \frac{a + e + i}{N}$$ is the proportion of studies for which there

was agreement, and

$$P_E = \frac{I_1 \times I_2 + E_1 \times E_2 + U_1 \times U_2}{N^2}$$ is the proportion of studies

in which one would expect there was agreement by chance alone.

Table 3.2 Calculating Cohen's Kappa Statistic

		Review Author 2			
		Include	Exclude	Unsure	Total
Review Author 1	Include	a	b	c	I_1
	Exclude	d	e	f	E_1
	Unsure	g	h	i	U_1
	Total	I_2	E_2	U_2	N

For the data in Table 3.3:

$$P_o = \frac{10 + 14 + 6}{50} = 0.6$$

(Continued)

(Continued)

and

$$P_E = \frac{24 \times 10 + 20 \times 20 + 6 \times 20}{50^2} = 0.304$$

and so

$$\kappa = \frac{0.6 - 0.304}{1 - 0.304} = 0.43$$

Accordingly, for this example, we conclude that there is fair agreement between the two review authors.

Table 3.3 Calculating Cohen's Kappa Statistic: Numerical Example

		Review Author 2			
		Include	Exclude	Unsure	Total
Review Author 1	Include	10	6	8	24
	Exclude	0	14	6	20
	Unsure	0	0	6	6
	Total	10	20	20	50

Source: Higgins, J. P. T., & Deeks, J. J. (2011). Chapter 7: Selecting studies and collecting data. In J. P. T. Higgins & S. Green (Eds.), *Cochrane Handbook for Systematic Reviews of Interventions* Version 5.1.0 (updated March 2011). Retrieved from http://handbook.cochrane.org.

DOCUMENTING AND REPORTING THE SEARCH PROCESS AND RESULTS

To enhance transparency, it is of utmost importance to document every step in the MMRS search process: how the search strategy was developed (e.g., scoping searches; see Practical Tip 3.4) and what the final search strategy looked like. With regard to the final search strategy, you should keep track of:

- The sampling strategy (i.e., exhaustive, selective, or purposeful)
- Which resources were searched (e.g., which bibliographic databases, gray literature resources, journals, conference proceedings, reference lists, citation indexes, and/or experts, authors, or organizations were contacted) and all the details of the conducted searches (e.g., the date each search was performed, the interface used for each search, the period searched, the subject headings and keywords used, Boolean operators, truncation, double quotes, and search limits)
- The number of retrieved publications for each resource
- The number of duplicate publications excluded (by reference management software and manually)
- The number of duplicate studies excluded (see Box 3.1 on *multiple publication bias*)
- The inclusion and exclusion criteria (i.e., the eligibility criteria)
- The number of publications and studies that were included and excluded (along with the reasons for exclusion) in every screening stage

In Practical Tip 3.8, we discuss how you can document and report the search process and results.

In addition to reporting on the search details in the MMRS report, we recommend describing how several review authors were involved in the (search and) screening process. The MMRS report can include information on (a) whether more than one review author independently examined each title and abstract to exclude obviously irrelevant reports (i.e., initial screening); (b) how many review authors were involved in the final screening stage, and whether these review authors conducted this screening of full texts independently; (c) whether the review authors involved in (a) and (b) are content area experts, methodologists, or both; (d) whether the review authors assessing the relevance of the studies knew the names of the authors, institutions, journal of publication, and results when they applied the eligibility criteria (i.e., blinded or nonblinded assessment); and (e) how disagreements were handled (Higgins & Deeks, 2011).

A detailed description of the search strategy and eligibility criteria allows a clear audit trail that can be followed by review authors who want to replicate or update the MMRS search process. It can also help the readers to judge the quality of the MMRS.

Practical Tip 3.8: Documenting and Reporting the Search Process and Results

We advise you to use a **flowchart** or **study retrieval diagram** to report on the MMRS search process. In addition, we recommend you include a sample search strategy (e.g., for one bibliographic database searched) as an appendix to the final report. Figures 3.1–3.3 present examples of how you can document an exhaustive, a selective, and a purposeful MMRS search process, respectively. Another example of how to visualize the MMRS search process and results can be found on the website of the PRISMA (i.e., Preferred Reporting Items for Systematic Reviews and Meta-Analyses) group (http://www.prisma-statement.org/). Furthermore, Booth (2006) developed the STARLITE mnemonic as a proposal toward a standard for reporting literature searches. He suggests reporting on the Sampling strategy, Type of study, Approaches, Range of years, Limits, Inclusion and exclusions, Terms used, and Electronic resources, and he provides an outline example of a report of a literature search structured according to STARLITE principles (Booth, 2006, p. 424).

CHALLENGES OF DATA COLLECTION AND ELIGIBILITY CRITERIA FOR MMRS LITERATURE REVIEWS

Throughout this chapter we mentioned several issues that can be taken into account with regard to the data collection process in MMRS literature reviews. In this section, we discuss some general challenges related to the search for studies to be included in the MMRS and the process of defining the eligibility criteria.

First, there are a number of challenges related to the search for studies to be included in MMRS literature reviews. A general drawback is that the data collection process requires a large amount of time and, thus, resources. Depending on whether an exhaustive, a selective, or a purposeful MMRS sampling strategy is selected, a smaller or larger amount of resources has to be scrutinized. Technical advancements like reference management software can enhance the work and time efficiency of conducting MMRS literature reviews. However, there remains a lot of *reflective* and *manual* work that has to be done by the review authors themselves, including planning the search and tailoring the search strategy to the topic of the MMRS; conducting scoping searches and developing an optimal search strategy; conducting the actual search; manually removing remaining duplicate publications from the search results; and linking together multiple publications on a single study (see *multiple publication bias*).

Another issue concerns the importance of following the review protocol when conducting the MMRS search process. At the beginning of this chapter, we stated that the search for studies to be included in the MMRS should be conducted in accordance with the strategy that is described in the review protocol (see Chapter 2). However, some scholars argue that review authors should not rely solely on predefined, protocol-driven search strategies. Strategies that might seem less efficient (e.g., browsing library shelves, asking colleagues, and simply being alert to serendipitous discovery) may have a better yield per hour spent and can identify important sources that would otherwise be missed (Greenhalgh & Peacock, 2005).

With regard to the process of defining the eligibility criteria, review authors might face several pitfalls too: (a) Inclusion criteria may be too broad, resulting in an MMRS including heterogeneous studies that are only marginally related to the review question(s); (b) exclusion criteria may be associated with the magnitude, direction, and statistical significance of the effect, resulting in biased conclusions (e.g., if studies that are not published in peer-reviewed journals are excluded); (c) the opportunity to explore certain study characteristics as related to divergent results later in the MMRS could be lost due to the use of these characteristics as exclusion criteria; and above all (d) arbitrary exclusions may be stipulated based on the data, for instance, because the content experts of the review team are familiar with the available evidence and/or are biased against certain perspectives or methodologies (Montori et al., 2003).

Summary Points

- The aim of the search process is to generate a list of primary-level studies that may be relevant for answering the review question(s).
- The sampling units included in an MMRS are primary-level qualitative, quantitative, and mixed methods studies, and the data included in the review are the data reported in these primary studies.

- The MMRS search process should be conducted and reported in a transparent way.
- You should carefully document every step in the MMRS search process: how the search strategy was developed and what the final search strategy looked like.
- Depending on the topic and goal of the MMRS and the selected MMRS design, you have to decide whether the search strategies you develop will be different for the separate strands of the MMRS or whether there will be one overall data collection phase covering all strands.
- There are three types of sampling strategies for MMRS literature reviews: exhaustive, selective, and purposeful sampling. The sampling strategy should be selected in accordance with the topic and purpose of the MMRS.
- Before starting the search process, you have to consider how you will store and save the search results. Using reference management software can be both work and time efficient.
- Biases such as publication bias, location bias, and multiple publication bias may influence which studies will be retrieved and included.
- To retrieve relevant studies, you can search bibliographic databases, gray literature databases, journals, reference lists, and citation indexes, and/or you can contact authors and experts.
- It is generally advised to consult multiple resources to retrieve potentially relevant studies and to search for published as well as unpublished studies.
- After having conducted the search for primary studies, you have to decide which studies will be included in the MMRS and which ones will be excluded.
- At least two independent review authors should screen the retrieved studies.
- It is recommended to use a formal screening form in the final screening stage.

Questions for Thought

- Would it be more appropriate for your MMRS to use diverse search strategies for the separate strands, or would it be more appropriate to use one overall data collection phase covering all strands of your MMRS?

- Depending on its topic and purpose, which sampling strategy would be most appropriate for your MMRS: an exhaustive, a selective, or a purposeful sampling strategy? Why?

- Think about how various types of bias (e.g., publication bias and location bias) may influence which studies will be retrieved and included in your MMRS. How might these different types of bias have affected the conclusions of your MMRS?

- Will you use methodological filters in your search strategy? What are possible advantages and limitations of using methodological filters for your MMRS?

- Based on the topic and goal of your MMRS, which resources would you search (e.g., bibliographic databases, gray literature databases, reference lists, citation indexes, contact authors and experts, and other resources)? Why?

- Will you develop a formal screening form for the initial as well as the final screening stage? Why (not)? What will the form look like?

- Will you quantify the (dis)agreements between the review authors who independently conducted the screening? Why (not)? How will you quantify the inter-rater agreement? What will be the role of the inter-rater agreement score for the remainder of your MMRS? What will be the consequences of a low inter-rater agreement score? Would you try to explain and account for the low inter-rater agreement score?

Exercises

- When developing the search strategy for interrogating bibliographic databases for your MMRS, try out index terms searches as well as free-text words searches. When developing the free-text words search strategy, try out several variations of your search string (e.g., different keywords, Boolean operators, truncation, double quotes, and search limits).

- Based on the topic of your MMRS, select a few gray literature databases and run a search for each of them. Afterward, evaluate how many of the studies retrieved by the gray literature databases were not retrieved by your bibliographic databases searches.

- Develop a formal screening form for the final screening stage (i.e., the screening of full texts). List the inclusion/exclusion criteria in order of importance on the form, so that the first *no/yes* response can be used as the primary reason for exclusion of a study, and the remaining criteria need not be assessed.

- Next, you can pilot the screening form. Let at least two review authors independently look at a small set of the publications retrieved for your MMRS, and let them use the form to decide which publications will be in/excluded. Afterward, compare in/exclusion decisions. Revise the screening form if there are any inconsistencies in the in/exclusion decisions and/or ambiguities in the form.

- After conducting the final screening stage for your MMRS, quantify the (dis)agreements between the two review authors, for instance, by using Cohen's kappa statistic or the agreement percentage.

- Create a flowchart to report on your MMRS search process and its results.

Suggestions for Further Reading

Cochrane handbook for systematic reviews of interventions. Retrieved from http://www.cochrane-handbook.org.

Hammerstrøm, K., Wade, A., & Jørgensen, A. M. K. (2010). *Searching for studies: A guide to information retrieval for Campbell Systematic Reviews: Supplement 1.* doi:10.4073/csrs.2010.1

University of York. (2014). *Finding studies for systematic reviews: A resource list for researchers*. Retrieved from http://www.york.ac.uk/inst/crd/finding_studies_systematic_reviews.htm

References

Booth, A. (2006). "Brimful of STARLITE": Toward standards for reporting literature searches. *Journal of the Medical Library Association, 94,* 421–429.

Butler, G., Deaton, S., Hodgkinson, J., Holmes, E., & Marshall, S. (2005). *Quick but not dirty: Rapid evidence assessments as a decision support tool in social policy.*

Retrieved from https://www.researchgate.net/publication/255580850_Quick_ but_Not_Dirty_Rapid_Evidence_Assessments_as_a_Decision_Support_Tool_ in_Social_Policy

Cooper, H. M., Hedges, L. V., & Valentine, J. C. (Eds.). (2009). *The handbook of research synthesis and meta-analysis* (2nd ed.). New York, NY: Russell Sage Foundation.

Dundar, Y., & Fleeman, N. (2014). Developing my search strategy and applying inclusion criteria. In A. Boland, M. G. Cherry, & R. Dickson (Eds.), *Doing a systematic review* (pp. 35–59). Thousand Oaks, CA: Sage.

Egger, M., & Smith, G. D. (1998). Meta-analysis—Bias in location and selection of studies. *BMJ, 316*, 61–66. doi:10.1136/bmj.316.7124.61

Farace, D. J., Frantzen, J., Schöpfel, J., Stock, C., & Boekhorst, A. K. (2006). Access to grey content: An analysis of grey literature based on citation and survey data. In *Seventh International Conference on Grey Literature: Open Access to Grey Resources. GL7 Conference Proceedings.* Retrieved from http://www.opengrey. eu/data/69/78/12/GL7_Farace_et_al_2006_Abstract_and_Bionotes.pdf

Ganann, R., Ciliska, D., & Thomas, H. (2010). Expediting systematic reviews: Methods and implications of rapid reviews. *Implementation Science, 5*, 56. doi:10.1186/1748-5908-5-56

Grant, M. J., & Booth, A. (2009). A typology of reviews: An analysis of 14 review types and associated methodologies. *Health Information & Libraries Journal, 26*, 91–108. doi:10.1111/j.1471-1842.2009.00848.x

Greenhalgh, T., & Peacock, R. (2005). Effectiveness and efficiency of search methods in systematic reviews of complex evidence: Audit of primary sources. *BMJ, 331*, 1064–1065. doi:10.1136/bmj.38636.593461.68

Hammerstrøm, K., Wade, A., & Jørgensen, A. M. K. (2010). *Searching for studies: A guide to information retrieval for Campbell Systematic Reviews: Supplement 1.* doi:10.4073/csrs.2010.1

Hannes, K., & Harden, A. (2011). Multi-context versus context-specific qualitative evidence syntheses: Combining the best of both. *Research Synthesis Methods, 2*, 271–278. doi:10.1002/jrsm.55

Harris, M. R. (2005). The librarian's roles in the systematic review process: A case study. *Journal of the Medical Library Association, 93*, 81–87.

Heyvaert, M., Hannes, K., Maes, B., & Onghena, P. (2013). Critical appraisal of mixed methods studies. *Journal of Mixed Methods Research, 7*, 302–327. doi:10.1177/1558689813479449

Heyvaert, M., Maes, B., Van den Noortgate, W., Kuppens, S., & Onghena, P. (2012). A multilevel meta-analysis of single-case and small-n research on interventions for reducing challenging behavior in persons with intellectual disabilities. *Research in Developmental Disabilities, 33*, 766–780. doi:10.1016/j. ridd.2011.10.010

Higgins, J. P. T., & Deeks, J. J. (2011). Chapter 7: Selecting studies and collecting data. In J. P. T. Higgins & S. Green (Eds.), *Cochrane handbook for systematic reviews of interventions Version 5.1.0* (updated March 2011). Retrieved from http://www.cochrane-handbook.org

Hopewell, S., Loudon, K., Clarke, M. J., Oxman, A. D., & Dickersin, K. (2009). Publication bias in clinical trials due to statistical significance or direction of trial results. *Cochrane Database of Systematic Reviews, 1.* doi:10.1002/14651858. MR000006.pub3

Jesson, J. K., Matheson, L., & Lacey, F. M. (2011). *Doing your literature review. Traditional and systematic techniques.* London, England: Sage.

Kemper, E. A., Stringfield, S., & Teddlie, C. (2003). Mixed methods sampling strategies in social science research. In A. Tashakkori & C. Teddlie (Eds.), *Handbook of mixed methods in social and behavioral research* (pp. 273–296). Thousand Oaks, CA: Sage.

Lefebvre, C., Manheimer, E., & Glanville, J. (2011). Chapter 6: Searching for studies. In J. P. T. Higgins & S. Green (Eds.), *Cochrane handbook for systematic reviews of interventions Version 5.1.0.* Retrieved from http://www.cochrane-handbook.org

Lorenzetti, D. L., & Ghali, W. A. (2013). Reference management software for systematic reviews and meta-analyses: An exploration of usage and usability. *BMC Medical Research Methodology, 13,* 141. doi:10.1186/1471-2288-13-141

Mokkink, L. B., Terwee, C. B., Gibbons, E., Stratford, P. W., Alonso, J., Patrick, D. L., . . . De Vet, H. C. (2010). Inter-rater agreement and reliability of the COSMIN checklist. *BMC Medical Research Methodology, 10,* 82. doi:10.1186/ 1471-2288-10-82

Montori, V. M., Swiontkowski, M. F., & Cook, D. J. (2003). Methodologic issues in systematic reviews and meta-analyses. *Clinical Orthopaedics and Related Research, 413,* 43–54. doi:10.1097/01.blo.0000079322.41006.5b

Oancea, A. (2005). Criticisms of educational research: Key topics and levels of analysis. *British Educational Research Journal, 31,* 57–183. doi:10.1080/ 0141192052000340198

Onghena, P. (2005). Single-case designs. In B. Everitt & D. Howell (Eds.), *Encyclopedia of statistics in behavioral science,* vol. 4 (pp. 1850–1854). Chichester, England: Wiley.

Orwin, R. G. (1994). Evaluating coding decisions. In H. Cooper & L. V. Hedges (Eds.), *The handbook of research synthesis* (pp. 139–162). New York, NY: Russell Sage Foundation.

Paterson, B. L., Thorne, S. E., Canam, C., & Jillings, C. (2001). *Meta-study of qualitative health research: A practical guide to meta-analysis and meta-synthesis.* Thousand Oaks, CA: Sage.

Patton, M. (1990). *Qualitative evaluation and research methods* (pp. 169–186). Beverly Hills, CA: Sage.

Petticrew, M., Egan, M., Thomson, H., Hamilton, V., Kunkler, R., & Roberts, H. (2008). Publication bias in qualitative research: What becomes of qualitative research presented at conferences? *Journal of Epidemiology and Community Health, 62,* 552–554. doi:10.1136/jech.2006.059394

Saini, M., & Shlonsky, A. (2012). *Systematic synthesis of qualitative research*. New York, NY: Oxford University Press.

Shaw, R. L., Booth, A., Sutton, A. J., Miller, T., Smith, J. A., Young, B., ..., & Dixon-Woods, M. (2004). Finding qualitative research: An evaluation of search strategies. *BMC Medical Research Methodology*, *4*, 5. doi:10.1186/1471-2288-4-5

Suri, H. (2011). Purposeful sampling in qualitative research synthesis. *Qualitative Research Journal*, *11*, 63–75. doi:10.3316/QRJ1102063

University of York. (2014). *Finding studies for systematic reviews: A resource list for researchers*. Retrieved from http://www.york.ac.uk/inst/crd/finding_studies_systematic_reviews.htm

QUALITY ASSESSMENT OF PRIMARY RESEARCH STUDIES

======================== ∂∞∾ ========================

Chapter Outline

Quality assessment of primary studies is generally perceived as a valuable asset in the development of a literature review. A plethora of instruments to assess the quality of primary research studies is currently available in the scientific literature. Although there is a general consensus on what constitutes quality for several research designs, academic debates on what an acceptable degree of methodological quality is for different types of quantitative, qualitative, and MMR studies are ongoing. In this chapter, we offer guidance on (a) whether we should consider quality assessment in a literature review and why, (b) what the different approaches to quality assessment are for different study designs including how we can motivate our choice for a particular approach to judging quality, and (c) how we are going to deal with the outcome of a quality assessment in terms of including or excluding primary studies from our MMRS and in terms of controlling for differences in methodological quality between studies.

======================== ∂∞∾ ========================

DEFINING QUALITY ASSESSMENT

Quality assessment (also called "quality appraisal" or "critical appraisal") refers to the process of systematically examining research evidence to assess its validity and its relevance before including it into MMRS that feed into our daily decision-making processes (Hill & Spittlehouse, 2003). In essence, quality assessment assists us in evaluating whether a primary research study has properly been conducted and whether the evidence it produced can be trusted. At some point in your career, you may have come across primary research studies that address a similar topic but reach fundamentally different conclusions. If you did, think about the strategy you have used to deal with this issue. You may have looked at who wrote the studies, or in which journal they have been published, to evaluate the trustworthiness of the author or the journal. You may have been tempted to follow the arguments of the most famous (and therefore most credible?) researcher or journal. The argument of "authority" has long been used to help people decide on which findings they were more likely to believe. However, it is an inaccurate measure of quality that builds on the belief that authorities are "right." This particular idea has been challenged by recent cases of scientific fraud from respected research authorities (Crocker & Cooper, 2011). This chapter outlines some of the core principles of quality assessment. Should we assess the quality of each type of study in order to include them in our MMRS? And if we do, what sort of frameworks or instruments are available to us, what are the consequences of our choices for a particular instrument, and how do we deal with the outcome of a quality assessment exercise? Should we exclude particular studies in our MMRS based on such a quality assessment, or should we assign more weight to those that obtain a higher score from a review author? Is there a merit in describing the limitations of a study that we have observed from reading the research report without excluding any of them, and what are the potential risks of doing so?

By the end of this chapter, you will be able to reach your own judgment about what constitutes quality in primary research. In a best-case scenario, it will allow you to detect potential methodological flaws in your set of primary studies that may explain the differences in conclusions reached. Beware of the fact that what is critically appraised in the context of an MMRS is the research report of a primary study, rather than the study itself. It follows that we can only judge what has been written up by the researchers. A good research report featuring a transparent methodological audit trail is the basis for all quality assessment procedures.

SHOULD WE APPRAISE THE
QUALITY OF STUDIES AND WHY?

Several review authors and nonprofit organizations involved in the production and dissemination of systematic reviews have contributed to the debates on whether we should appraise and, if so, how. Opinions on the type of criteria that should generally be promoted differ between research traditions and between individual authors. Review authors subscribe to a variety of ontological and epistemological positions that may lead them into agreeing on a basic set of quality criteria but disagreeing on another (see Chapter 1 for a more extensive explanation of potential philosophical stances of review authors). There is little disagreement among review authors on the importance of judging the overall quality of a research study in terms of providing a neutral research account, which brings clarity, consistency, and added value in terms of implications provided for policy and practice. However, there is considerable disagreement about how these values should be translated into criteria that do justice to the quality of research studies. Over time, and in a general move toward developing the scientific method, concepts such as neutrality, consistency, and applicability of research have been transformed into objectivity, validity, reliability, and generalizability. These measures now serve as guiding principles in determining the quality of studies conducted in a quantitative research tradition. Reactions have been mixed in relation to whether such measures should be applied to qualitative studies included in an MMRS (Cohen & Crabtree, 2008). In what follows we will provide insight into this ongoing debate.

The major aim in assessing the quality of a primary study for inclusion in an MMRS is to evaluate whether a study has been conducted according to the methodological state of the art. It helps review authors to distinguish sound from poor studies and delineates what it takes for an intervention or program to be considered empirically supported (Schlosser, 2009). Early pioneers, such as the first generation of Cochrane and Campbell review authors, have emphasized the importance of "risk of bias" in critically appraising experimental and quasi-experimental study designs (Turner, Boutron, Hróbjartsson, Altman, & Moher, 2013). They mainly evaluated the extent to which a study succeeded in controlling issues of bias that may impact the research results or distort the results. A researcher conducting a study that is free from bias is then able to answer a research question "correctly." This is crucially important because we know that systematic reviews in which the findings of invalid studies are statistically pooled may produce misleading results, yielding a narrow confidence interval around the wrong intervention effect estimate (Higgins et al., 2008). This potential over- or underestimation of an effect is often referred to as **risk of bias**. Critically appraising a primary study in terms of its validity is therefore considered an essential component of any MMRS and has played a dominant role in decisions to include or exclude studies from an MMRS. However, the principles outlined by major review organizations such as Campbell and Cochrane are limited in the sense that they have specifically been developed for experimental designs. Claiming that the debate on what constitutes quality in quantitative research is currently closed would therefore be inappropriate. For a lot of other quantitative study designs now considered for inclusion in systematic reviews, there is no internationally consolidated consensus yet on what the dominant quality criteria should be and how they should be dealt with in terms of in- or excluding studies for an MMRS (Evers, Goossens, de Vet, van Tulder, & Ament, 2005; Tate et al., 2008; Vandenbroucke, 2004). We invite you to remain sensitive to arguments raised in old and new debates that will appear in upcoming literature.

The development of a coherent vision on quality assessment for qualitative studies considered for inclusion in an MMRS is even more complicated. Review authors engaged in qualitative evidence synthesis may take radical philosophical positions toward quality assessment that sometimes oppose each other. A first group of qualitatively oriented review authors would argue that the focus on limiting bias to establish validity is antithetical to the philosophical foundations of qualitative approaches to inquiry. They are located in diverse understandings of knowledge and do not distance the researcher from the researched. The researcher is the instrument through which data are collected and analyzed. Consequently, the data analysis is legitimately influenced by the researchers when they interpret the data. These researchers would emphasize the important aspect of "relevance" of an insight from a primary study to complete their understanding of an issue. They generally downsize the importance of methodological quality (Morse, Barett, Mayan, Olson & Spiers, 2002; Smith, 1984). This point of view is more likely to occur in review authors subscribing to a postmodern, idealist discourse in qualitative research.

A second group of qualitative review authors promotes the principle that qualitative research studies should be assessed using the same criteria as used in appraising quantitative research; that is, the quality of original research should first of all be evaluated in terms of its ability to produce valid, reliable, and generalizable research findings (Kirk & Miller, 1986). This point of view is mostly associated with review authors taking a realist stance to synthesis (see Chapter 1). There are many positions in between both ends of the philosophical spectrum applied to qualitative research methods. The balance between relevance of an insight for an MMRS as an inclusion criterion and a lack of methodological quality as an exclusion criterion is fragile. A recent update of a review on published qualitative evidence syntheses in the field of health care has shown an increase in the number of review authors conducting a quality assessment exercise as part of their review. So the number of health care–oriented review authors openly rejecting quality assessment as part of evaluating the merit of qualitative strands of evidence is decreasing (Hannes & Macaitis, 2012). Authors of a similar study in progress looking into social science literature indicate that a quality assessment of primary studies is less likely embedded in the review process (personal communication with Parylo & Hannes, 2015). The strong impact of the Cochrane Collaboration and the evidence-based practice movement promoting the "risk of bias" discourse may explain why review authors in the field of health care are generally more sensitive toward the idea of quality assessment.

How do we need to respond to the variety in epistemological positions toward quality assessment when primary MMR studies are part of our set of included articles? Review authors can draw inspiration from a review from Mieke Heyvaert, Karin Hannes, Bea Maes, and Patrick Onghena (2013), outlining different strategies for quality assessment, with two main positions reported on: (a) Authors should critically appraise each of the evidence strands separately or (b) MMR studies are more than just the sum of their individual qualitative and quantitative strands of evidence and require specific criteria. Therefore, MMR studies should best be appraised according to review authors' judgments of what constitutes "good" MMR. We promote an assessment framework that emphasizes specific characteristics of MMR studies, for example, the author's level of attention paid to justifying an MMR approach and the reporting of how and why qualitative and quantitative data collection and analytical techniques have been combined. In addition, it is worthwhile to look into how the research findings from quantitative and qualitative data have been integrated to formulate conclusions to be drawn from the study and whether it has been done adequately (Heyvaert et al., 2013).

A helpful framework to familiarize yourself with the core principles related to quality assessment is the one produced by Yvonna Lincoln and Egon Guba (1985), in which efforts have been made to translate a quantitative jargon into a set of concepts that is more sensitive to the specific nature of qualitative research. In the absence of a consolidated conceptual framework for the quality assessment of MMR studies, we added specific criteria for primary MMR studies to the list (see Box 4.1). This jargon can be used to facilitate communication on the sort of criteria that may assist a quality assessment of primary MMR studies.

Box 4.1. Basic Methodological Jargon to Discuss Quality Assessment of Primary Studies

Aspect	Qualitative Studies	MMR Studies	Quantitative Studies
Truth value/ Bias	Credibility: the extent to which the representation of data fits the views of the participants studied, whether the findings hold true.	Meta-validity: the extent to which the overarching arguments or inferences made remain sensitive to the original ideas as expressed in both the quantitative and qualitative strands of evidence.	Internal Validity: the extent to which you are able to say that no other variables except the one you are studying caused the result.
Applicability	Transferability: the extent to which research findings are transferable to other specific persons, settings, situations, or timeframes.	Meta-transfer: the extent to which the complexity level featured in a primary MMR study and addressed by the different strands of evidence is of a similar nature than in other persons, settings, situations or timeframes.	External Validity or Generalizability: the extent to which the conclusions in a study would hold for other persons, settings, situations, or timeframes.

Aspect	Qualitative Studies	MMR Studies	Quantitative Studies
Consistency	Dependability: the extent to which the process of research is logical, traceable, and clearly documented, particularly on the methods chosen and the decisions made by the researchers.	Mixing Rationale: the extent to which the mixing of the results and findings is clearly illustrated, motivated, and documented in terms of additional value of the mixed component.	Reliability: the extent to which the results or findings are consistent or repeatable.
Neutrality	Confirmability: the extent to which findings are qualitatively confirmable through the analysis being grounded in the data and through examination of the audit trail.	Meta-inference: the extent to which the inferences made in the findings or conclusion sections incorporate and are grounded in the inferences made in the separate strands of evidence.	Objectivity: the extent to which a person has the quality of being true or bias-free, outside of his or her individual biases, interpretations, feelings, and imaginings.

APPROACHES TO QUALITY ASSESSMENT

A few choices have to be made within an MMRS review team before it can actually start a quality assessment of relevant studies. First, review authors need to decide whether they are going to use an overall judgment approach or some form of criterion-based judgment approach. Although the second strategy is more commonly used and promoted, expert judgment may play a role in teams that decide to include studies based on relevance of their content to ensure a baseline measurement of quality. Second, the team needs to decide whether it will opt for an integrative quality assessment framework with generic criteria cutting across the different strands of evidence or whether a design-specific tool would be more appropriate to judge the quality of the studies included.

Expert Judgment Versus Criterion-Based Judgment

Judging the quality of other people's research has been an important part of our scientific research history and is generally known under the term **peer review**. Peer review, in its original meaning, is a method to improve the quality of scientific work in progress by submitting it to a critical assessment usually done by peers or colleagues working in a similar domain. Peer review processes are based on the presumption that peers and colleagues will notice several errors, increasing the chance that an error or shortcoming of the author will be discovered and corrected before publication. Some editors provide their peer reviewers with guidance on what exactly to assess, whereas others give their peer reviewers the freedom to submit an overall judgment on the quality, relevance, and importance of the paper for their particular discipline. Critical assessment processes in systematic reviews do not differ substantially from peer review processes, except that the quality assessment procedures occur post hoc, after the study has been published. This suggests that we potentially correct for methodological flaws that have not previously been picked up or for quality criteria that have not been considered in the pre–post peer review processes.

Like editors, review authors critically assessing the quality of relevant articles need to decide whether they are going to stick to a predefined set of quality markers or whether they will prefer an overall judgment approach. Review authors may vary in their viewpoint about the level of detail required in an appraisal framework. Experienced review authors may prefer to work with a minimum set of criteria for concomitantly appraising the methodological quality of the qualitative, quantitative, and MMR studies in an MMRS. They may actively search for a selection without which a judgment about quality cannot be made (see Pluye, Gagnon, Griffiths, & Johnson-Lafleur, 2009). These review authors most likely have the knowledge to supplement their checklist approach with an expert judgment that will implicitly be used when discussing the outcome of the quality assessment exercise with fellow review authors. Other, less experienced review authors may feel more comfortable with an extensive list of criteria, supplemented with a user guide on what exactly to look for in the article text. An assessment of the available levels of expertise in your review team is crucial to a successful endeavor in critically appraising research and in choosing the instruments that will be more likely to provide the right guidance.

Although checklist approaches outlining clear criteria have gained popularity in the last couple of years, the power of an overall judgment approach conducted by methodological experts should not be underestimated. Experienced methodologists have valuable insights, for example, into potential flaws in the logic of conceptualizing a study that are not at first apparent when quality is evaluated through a checklist approach. In essence, checklists are no more than technical tools that assist us in appraising original research. They provide us with a set of indicators to look for in the methods or discussion sections. These indicators are chosen based on general agreements between researchers on what constitutes quality in a particular research tradition. Some would only include criteria that evaluate the level of methodological soundness of a study. Other instruments stimulate review authors to assess the importance and value of a particular article for progressing the knowledge base in our field of interest. Overall, our judgments based on criteria outlined in checklists determine the extent to which we have confidence in the competence of the authors to conduct research that follows established norms (Morse et al., 2002). However, the use of checklists does not decrease discrepancies in judgment between different review authors, nor does it allow us to identify the quality of the decisions made by the researchers, the rationale behind these decisions, and the responsiveness or sensibility of the researcher to the data (Hannes, 2011). They do invite us, though, to clarify for which particular criterion a study fails to convince us and why it should be excluded from our MMRS. This level of transparency gives structured or checklist approaches to quality assessment an advantage over expert judgment in further discussions within the team. In any case, review authors need to have a general understanding of the methodological principles underpinning the study designs under evaluation. Alternatively, they may want to consider compiling a team of evaluators that do cover for the necessary expertise.

Given the variety of paradigms used in qualitative and MMR studies, an overall judgment approach may be useful to consider, for instance, when trying to evaluate the consistency of the research paradigm adopted in relation to the findings presented. In the case of MMR studies, an in-depth evaluation of methodological coherence or congruity between paradigms and methods that guide the research project should be conducted. This includes an evaluation of the analytic stance and theoretical position of the researcher and his or her responsiveness, openness, and grounding of the data in the study. The latter includes a systematic check and confirmation of the fit between the data gathered and the conceptual work involved in the analysis and interpretation. Overall, review teams benefit from involving people with content expertise for such an evaluation exercise. It increased the chance to end up with a consistent assessment. Piloting the chosen instrument is always a good idea (see Practical Tip 4.1) to evaluate whether potential conflicts between review authors are related to the lack of clarity in criteria promoted in the instrument used or to disciplinary, country, epistemological, or other differences between review authors in how to interpret certain criteria.

Generic Versus Design-Specific Frameworks for Quality Assessment

Whether to use a generic framework to conduct a quality assessment or a design-specific one for each of the included strands of evidence currently is subject to the personal preference of the authors involved in a review project. Some authors plead for an approach in which a unique set of criteria is used for each different strand of evidence. This is generally referred to as a "separate approach" (Bryman, 2006). Review authors opting for a segregated or a contingent MMRS (see Chapter 2) are generally more likely to use checklists that have been developed with a particular (quantitative or qualitative) study design in mind. Although the same strategy can be used by review authors opting for an integrative MMRS, these authors may potentially benefit from a generic quality assessment instrument, outlining general criteria that can be

---

Practical Tip 4.1: Piloting the Quality Assessment Instrument

It is helpful to test the quality assessment approach opted for within a review team on a pilot sample of articles to ensure that selected criteria are applied consistently, and that consensus can be reached. Three to six papers that, based on an initial familiarization with their content and methodology, span a range from low- to high-quality papers in the different strands of evidence provide a suitable sample for this. Ideally, this pilot is done by two independent review authors to allow for cross checking of the individual results and to spot potential areas of misunderstanding or conflict between review authors.

applied to all of the study designs included. The most appealing advantage of using a single, all-inclusive tool is the comparability of the quality assessment scores or judgments across all studies, including MMR studies. However, such an ideal instrument is hard to achieve and potentially undesirable, for reasons outlined in previous sections of this chapter, for example, the potential incompatibility of quality criteria for qualitative and quantitative research designs. Several arguments may support such a viewpoint. Although it is theoretically possible to generate a generic set of criteria that will enable us to cut across study designs, it may risk coming too close to common sense and, therefore, hardly support us in judging the merit of a study from a quality point of view. In another potential scenario, a generic set of criteria may cover at least one strand of evidence and the overall MMR study design well enough, but it will fail to be relevant or will be far too general for designs related to the other strand of evidence included. In addition, such a quality framework is less likely to provide clear instructions on what to look for in a study report and requires a substantial level of methodological expertise to be used accurately. A worthwhile compromise is a more comprehensive instrument, such as the one developed by Pluye and colleagues (2009). Their appraisal tool contains a unique set of quality indicators that allows review authors to assess the interdependent qualitative and quantitative components of a primary MMR study. In addition, the instrument outlines additional criteria that need to be taken into account when dealing with an MMR study (see Box 4.2).

The framework of Pluye et al. (2009) only outlines criteria for experimental and observational quantitative studies on a group level. Review authors including, for example, experimental single-subject research designs are advised to add an additional set of design-specific criteria to facilitate the appraisal process (e.g., Tate et al., 2008). The list with criteria for qualitative research is also fairly general and could be replaced by more specific criteria related to grounded theory, phenomenological, or other types of qualitative study designs.

We believe the use of a comprehensive framework currently is the most sensible approach in the conduct of MMRS, particularly because it includes overarching criteria for MMR studies. This has several advantages in terms of shaping the analytical part of the synthesis. First, judging the quality of decisions made and rationales provided by authors of MMR studies may inform us on how potential areas of agreement or conflict between different strands of evidence have been dealt with in the primary study, and how we

Box 4.2 Example of a Quality Assessment Framework Adopting a Design-Specific, Minimal-Criteria Approach (Pluye et al., 2009)

Types of mixed methods study components or primary studies in a SMSR context[a]	Methodological quality criteria[b]
1. Qualitative	• Qualitative objective or question • Appropriate qualitative approach or design or method • Description of the context • Description of participants and justification of sampling • Description of qualitative data collection and analysis • Discussion of researchers' reflexivity
2. Quantitative experimental	• Appropriate sequence generation and/or randomization • Allocation concealment and/or blinding • Complete outcome data and/or low withdrawal/drop-out
3. Quantitative observational	• Appropriate sampling and sample • Justification of measurements (validity and standards) • Control of confounding variables

4. Mixed methods	• Justification of the mixed methods design
	• Combination of qualitative and quantitative data collection-analysis techniques or procedures
	• Integration of qualitative and quantitative data or results

Source: Reprinted from Pluye, P., Gagnon, M. P., Griffiths, F., & Johnson-Lafleur, J. (2009). A scoring system for appraising mixed methods research, and concomitantly appraising qualitative, quantitative, and mixed methods primary studies in mixed studies reviews. *International Journal of Nursing Studies, 46,* 529–546 with permission from Elsevier.

Caution notice: Outside quantitative experimental studies, the implication of clustering primary studies or study components by quality score has not been critically examined. With respect to systematic reviews of quantitative experimental studies, the clustering of primary studies and the weighting of quantitative results by quality score are discouraged.

[a] Potential applications: *With respect to mixed methods research in general:* Appraisal of the methodological quality of qualitative, quantitative and mixed methods components. With respect to systematic mixed studies reviews: Concomitant appraisal of the methodological quality of primary qualitative, quantitative and mixed methods studies.

[b] Procedure for planning, reporting and assessing mixed methods research or mixed studies reviews. For each type of study component or primary study, describe the methodological quality by criterion. Score presence/absence of criteria respectively 1/0 (complement the retained publication with related documents, and contact authors when more information is needed). Calculate a 'quality score' [(number of 'presence' responses divided by the number of 'relevant criteria') x 100]. Use this score as a rationale for excluding 'poor quality' study components or primary studies. Use the criteria for describing the quality of retained components or studies (qualitative quality appraisal).

could be dealing with them when working on the meta-level. Second, it may provide insights into the arguments used to motivate why different strands of evidence could not fully be integrated into the primary study and what the analytic consequences are for our MMRS review. Third, it allows us to evaluate the claim that quantitative and qualitative strands of evidence provide a more comprehensive picture of a research phenomenon. It also allows review authors to assess whether the inclusion of both quantitative and qualitative evidence mattered or was appropriate at all, in producing the final conclusions of the study. Review authors are encouraged to choose the most appropriate instrument, in line with their goal and the inclusion and exclusion criteria outlined in their review protocol. Several tools will be presented in the next section.

WHAT SORT OF TOOLS ARE AVAILABLE TO SUPPORT QUALITY ASSESSMENT OF PRIMARY STUDIES?

Once the overall approach to judging the quality of studies has been clarified and motivated, we can start thinking about which particular criteria would be relevant to be considered in a quality assessment instrument or framework. Whatever list of criteria review authors decide on using in their review, they can and will be subject to critique because they are used to decide which articles are "good enough" to be part of our MMRS and which are not. We advise you to think carefully about which instrument you choose, how you intend to use it, and what motivates you to opt for a particular set of criteria (Crowe & Sheppard, 2011; Hannes & Aertgeerts, 2014). If methodological quality is more important to you than relevance, focus on criteria that allow you to distinguish fatal methodological flaws in a research study (that is, impacting on the trustworthiness of a study) from methodological compromises that each researcher has to make to be able to complete a study.

Most review authors adopt an existing quality framework. It saves them valuable time that can be spent on the actual data extraction and synthesis phase. Also, most of these instruments have been developed by experts that have given their selection considerable thought. It provides a better guarantee in terms of the consistency of the instrument, regardless of who uses it. Some other review authors, however, may find existing instruments too restrictive or potentially unsuitable for their review. In that case, you may want to consider an adaptation of an existing instrument to fit your goals better. Alternatively, you may want to develop your own. Reasons for adapting existing instruments or developing new ones may be epistemologically inspired or design related. Ideally, the final instrument resulting from what could be perceived as a "cherry-picking strategy" should best be validated. In any of these three cases, you should justify not only your choice for an instrument but also for the selection of criteria you will work with.

We already discussed design-specific, generic, and comprehensive instruments for quality assessment. In what follows, we present a selection of such appraisal instruments and focus on their content. Those conducting a segregated MMRS or a contingent MMRS in which different strands of evidence are synthesized in different phases of the review process can select several instruments and match them with the types of studies retrieved. If your intention is to integrate different strands of evidence, we suggested previously that you would probably benefit more from a generic tool presenting criteria that cut across different designs. We will discuss the particularities of relevant criteria of a limited set of instruments currently used in critically appraising quantitative, qualitative, and MMR primary studies.

Quality Assessment Criteria for Quantitative Studies

Given the range of different quantitative study designs, one can imagine that there is a large variability in the sort of criteria put forward within each of these methodological traditions. However, in the whole debate on potential frameworks to support the quality assessment of quantitative research, there are two dominant positions. The first one reduces assessment of quality to evaluating the risk of bias of a particular study. Proponents of such an approach have critiqued authors that use the phrase "assessment of methodological quality" and "risk of bias" interchangeably. "Assessment of methodological quality" refers to the extent to which study authors conduct their research to the highest possible standards, whereas "bias" refers to the potential negative impact of (a) the subjective lens of the review author in judging studies or (b) systematic differences between groups compared in a study or between reported and unreported findings. Both of these may influence the final results or findings of a study and as such the outcome of a meta-synthesis. Proponents of a risk of bias discourse mainly stress the fact that some markers of quality currently used in existing checklists are unlikely to have direct implications on the robustness of a study result and should therefore not be promoted. For example, whether a power calculation was done in a basic research study relates to the precision of results, but it does not compromise on the robustness of the results. Likewise, a clear description of inclusion and exclusion criteria in a checklist assessing the quality of published systematic reviews mainly increases the applicability of the findings of the review, rather than impacting the validity of the review outcome (Higgins et al., 2008). A description of different types of bias that has been proposed in the Cochrane framework for quality assessment of randomized controlled trials (RCTs; and to some extent quasi-RCTs) can be consulted in Box 4.3. The instrument described allows review authors to assess the extent to which a quantitative part of their review draws valid conclusions about the effects of the intervention promoted. It addresses five different types of potential bias: selection bias, performance bias, detection bias, attrition bias, and reporting bias (column 1). Invalid studies may produce a misleading result, yielding a narrow confidence interval around the wrong intervention effect estimate. The judgement for each entry (column 3), according to Higgins and colleagues (2008), involves assessing the presented risks of bias that follows as "low risk," as "high risk," or as "unclear risk," with the last category indicating either lack of information or uncertainty over the potential for bias. The judgement is largely based on the type of info authors of primary studies provide in their reports (column 2). Review authors generally decide on their own cut-off point for inclusion or exclusion of studies based on the quality assessment.

The type of studies included in an MMRS largely depends on the type of questions that need to be answered and on the sort of research evidence that is available for synthesis. For each type of study, a different set of criteria applies. For example, an important criterion to consider in the context of judging the quality of observational, longitudinal studies could be a risk of bias introduced by confounding variables. Deeks and colleagues (2003) selected six potentially useful assessment frameworks for nonrandomized studies. Two of them were perceived as the most useful for review authors: the Downs and Black instrument (Downs & Black, 1998) and the Newcastle-Ottawa Scales (Wells et al., 2008). The Downs and Black instrument generally requires considerable epidemiological expertise, is time-consuming, and is difficult to

Box 4.3 Description of Different Types of Bias*

Domain	Support for judgment	Review authors' judgment
Selection bias: Systematic differences between baseline characteristics of the groups that are compared.		
Random sequence generation	Describe the method used to generate the allocation sequence (also referred to as blocking in randomization) in sufficient detail to allow an assessment of whether it should produce comparable groups.	Selection bias (biased allocation to interventions) due to inadequate generation of a randomized sequence.
Allocation concealment	Describe the method used to conceal the allocation sequence in sufficient detail to determine whether intervention allocations could have been foreseen in advance of, or during, enrollment.	Selection bias (biased allocation to interventions) due to inadequate concealment of allocations prior to assignment.
Performance bias: Systematic differences between groups in the program that is provided, or in exposure to, factors other than the interventions of interest.		

(Continued)

(Continued)

Domain	Support for judgment	Review authors' judgment
Blinding of participants and personnel *Assessments should be made for each main outcome (or class of outcomes).*	Describe all measures used, if any, to blind study participants and personnel from knowledge of which intervention a participant received. Provide any information relating to whether the intended blinding was effective.	Performance bias due to knowledge of the allocated interventions by participants and personnel during the study.
Detection bias: Systematic differences between groups in how outcomes are determined.		
Blinding of outcome assessment *Assessments should be made for each main outcome (or class of outcomes).*	Describe all measures used, if any, to blind outcome assessors from knowledge of which intervention a participant received. Provide any information relating to whether the intended blinding was effective.	Detection bias due to knowledge of the allocated interventions by outcome assessors.
Attrition bias: Systematic differences between groups in withdrawals from a study.		
Incomplete outcome data *Assessments should be made for each main outcome (or class of outcomes).*	Describe the completeness of outcome data for each main outcome, including attrition and exclusions from the analysis. State whether attrition and exclusions were reported, the numbers in each intervention group (compared with total randomized	Attrition bias due to amount, nature, or handling of incomplete outcome data.

	participants), reasons for attrition/exclusions where reported, and any re-inclusions in analyses performed by the review authors.	
Reporting bias: Systematic differences between reported and unreported findings.		
Selective reporting	State how the possibility of selective outcome reporting was examined by the review authors, and what was found.	Reporting bias due to selective outcome reporting.
Other bias: e.g., carry-over in cross-over trials and recruitment bias in cluster-randomized trials. Contamination whereby the experimental and control interventions get "mixed," etc.		
Other sources of bias	State any important concerns about bias not addressed in the other domains in the tool. If particular questions/entries were prespecified in the review's protocol, responses should be provided for each question/entry.	Bias due to problems not covered elsewhere in the table.

*Based on the Cochrane Collaboration's tool for assessing risk of bias (http://handbook.cochrane.org/).

apply to case-control studies (MacLehose et al., 2000). The Newcastle-Ottawa Scales contain only eight items, and the tool is simpler to apply (Wells et al., 2008). A version to be used in critically appraising cohort studies is presented in Box 4.4. A similar version for the assessment of case-control studies is available from http://www.ohri.ca/programs/clinical_epidemiology/oxford .asp. As with countless other frameworks, you may want to customize the items to your review questions of interest.

Assessing what researchers actually did to control for confounding factors may be difficult because very often the information provided by authors of

---

Box 4.4   Newcastle-Ottawa Scale for the Quality Assessment of Cohort Studies (Wells et al., 2008)

Note: A study can be awarded a maximum of one star for each numbered item within the Selection and Outcome categories. A maximum of two stars can be given for Comparability.

Selection

1) Representativeness of the exposed cohort
   a) truly representative of the average _____
      (describe) in the community *
   b) somewhat representative of the average _____ in
      the community *
   c) selected group of users eg nurses, volunteers
   d) no description of the derivation of the cohort

2) Selection of the non exposed cohort
   a) drawn from the same community as the exposed
      cohort *
   b) drawn from a different source
   c) no description of the derivation of the non exposed
      cohort

3) Ascertainment of exposure
   a) secure record (eg surgical records) *
   b) structured interview *
   c) written self report
   d) no description

4) <u>Demonstration that outcome of interest was not present at start of study</u>
   a) yes *
   b) no

Comparability

1) <u>Comparability of cohorts on the basis of the design or analysis</u>
   a) study controls for _____ (select the most important factor) *
   b) study controls for any additional factor * (These criteria could be modified to indicate specific control for a second important factor.)

Outcome

1) <u>Assessment of outcome</u>
   a) independent blind assessment *
   b) record linkage *
   c) self report
   d) no description

2) <u>Was follow-up long enough for outcomes to occur</u>
   a) yes (select an adequate follow up period for outcome of interest)*
   b) no

3) <u>Adequacy of follow up of cohorts</u>
   a) complete follow up - all subjects accounted for *
   b) subjects lost to follow up unlikely to introduce bias - small number lost - > _____ % (select an adequate %) follow up, or description provided of those lost *
   c) follow up rate < _____ % (select an adequate %) and no description of those lost
   d) no statement

Source: Wells, G. A., Shea, B., O'Connell, D., Peterson, J., Welch, V., Losos, M., & Tugwell, P. (2008). *The Newcastle-Ottawa Scale (NOS) for Assessing the Quality of Nonrandomised Studies in Meta-Analyses*. Ottawa, Ontario: Ottawa Hospital Research Institute.

primary studies is sparse. Practical Tip 4.2. should get you started with detecting relevant accounts for assessing the impact of confounding factors on the study under evaluation.

The list with quantitative study designs potentially covered in MMRS we have addressed in this section is far from complete. More design-related appraisal instruments have been developed, for instance, to assess the methodological quality of economic studies (e.g., Drummond & Jefferson, 1996; Evers et al., 2005) and single-subject designs (e.g., Tate et al., 2008). A box with criteria that are relevant to consider in the context of cross-sectional designs, diagnostic studies, and case studies has been made available in an article from Young and Solomon (2009). Alternatively, the Quality Assessment Skills Program (CASP) hosts a website that provides several quality assessment instruments for a broad variety of different study designs including, for example, randomized controlled trials, cohort studies, case control studies, economic evaluations, and diagnostic studies (http://www.casp-uk.net/#!casp-tools-checklists/c18f8). It also contains a checklist to assess qualitative studies that will be discussed in the next section.

Practical Tip 4.2: Confounding Factors

A good way to start is (a) checking whether confounding factors were listed up front in the protocol phase, (b) trying to identify the confounding factors that the researchers have considered and those that have been omitted, and (c) looking into how they have been measured. The ability to control for a confounding factor depends on the precision with which the factor is measured (Concato, Horwitz, Feinstein, Elmore, & Schiff, 1992). Other suggested strategies include an assessment of the balance between comparator groups at baseline, with respect to the main prognostic or confounding factors, and an identification of what researchers did to control for selection bias. This could include, for example, matching or restriction to particular subgroups, as well as stratification or regression modeling with propensity scores or covariates in the analytic sections (Higgins et al., 2008).

Quality Assessment Criteria for Qualitative Studies

Earlier in this chapter we presented a few core concepts related to the quality assessment of qualitative studies, with **credibility** referring to an evaluation of the trustworthiness of the study findings, with a focus on whether the representation of data fits the views of the participants studied (see Box 4.1). Other concepts introduced were **transferability** evaluating whether research findings are transferable to other specific settings; **dependability** evaluating whether the process of research, methods, and decisions made is logical, traceable, and clearly documented; and **confirmability** evaluating the extent to which findings are qualitatively confirmable through the analysis being grounded in the data and through examination of the audit trail (see Box 4.1). In contrast with the quantitative research community, qualitative review authors have not promoted an appraisal based solely on aspects related to validity of research. However, the number of qualitative review authors emphasizing the importance of evaluating the trustworthiness of qualitative studies has increased in the last couple of years (Hannes & Macaitis, 2012). A range of appraisal instruments and frameworks is available for use in the assessment of the quality of qualitative research. Some of these frameworks are generic, being applicable to almost all qualitative research designs. An example of such a generic quality framework is the list of criteria proposed by Garside (2014; see Box 4.5).

Box 4.5   Generic Quality Assessment Framework for Qualitative Studies (Garside, 2014)

- Trustworthiness – considering such elements such as:
  - Are the design and execution appropriate to the research question?
  - What evidence of reflexivity is there?
  - Do the voices of the participants come through?
  - Are alternative interpretations, theories, etc. explored?
  - How well supported by the data are any conclusions?
  - Are ethical considerations given appropriate thought?

(Continued)

(Continued)

- Theoretical considerations – considering such elements such as:
  - Does the report connect to a wider body of knowledge or existing theoretical framework?
  - If so, is this appropriate (e.g., not uncritical verification)?
  - Does the paper develop explanatory concepts for the findings?
- Practical considerations – considering such elements such as:
  - Does this study usefully contribute to the policy question?
  - Does this study provide evidence relevant to the policy setting?
  - Does this study usefully contribute to the review?

Source: Reprinted from Garside, R. (2014). Should we appraise the quality of qualitative research reports for systematic reviews, and if so, how? *Innovation: The European Journal of Social Science Research, 27,* 67–79. Reprinted by permission of the publisher (Taylor & Francis Ltd, http://www.tandfonline.com).

This quality framework can be applied to a broad range of qualitative studies and is sensitive to some of the more distinguished features of qualitative research studies, such as their capacity to illuminate and to explore a diverse range of possible interpretations. The contribution of qualitative studies to MMRS often relates to increasing the level of conceptual clarity. From this point of view, it seems logical that the extent to which an author is able to articulate a particular concept is taken into account when deciding on the merit of an article for inclusion in the review. An example of a checklist with a minimalistic set of general criteria has been developed by Francine Toye and colleagues (2013). It contains a few overarching guiding questions that may assist you in judging the interpretive rigor of most qualitative study designs, including the following: (a) What is the context of the interpretation? (b) How inductive is the interpretation? (c) Has the researcher challenged his or her interpretation? These questions may be useful to consider if you would opt for an expert judgment approach instead of a checklist or framework approach.

Other frameworks have specifically been developed for use with certain methods or techniques, including, for example, the framework to assess the quality of action research proposed by Kathryn Herr and Gary Anderson (2005), the quality criteria proposed by Tom Barone and Elliot Eisner (2012) to make sense of arts-based research, or the framework proposed by

Etienne Vermeire and colleagues (2002) to judge the quality of focus group research. The criteria used to judge the quality of original research studies may vary substantially across designs. However, a large number of frameworks rely—implicitly or explicitly—on a particular understanding of validity or trustworthiness of research. The underlying principle that cuts across all these different frameworks is that validity refers primarily to accounts identified by researchers of original studies and is, therefore, relative to purposes and circumstances. We know from previous comparative research on the sensitivity of frameworks to the aspect of validity that some do more justice to this criterion than others (Hannes, Lockwood, & Pearson, 2010). An example of a framework that highly supports validity criteria is the QARI instrument developed by the Joanna Briggs Institute, presented in Box 4.6.

Box 4.6   Joanna Briggs Quality Assessment Instrument (Joanna Briggs Institute, 2014)

QARI Critical Appraisal Instrument

Criteria	Yes	No	Unclear
1) There is congruity between the stated philosophical perspective and the research methodology.			
2) There is congruity between the research methodology and the research question or objectives.			
3) There is congruity between the research methodology and the methods used to collect data.			
4) There is congruity between the research methodology and the representation and analysis of data.			
5) There is congruity between the research methodology and the interpretation of results.			

(Continued)

(Continued)

Criteria	Yes	No	Unclear
6) There is a statement locating the researcher culturally or theoretically.			
7) The influence of the researcher on the research, and vice-versa, is addressed.			
8) Participants, and their voices, are adequately represented.			
9) The research is ethical according to current criteria or, for recent studies, there is evidence of ethical approval by an appropriate body.			
10) Conclusions drawn in the research report do appear to flow from the analysis, or interpretation, of the data.			
TOTAL			

Reviewers' Comments:

_____

_____

_____

Source: Reprinted from Joanna Briggs Institute (2014). *Joanna Briggs Institute Reviewers' Manual: 2014 edition*. The Joanna Briggs Institute, the University of Adelaide, Australia, with permission of the publisher.

The QARI instrument requires a substantial amount of qualitative research expertise mainly because it looks into the congruity of different components of a research study rather than evaluating the presence or absence of a particular research component like many other instruments do. The CASP instrument to assess qualitative studies offered by the Quality Assessment Skills Program already mentioned is commonly perceived as a more user-friendly tool. It can be used by those unfamiliar with qualitative research and its theoretical perspectives. This tool presents several questions that deal very broadly with some of the principles or assumptions that characterize qualitative research. It provides relevant cues on what to look for in a research study (see Box 4.7).

Box 4.7 Critical Appraisal Skills Tool (CASP) for Qualitative Research Studies

The CASP tool offers 10 questions to make sense of qualitative research. For each question, it provides cues on what exactly to look for. We provide one example of such cues for question 8 in the tool.

1. Was there a clear statement of the aims of the research?

2. Is a qualitative methodology appropriate?

3. Was the research design appropriate to address the aims of the research?

4. Was the recruitment strategy appropriate to the aims of the research?

5. Were the data collected in a way that addresses the research issue?

6. Has the relationship between researcher and participants been adequately considered?

7. Have ethical issues been taken into consideration?

8. Was the data analyses sufficiently rigorous?

9. Is there a clear statement of the findings?

10. How valuable is the research?

Example of cues for question 8:

a. Is there an in-depth description of the analysis process?

b. Is it clear how the categories/themes were derived from the data?

c. Does the researcher explain how the data presented were selected from the original sample to demonstrate the analysis process?

d. Are there sufficient data presented to support the findings?

e. To what extent are contradictory data taken into account?

f. Does the researcher critically examine his or her own role, potential bias, and influence during analysis and selection of data for presentation?

Source: Based on the CASP tool, produced by the Critical Appraisal Support Program (http://media.wix.com/ugd/dded87_29c5b002d99342f788c6ac670e49f274.pdf).

The checklists presented mainly provide review authors with an indication about whether a research project has been conducted according to the state of the art. To be judged as "good enough," qualitative papers should move beyond basic methodological requirements such as providing citations to demonstrate the credibility of the author's statement to the reader. Apart from providing a clear audit trail of the methodological process, they should contribute to advancing the wider knowledge or understanding on the practice, policy, or theory in a particular field and the arguments offered by the authors should be grounded in the data. This will allow us to unfold plausible lines of argument about the significance of qualitative evidence in our MMRS. The list with examples presented is not exclusive, with many instruments still in development or yet to be validated and others not yet commonly used in practice. You may want to draw on the list of appraisal instruments outlined in Practical Tip 4.3.

The ongoing debates on what constitutes quality in research and which criteria to opt for in the assessment of quantitative and qualitative studies show that quality is a multidimensional concept. The number of researchers opting for an MMR study is increasing, and they have certainly become more prevalent in scientific literature. It warrants the use of instruments assessing the particularities of MMR studies. Also, we have previously promoted instruments that integrate appraisal criteria from a quantitative and a qualitative research tradition or cut across these traditions in the context of conducting integrated reviews. In what follows, we will discuss how quality assessment can be dealt with for MMR studies.

Quality Assessment Criteria for MMR Studies

What we have learned so far from the whole debate on quality assessment in quantitative and qualitative research is that methods alone will not determine the quality of research for inclusion into an MMRS. The way we approach quality assessment is largely influenced by the philosophical stance (implicitly or explicitly) underpinning our choice for particular study designs. The way we position ourselves in research largely defines what we value and influences our choice for particular quality criteria and frameworks. Review authors working on a segregated MMRS would most likely opt for instruments specifically designed for assessing the quality of quantitative or qualitative research projects. Preferably, these criteria align well with our definition of what constitutes good quality in scientific research.

Practical Tip 4.3: Quality Assessment Criteria for Qualitative Studies

We identified several quality appraisal instruments in a review of published qualitative evidence syntheses (Hannes & Macaitis, 2012) including, but not limited to, the following: the Nancy Burns standards for qualitative research (1989), the Nicholas Mays and Catherine Pope criteria (2000), and the criteria developed by Jennie Popay, Anne Rogers, and Gareth Williams (1998). Various scientific disciplines may promote different instruments. Those working in the area of education can explore the standards established by the What Works Clearinghouse, to be found on the following website: http://ies.ed.gov/ncee/wwc/DocumentsSum .aspx?sid=19. You will need to decide for yourselves which instrument seems to be most appropriate in the context of your MMRS and use your own judgment to determine your choice. However, the following tips might help you to decide, if you are new to the field:

(1) Check the availability of a user guide that defines the criteria and provides suggestions on what to look for in an article. An example of a tool that comes with a user guide is the CASP tool (see Box 4.7).

(2) Most checklists have not been validated. However, information on the pilot phase often is available. Check on potential incongruences in how different raters have interpreted a particular criterion. Discuss these issues before you start the appraisal process. If your background is mainly quantitative, consider an input from a researcher familiar with qualitative research, even when an appraisal instrument suitable for novices in the field is opted for.

Most review authors conducting a segregated MMRS would choose a different framework or set of criteria to assess the quality of qualitative and quantitative studies. When MMR studies are part of the set, review authors evaluate whether the quantitative and qualitative parts can be pulled apart for the quality assessment and data extraction phase. However, several experts in MMR have pleaded against an approach that totally neglects the MMR framework outlined in such studies (Creswell & Plano Clark, 2011; O'Cathain, 2010) or an approach that is based on very generic criteria that can be applied to all sorts of study designs (Katrak, Bialocerkowski, Massy-Westropp, Kumar, & Grimmer, 2004; Young & Solomon, 2009). Instead, we should think about how these designs differ from purely quantitative and qualitative designs and thoroughly evaluate the choices made by the authors of such studies. The instrument from Pluye and colleagues (2009; see Box 4.2) already introduced us to criteria that assess the justification for an MMR approach as well as whether and how quantitative and qualitative criteria have been combined and integrated. Other authors have proposed similar, overarching criteria introducing, for example, the concept of integrative efficacy as a criterion pertaining to the mixing and integration of methods (Teddlie & Tashakkori, 2009). It evaluates whether meta-inferences adequately incorporate the inferences made in the quantitative and qualitative strands of the study. In a good-quality MMR study, authors should be able to provide the reader with theoretical explanations for potential inconsistencies that exist between the inferences made. If, for example, a quantitative study offers a beneficial effect measure for removing kids out of their home setting to improve their academic achievement, qualitative studies may present ethical reasons about why such a strategy should best be avoided. A lot of criteria to consider in MMR primary studies have been proposed lately and have been discussed in the systematic review from Heyvaert et al. (2013). Nine out of the thirteen quality frameworks retrieved by Heyvaert et al. included criteria pertaining to the mixing and integration of methods (see Box 4.8). It is assumed that at the point where the mixed method potential of a study is evaluated, quality criteria for both the qualitative and the quantitative components are met.

Box 4.8   Overview of Questions for Assessing the Quality of MMR Studies

1. Was it appropriate or adequate to opt for an MMR study?
2. Was it legitimate, and if so, has the rationale been provided?
3. Have both strands adequately been integrated?
4. Did the authors provide a clear and defensible rationale for mixing the findings of studies (see Practical Tip 4.4)?

5. Was there an overall benefit of triangulating designs or combining quantitative and qualitative strands of evidence?

6. Did the combination of quantitative and qualitative evidence minimalize bias, and if so, has it clearly been documented?

Example of cues for question 3 (based on O'Cathain, 2010):

a. Is the type of integration stated?

b. Is the type of integration appropriate to the design?

c. Is enough time allocated for integration?

d. Is the approach to integration detailed in terms of working together as a team?

e. Is the personnel who participated in the integration clearly identified?

f. Did appropriate members of the team participate in the integration?

g. Is there evidence of communication within the team?

h. Has rigor been compromised by the process of integration (similar to criterion 6 reported earlier and referred to as integrative efficacy by Teddlie & Tashakorri, 2009)?

Practical Tip 4.4: Rationales for MMR Studies

If you want to know what a defensible rationale for an MMR study could be, check the findings from a content analysis on MMR studies produced by Alan Bryman (2006), who identified 16 rationales: triangulation, offset, completeness, process, different research questions, explanation, unexpected results, instrument development, sampling, credibility, context, illustration, utility, confirm and discover, diversity of views, and enhancement.

(Continued)

(Continued)

The sort of criteria outlined in Box 4.8. facilitate a thoughtful decision process concerning the design and implementation of a primary MMR study. The claim we make here is that qualitative and quantitative strands of an MMR study should not only be answering to design-specific criteria but also be appropriately mixed to answer accurately multilayered research questions. It follows that a study's capacity to provide a better "insight" into a research phenomenon should drive researchers to conduct an MMR study. Notice the emphasis on the team work to be able to meet an adequate integration of evidence strands that nicely matches our plea for pulling together the right stakeholders to be able to conduct MMR in Chapter 2. In documenting the quality assessment process, it is important to provide a transparent outline of which particular criteria were judged as not fulfilled by which evaluator and what the final score was for an article on a particular criterion after having discussed any disagreements between review authors (see Practical Tip 4.5).

Practical Tip 4.5: Quality Assessment Categories

The quality assessment sheets for each study could be included as an annex to your MMRS report or summarized in a frequency table (see also Chapter 9). Check the scoring or judging system developed for the instrument. Several review authors have borrowed a "Yes–No" binary approach to documenting their appraisal process. For example, in an assessment of a quantitative strand of an MMRS, the answer "Yes" indicates low risk of bias, "No" indicates high risk of bias, and "Unclear" indicates an unknown risk of bias. When no information is available from which to make such judgment, this should be stated explicitly. Those who are able to contact the authors of the primary studies under assessment should consider this prior to judging a study, to tackle issues related to incomplete reporting. If you intend to review a topic that is broad or complex in its focus, choose an instrument that includes a category "Unclear" or a category

"Probably done" or "Probably not done." Some instruments provide a box to include narrative comments on what exactly the doubts of the evaluator are. This facilitates the discussion between review authors. An evaluation of connectivity with a wider theoretical background or thickness of description in terms of conceptual clarity, for example, may be harder to judge in terms of a yes or a no, particularly when the concepts have not been defined prior to the study and the development of these concepts is part of the research process. Such items require an extensive discussion between review authors.

DEALING WITH THE OUTCOME OF A QUALITY ASSESSMENT EXERCISE

There is little chance that an original research study will achieve a positive score for each of the criteria listed in the chosen framework(s) against which it has been assessed. Consequently, in the process of conducting our quality assessment, we need to think about how we plan to use and report on the outcome of our quality assessment exercise. Will we include studies that fail to report sufficient information or fail to comply with some design-related quality criteria? Do we need to decide on a cut-off point, or more specifically, does a score of 7/10 equal good quality? The answer is not straightforward. Review authors have used different strategies in dealing with the outcome of quality assessment exercises. Three core strategies on the use of quality assessment outcomes have been reported in the Cochrane Qualitative and Implementation Methods Group's online supplemental guidance (Hannes, 2011): (1) using the outcome to in- or exclude particular studies in our MMRS; (2) assigning more weight to studies that scored high on quality; and (3) describing what we have observed in the studies without excluding any of the studies from our MMRS.

Using the Quality Assessment Outcome to Include or Exclude a Study

A first strategy is to use the quality assessment outcome to include or exclude particular studies from the MMRS. This is the most radical decision review authors can make. In this particular case, only high-quality studies will be included in our MMRS. The most important issue to think about when adopting such as strategy is when do we consider a study "good enough"? There are several decisions we need to make in advance. First, review authors need to decide whether they are going to assign more weight to certain criteria on their quality assessment list. For example, they might want to exclude RCTs from their MMRS as soon as the criterion for blinding of treatment is not fulfilled, whereas other methodological flaws might be perceived as having a smaller impact on the robustness of the results. Likewise, they might want to exclude a qualitative study from their MMRS when it does not show any proof of the findings being grounded in the data. All of these decision points are somehow subjective. It becomes even more difficult when a potential cut-off point needs to be decided on within a review team. Currently, there is no standard for a cut-off point that review authors agree on internationally. Even when we decide on a cut-off point of 7/10 criteria, we still need a judgment, particularly for those studies that are on the verge between inclusion and exclusion.

Reasons for excluding an original study from the MMRS based on quality criteria should best be justified, either in the MMRS report itself or in an online annex that can be consulted by the readers. A potential risk related to this "inclusion and exclusion strategy" is that review authors may end up with an empty review because none of the studies selected for inclusion reaches the level of high methodological quality (see also Chapter 9). Furthermore, this strategy is highly debated among qualitative review authors. Often, the issue of relevance of particular insights from a primary study for the further development of a line of argument at the meta-synthesis level is used to motivate the inclusion of lower quality studies (Dixon-Woods et al., 2007). Other review authors state that primary studies must meet minimum criteria of rigor to be retained and synthesized in MMRS (Pawson, 2005). A good compromise would be to opt for a quality assessment instrument that evaluates conceptual depth and breadth of findings as well as methodological rigor. Review authors that are more sensitive to the first issue will most likely use the score on methodological rigor as a baseline measure for quality rather than as a criterion for inclusion or exclusion.

Assigning More Weight to Studies That Score High on Quality

A second strategy is to assign more weight to primary studies that score high on methodological quality. Review authors that use this particular strategy stress the importance of including all valuable insights of the original studies but agree on the fact that some studies would be featured more prominently than others. This strategy provides a solution for potential empty reviews, or reviews for which only a low number of studies are available for synthesis. An important downside of assigning different weights to studies is the complexity with which to report on the findings of the MMRS. One option is to describe the results and findings of differently rated studies in separate sections in the MMRS report. This is far from ideal, particularly for qualitatively inspired sections of the MMRS in which new theory is generated. Such theory should ideally be based on all of the relevant and illuminating findings.

If you want to take into account the methodological quality of the primary studies when conducting a statistical meta-analysis for the quantitative strand of your segregated or contingent MMRS (which will be further elaborated in Chapter 6), one possible strategy is to assign weights to the primary studies based on the methodological quality scores. In most meta-analyses, relative weights are assigned to the included primary studies based on their sample size. Primary studies based on a higher sample size are assigned a higher weight in the meta-analysis, and they will to a greater extent influence the overall effect size (see Practical Tip 6.5 in Chapter 6). However, it is also possible to assign weights to the primary studies based on their methodological quality score. In such analyses, primary studies with a higher methodological quality score are assigned a higher weight in the meta-analysis, and they will to a greater extent influence the overall effect size.

However, if you conduct a statistical meta-analysis for the quantitative strand of your segregated or contingent MMRS, you might turn to alternative procedures than assigning weights based on the methodological quality scores. A first alternative approach to take into account the methodological quality of the primary studies is using quality as **predictor** or **explanatory variable** for the intervention effect. By considering the total methodological quality score assigned to each primary study to be a continuous variable, you can perform a meta-regression analysis. For instance, by using *Comprehensive Meta-Analysis (CMA)* for conducting the statistical meta-analysis within the quantitative strand of your MMRS (see Chapter 6), you can examine the relationship between the total methodological quality score (as predictor variable) and the intervention effect (as dependent variable). If you use meta-regression to study the effect of the methodological quality of the primary studies on the intervention effect, you will likely be interested in the regression coefficient itself as well as in the statistical significance of the regression coefficient. First, the regression coefficient obtained from a meta-regression analysis describes how the outcome variable (i.e., the intervention effect) changes with a unit increase in the predictor variable (i.e., the total methodological quality score) (Deeks, Higgins, & Altman, 2011). Second, the statistical significance test of the regression coefficient obtained from a meta-regression analysis is a test of whether there is a linear relationship between the intervention effect and the predictor variable (Deeks et al., 2011). We refer to Chapter 20 of Michael Borenstein, Larry Hedges, Julian Higgins, and Hannah Rothstein (2009) for various worked examples of meta-regression conducted within the context of fixed and random effects meta-analyses (we will engage in a more profound discussion of these issues in Chapter 6).

A second alternative approach to take into account the methodological quality of the primary studies in the statistical meta-analysis for the quantitative strand of your segregated or contingent MMRS is to conduct a **sensitivity analysis**. Sensitivity analyses are meant to examine how the results and conclusions of the analyses might be affected if studies with a low methodological quality were excluded. If you consider conducting a sensitivity analysis in the context of the statistical meta-analysis within the quantitative strand of your MMRS, you may draw on supporting software programs (e.g., *CMA*). These programs allow you to exclude the set of studies with the lowest methodological quality scores from the analyses (e.g., the primary studies that did not reach a certain cut-off score), and to evaluate how the results of the meta-analysis are affected by excluding these studies. You can investigate the robustness of your meta-analysis by comparing the results for the set of high-quality studies with the results for the full set of primary studies (see Practical Tip 4.6 for a discussion of high- versus low-quality studies).

Sensitivity analyses can also be applied in qualitative evidence synthesis procedures that are used within qualitative strands of segregated and contingent MMRS. Review authors can first analyze the findings from all primary studies and then evaluate whether there are particular insights that would not be found if low-quality studies were excluded. Such an analysis is used to assist future review authors in deciding on whether to include low-quality studies. The findings of studies that have applied a sensitivity analysis to qualitative parts of a review are not straightforward. James Thomas and colleagues (2004) and Jane Noyes and Jennie Popay (2007) claimed that the findings of the studies rated as low quality did not contradict those from

> **Practical Tip 4.6: Quantitative Strand of a Segregated or Integrated MMRS: High- Versus Low-Quality Studies**
>
> When you conduct a sensitivity analysis, you can make the decision to exclude studies temporarily based on their total methodological quality scores, as discussed earlier. Such a decision is informed by the quality assessment tool you applied, and by the cut-off score described by the developers of the tool. The null hypothesis you test with this sensitivity analysis is that there is no relationship between the primary studies' total methodological quality scores and the primary studies' effect sizes. However, other hypotheses as well could inform your sensitivity analysis. For instance, randomized experimental studies are often perceived to be of higher methodological quality than nonrandomized experimental studies (e.g., Concato, Shah, & Horwitz, 2000). You might hypothesize that the effect sizes reported in the nonrandomized experimental studies included in your meta-analysis might be systematically different from the effect sizes reported in the randomized experimental studies included in your meta-analysis. To test this hypothesis, you can conduct a sensitivity analysis in which you compare the results for the set of randomized experimental studies with the results for the full set of primary studies.

studies rated as high quality. In other words, their synthesis would have come to the same conclusion.

Chris Carroll, Andrew Booth, and Myfanwy Lloyd-Jones (2012) support this line of argument. They evaluated the impact of a sensitivity analysis on qualitative data and concluded that exclusion of so-called inadequately reported studies had no meaningful effect on the overall findings of their synthesis. They also identified a correlation between quality of reporting of a study and its value as a source for the final synthesis and proposed that there is a possible case for excluding inadequately reported studies from qualitative evidence synthesis. However, they also reported on the partial loss of information in their review due to exclusion of low-quality articles. More research is needed to provide readers with any firm conclusion on the relevance of low-quality studies in MMRS. Review authors feeling uncomfortable about excluding potentially relevant insights can analyze findings from high-quality studies and then scan the low-quality studies for any missing insights that may help them to develop a more comprehensive theoretical model or line of argument. This strategy is comparable to the active search for deviant cases that basic qualitative researchers would consider to test the model that has been developed.

Describing What Has Been Observed in the Quality Assessment Without Excluding Any Studies

A third strategy is to describe what has been observed in the quality assessment exercise without excluding any studies from the MMRS. In this case, all potential valuable insights remain included because the worth of individual studies might only become recognizable at the point of synthesis rather than in the phase of quality assessment. Review authors still have the option to separate the findings from lower and higher quality studies and discuss them in different tables or parts in a review report (see the strategies for sensitivity analysis mentioned earlier). However, a more commonly found strategy is to devolve the evaluating of the quality of the studies to the reader. Review authors then rely on the judgment of their end-user to evaluate whether the findings are trustworthy in the context in which they have been generated. Review authors that synthesize evidence on more recent phenomena of interest, for which scientific evidence is still scarce, may not have another option, then, to include everything to build a meaningful storyline.

Regardless of the approach chosen for the quality assessment stage of the MMRS, review authors should be sufficiently transparent about the choices that have been made. In line with the guidance outlined by international non-profit organizations such as the Cochrane and Campbell collaborations, we suggest adopting the convention of using at least two review authors for the quality assessment process. This is a useful legacy from quantitative-based review processes that has relevance for MMRS as well. The opinion of others on whether particular criteria are fulfilled may assist review authors in seeing and experiencing a broader range of possible interpretations.

REMAINING CHALLENGES FOR THE QUALITY ASSESSMENT STAGE

A key difficulty in the assessment of study quality is the obstacle provided by incomplete reporting. Although the emphasis should be on potential methodological flaws in the actual design and conduct of a primary study, it can be tempting to resort to assessing the adequacy of reporting. And even if authors of a study are aware of the relevance of, for instance, blinding in the context of a methodological quality assessment of an RCT, in some cases, it may be impractical or impossible to blind participants or study personnel to the intervention. Consequently, it would be an inappropriate judgment to categorize all such studies as "low quality." Rather, it shows that our methods base currently still is incomplete in terms of providing us with an elegant solution for all types of projects and problems. The different opinions about how to approach quality assessment indicate that the whole debate on what constitutes quality has a normative flavor to it. Any compilation of criteria in a checklist is most likely inspired by ideological and methodological preferences that are mainly theoretical in nature and may not fully allow review authors to adapt methodological features to create a contextually inspired "fit for purpose." This would imply that newly developed approaches to researching complex phenomena may risk being excluded from a synthesis based on reasonable but potentially inappropriate doubts about a study's quality. This may eventually lead to a potential lack of innovation in research.

Summary Points

- Quality is a multidimensional concept that usually covers several dimensions, including methodological soundness, relevance, and transparency of reporting.
- Quality assessment is a highly debated area, so choose wisely from the number of instruments and frameworks available. Take into account the nature of the studies you will be working with in your MMRS, your personal viewpoints in terms of what constitutes good quality, and how these are negotiated within your review team. Where necessary, adapt existing instruments to create a better fit for purpose.
- Consider the type of MMRS you are conducting in deciding on the right approach to quality assessment. You are probably better off with a design-specific approach to quality assessment if you are conducting a segregated MMRS. If you opt for an integrative type of MMRS, a framework that cuts across different designs could be a more

appropriate choice. In a contingent MMRS, the set of instruments can be negotiated during the process of conducting the review.

- The outcome of a quality assessment exercise can be used to include or exclude studies, to give more weight to high-quality studies, or as a baseline measure for quality without excluding any of the studies. Regardless of the approach eventually chosen, there is a need to pre-serve the transparency of the method through careful documentation of decisions made.

- Be aware of the fact that the summary or synthesis of findings in your MMRS is influenced by the type of instrument used and the criteria opted for, particularly when you decide on excluding lower quality studies. Also, whether a study meets the methodological standard might depend on the instrument used. Sensitivity analyses are promoted as an interesting approach to explore whether insights are lost when deciding on an exclusion approach based on quality.

- As a general principle, we believe that "the skill in quality assess-ment lies not in identifying problems, but in identifying errors that are large enough to affect how the result of the study should be interpreted" (Petticrew & Roberts, 2006, p. 128). Balance quality assessment outcomes against the relevance of an insight to develop a line of argument.

Questions for Thought

If you are ready to start your quality assessment exercise, think about the dif-ferent decision points you need to make, apply them consistently throughout the process of quality assessment, and motivate your choices. Provide a trans-parent audit trail of your answer to each of the following questions:

- Will you assess the methodological quality of the primary studies and, if so, for which particular strands of evidence in your set of included studies?

- If you decide to assess the quality of the primary studies, will you use an overall judgment approach, a domain-based approach, or a check-list-based approach?

- Will you opt for a generic tool or for a design-specific tool?

- Which criteria do you think should be part of your assessment framework or instrument?
- Will you limit the type of criteria to those that allow you to evaluate methodological rigor, or will you also assess the relevance of study results in the context of the storyline you develop in your MMRS? Will you weigh the studies based on their overall score on quality?
- How do the results apply to your specific question, population, and context?
- Once your quality assessment has been done, how are you going to report the outcome in your MMRS? Will you include or exclude papers based on the quality assessment? Will you weigh the findings or conduct a sensitivity analysis? Will you consider the outcome of the quality assessment exercise as a baseline measure of quality without having the intention to exclude papers?
- In any of the previous cases, will you use the same strategy for quantitative, qualitative, and MMR strands of evidence, or will you vary your approach according to the type of design outlined in a study?
- Most importantly, how does this all link into your overall vision on what constitutes good research?

Exercises

You may want to explore existing reviews of quality assessment instruments mentioned in this chapter and cross-compare several instruments in terms of the criteria they put forward. A useful exercise to decide among these instruments is to write down your philosophical stance toward quality assessment first. It will considerably speed up the choice process:

- Define what constitutes quality in an original research study, and investigate how much tolerance you have toward methodological flaws. Try to imagine how you would deal with potentially flawed studies that are rich in content and how you would tackle this issue on a meta-synthesis level.
- How does methodological quality relate to the relevance of a study in your personal opinion? Investigate what you naturally focus on when you read a report and what captures your attention. Then explicitly

focus on the aspects that generally get less of your attention. How does this change your opinion on the quality of an article?

- How much tolerance do you have toward the methodological compromises authors of original studies make in terms of, for instance, ethical issues that may be at play? Think ahead and develop an argument on why studies that are "compromised" should or should not end up in the pile of excluded studies.

- Think about how the heuristic options you currently take will inform your quality assessment process. And if you believe there is no such thing as a predefined position in terms of perceived quality, think again and ask yourself what the consequences might be of not identifying your personal or philosophical stance on "what constitutes good research."

Suggestions for Further Reading

Pace, R., Pluye, P., Bartlett, G., Macaulay, A. C., Salsberg, J., Jagosh, J., & Seller, R. (2012). Testing the reliability and efficiency of the pilot Mixed Methods Appraisal Tool (MMAT) for systematic mixed studies review. *International Journal of Nursing Studies, 49*, 47–53. doi:10.1016/j.ijnurstu.2011.07.002

Pluye, P., Robert, E., Cargo, M., Bartlett, G., O'Cathain, A., Griffiths, F., . . . Rousseau, M. C. (2011). *Proposal: A mixed methods appraisal tool for systematic mixed studies reviews.* Retrieved from http://mixedmethodsappraisaltoolpublic .pbworks.com

References

Barone, T., & Eisner, E. W. (Eds.). (2012). *Arts based research.* Thousand Oaks, CA: Sage.

Borenstein, M., Hedges, L. V., Higgins, J., & Rothstein, H. (2009). *Introduction to meta-analysis.* Chichester, England: Wiley.

Burns, N. (1989). Standards for qualitative research. *Nursing Science Quarterly, 2,* 44–52. doi:10.1177/089431848900200112

Bryman, A. (2006). Integrating quantitative and qualitative research: How is it done? *Qualitative Research, 6,* 97–113. doi:10.1177/1468794106058877

Carroll, C., Booth, A., & Lloyd-Jones, M. (2012). Should we exclude inadequately reported studies from qualitative systematic reviews? An evaluation of sensitivity analyses in two case study reviews. *Qualitative Health Research, 22*, 1425–1434. doi:10.1177/1049732312452937

Cohen, D. J., & Crabtree, B. F. (2008). Evaluative criteria for qualitative research in health care: Controversies and recommendations. *The Annals of Family Medicine, 6*, 331–339. doi:10.1370/afm.818

Concato, J., Horwitz, R. I., Feinstein, A. R., Elmore, J. G., & Schiff, S. F. (1992). Problems of comorbidity in mortality after prostatectomy. *JAMA, 267*, 1077–1082. doi:10.1001/jama.1992.03480080047025

Concato, J., Shah, N., & Horwitz, R. I. (2000). Randomized, controlled trials, observational studies, and the hierarchy of research designs. *New England Journal of Medicine, 342*(25), 1887–1892. doi:10.1056/NEJM200006223422507

Creswell, J. W., & Plano Clark, V. L. (2011). *Designing and conducting mixed methods research* (2nd ed.). Thousand Oaks, CA: Sage.

Crocker, J., & Cooper, M. L. (2011). Addressing scientific fraud. *Science, 334*(6060), 1182–1182. doi:10.1126/science.1216775

Crowe, M., & Sheppard, L. (2011). A review of quality assessment tools show they lack rigor: Alternative tool structure is proposed. *Journal of Clinical Epidemiology, 64*, 79–89.

Deeks, J. J., Dinnes, J., D'amico, R., Sowden, A. J., Sakarovitch, C., Song, F., . . . Altman, D. J. (2003). Evaluating non-randomised intervention studies. *Health Technology Assessment, 7*(27), 1–179.

Deeks, J. J., Higgins, J. P. T., & Altman, D. G. (2011). Chapter 9: Analysing data and undertaking meta-analyses. In J. P. T. Higgins & S. Green (Eds.), *Cochrane handbook for systematic reviews of interventions Version 5.1.0* (updated March 2011). Retrieved from http://www.cochrane-handbook.org

Dixon-Woods, M., Sutton, A., Shaw, R., Miller, T., Smith, J., Young, B., . . . Jones, D. (2007). Appraising qualitative research for inclusion in systematic reviews: A quantitative and qualitative comparison of three methods. *Journal of Health Services Research & Policy, 12*, 42–47. doi:10.1258/135581907779497486

Downs, S. H., & Black, N. (1998). The feasibility of creating a checklist for the assessment of the methodological quality both of randomised and non-randomised studies of health care interventions. *Journal of Epidemiology and Community Health, 52*, 377–384. doi:10.1136/jech.52.6.377

Drummond, M. F., & Jefferson, T. O. (1996). Guidelines for authors and peer reviewers of economic submissions to the BMJ. *BMJ, 313*(7052), 275–283. doi:10.1136/bmj.313.7052.275

Evers, S., Goossens, M., de Vet, H., van Tulder, M., & Ament, A. (2005). Criteria list for assessment of methodological quality of economic evaluations: Consensus on Health Economic Criteria. *International Journal of Technology Assessment in Health Care, 21*, 240–245. doi:10.1017.S0266462305050324

Garside, R. (2014). Should we appraise the quality of qualitative research reports for systematic reviews, and if so, how? *Innovation: The European Journal of Social Science Research, 27*, 67–79. doi:10.1080/13511610.2013.777270

Hannes, K. (2011). Chapter 4: Quality assessment of qualitative research. In J. Noyes, A. Booth, K. Hannes, A. Harden, J. Harris, S. Lewin, & C. Lockwood (Eds.), *Supplementary guidance for inclusion of qualitative research in Cochrane systematic reviews of interventions*. Version 1 (updated August 2011). Retrieved from http://cqrmg.cochrane.org/supplemental-handbook-guidance

Hannes, K., & Aertgeerts, B. (2014). Literature reviews should reveal the reviewers' rationale to opt for particular quality assessment criteria. *Academic Medicine, 89*, 370. doi:10.1097/ACM.0000000000000128

Hannes, K., Lockwood, C., & Pearson, A. (2010). A comparative analysis of three online appraisal instruments' ability to assess validity in qualitative research. *Qualitative Health Research, 20*, 1736–1743. doi:10.1177/1049732310378656

Hannes, K., & Macaitis, K. (2012). A move to more systematic and transparent approaches in qualitative evidence synthesis: Update on a review of published papers. *Qualitative Research, 12*, 402–442. doi:10.1177/1468794111432992

Herr, K., & Anderson, G. L. (Eds.). (2005). *The action research dissertation: A guide for students and faculty*. Thousand Oaks, CA: Sage.

Heyvaert, M., Hannes, K., Maes, B., & Onghena, P. (2013). Quality assessment of mixed methods studies. *Journal of Mixed Methods Research, 7*, 302–327. doi:10.1177/1558689813479449

Higgins, J. P. T., Altman, D. G., Sterne, J. A. C., the Cochrane Statistical Methods Group, & the Cochrane Bias Methods Group. (2008). Assessing risk of bias in included studies. In J. P. T. Higgins & S. Green (Eds.), *Cochrane handbook for systematic reviews of interventions* (Version 5.0.1). Retrieved from http://www.cochrane-handbook.org

Hill, A., & Spittlehouse, C. (2003). What is quality assessment? *Evidence Based Medicine, 3*, 1–8. Retrieved from http://www.evidence-based-medicine.co.uk/ebmfiles/WhatisCriticalAppraisal.pdf

Joanna Briggs Institute. (2014). *Joanna Briggs Institute Reviewers' Manual: 2014 edition*. Adelaide, Australia: Author.

Katrak, P., Bialocerkowski, A. E., Massy-Westropp, N., Kumar, V. S., & Grimmer, K. A. (2004). A systematic review of the content of quality assessment tools. *BMC Medical Research Methodology, 4*, 22. doi:10.1186/1471-2288-4-22

Kirk, J., & Miller, M. (1986). *Reliability and validity in qualitative research*. London, England: Sage.

Lincoln, Y., & Guba, E. (1985). *Naturalistic inquiry*. Beverly Hills, CA: Sage.

MacLehose, R. R., Reeves, B. C., Harvey, I. M., Sheldon, T. A., Russell, I. T., & Black, A. M. (2000). A systematic review of comparisons of effect sizes derived from randomised and non-randomised studies. *Health Technology Assessment, 4*(34), 1–154.

Mays, N., & Pope, C. (2000). Qualitative research in health care: Assessing quality in qualitative research. *BMJ, 320*(7226), 50–52.

Morse, J. M., Barrett, M., Mayan, M., Olson, K., & Spiers, J. (2002). Verification strategies for establishing reliability and validity in qualitative research. *International Journal of Qualitative Methods, 1*(2), 13–22.

Noyes, J., & Popay, J. (2007). Directly observed therapy and tuberculosis: How can a systematic review of qualitative research contribute to improving services? A qualitative meta-synthesis. *Journal of Advanced Nursing, 57*, 227–243. doi:10.11 11/j.1365-2648.2006.04092

O'Cathain, A. (2010). Assessing the quality of mixed methods research: Towards a comprehensive framework. In A. Tashakkori & C. Teddlie (Eds.), *Handbook of mixed methods in social and behavioral research* (2nd ed., pp. 531–555). Thousand Oaks, CA: Sage.

Pawson, R. D. (2005). Simple principles for the evaluation of complex programmes. *Cidades, Comunidades e Territorios, 8*, 92–107.

Petticrew, M., & Roberts, H. (2006). *Systematic reviews in the social sciences: A practical guide.* Oxford, England: Blackwell.

Pluye, P., Gagnon, M. P., Griffiths, F., & Johnson-Lafleur, J. (2009). A scoring system for appraising mixed methods research, and concomitantly appraising qualitative, quantitative, and mixed methods primary studies in mixed studies reviews. *International Journal of Nursing Studies, 46*, 529–546.

Popay, J., Rogers, A., & Williams, G. (1998). Rationale and standards for the systematic review of qualitative literature in health services research. *Qualitative Health Research, 8*, 341–351. doi:10.1177/104973239800800305

Schlosser, R. (2009). The role of single-subject experimental designs in evidence-based practice times. *National Center for the Dissemination of Disability Research (NCDDR), 22*. Retrieved from http://www.ncddr.org/kt/products/focus/focus22/

Smith, J. K. (1984). The problem of criteria for judging interpretive inquiry. *Educational Evaluation and Policy Analysis, 6*, 379–391.

Tate, R. L., McDonald, S., Perdices, M., Togher, L., Schultz, R., & Savage, S. (2008). Rating the methodological quality of single-subject designs and n-of-1 trials: Introducing the Single-Case Experimental Design (SCED) Scale. *Neuropsychological Rehabilitation, 18*, 385–401. doi:10.1080/09602010802009201

Teddlie, C., & Tashakkori, A. (Eds.). (2009). *Foundations of mixed methods research: Integrating quantitative and qualitative approaches in the social and behavioral sciences.* Thousand Oaks, CA: Sage.

Thomas, J., Harden, A., Oakley, A., Oliver, S., Sutcliffe, K., Rees, R., . . . Kavanagh, J. (2004). Integrating qualitative research with trials in systematic reviews. *BMJ, 328*(7446), 1010–2012. doi:10.1136/bmj.328.7446.1010

Toye, F., Seers, K., Allcock, N., Briggs, M., Carr, E., Andrews, J., & Barker, K. (2013). "Trying to pin down jelly." Exploring intuitive processes in quality assessment for meta-ethnography. *BMC Medical Research Methodology, 13*, 46. doi:10.1186/1471-2288-13-46

Turner, L., Boutron, I., Hróbjartsson, A., Altman, D. G., & Moher, D. (2013). The evolution of assessing bias in Cochrane systematic reviews of interventions: Celebrating methodological contributions of the Cochrane Collaboration. *Systematic Reviews, 2*(79).

Vandenbroucke, J. P. (2004). When are observational studies as credible as randomised trials? *The Lancet, 363*(9422), 1728–1731.

Vermeire, E., Van Royen, P., Griffiths, F., Coenen, S., Peremans, L., & Hendrickx, K. (2002). The quality assessment of focus group research articles. *European Journal of General Practice, 8*, 104–108.

Wells, G. A., Shea, B., O'Connell, D., Peterson, J., Welch, V., Losos, M., & Tugwell, P. (2008). *The Newcastle-Ottawa Scale (NOS) for Assessing the Quality of Non-randomised Studies in Meta-Analyses.* Ottawa, Ontario, Canada: Ottawa Hospital Research Institute.

Young, J. M., & Solomon, M. J. (2009). How to critically appraise an article. *Nature Clinical Practice Gastroenterology & Hepatology, 6*, 82–91. doi:10.1038/ncpgasthep1331

☙ 5 ☚

EXTRACTING DESCRIPTIVE DATA

Chapter Outline

In this chapter, we discuss how descriptive data can be extracted from the primary studies included in MMRS literature reviews. The descriptive data extraction process consists of four steps: (1) deciding which data will be extracted and developing a preliminary data extraction form and coding guide, (2) piloting the form and the guide, (3) conducting the data extraction, and (4) identifying and discussing differences in extraction between review authors. We will describe, discuss, and illustrate these four steps.

RATIONALE FOR DESCRIPTIVE DATA EXTRACTION

In this chapter, we will discuss how you can extract descriptive data from primary studies included in your MMRS. **Descriptive data** refer to important characteristics of the primary studies included in the MMRS. Examples of descriptive data include characteristics relating to the phenomenon or intervention under study, sample and participant characteristics, outcome or evaluation measures, geographical location and setting characteristics, characteristics relating to the design and methods used in the primary studies, and process and implementation characteristics.

The role of descriptive data for the MMRS process is twofold. First, for the review authors themselves it can be interesting to extract descriptive data to get an overview of the primary studies included in the MMRS and their most important characteristics. This helps them to become more familiar with the primary studies and the empirical data included in these studies. The descriptive data extraction can also inform the data synthesis process, which will be discussed in Chapters 6, 7, and 8. For instance, the descriptive data can inform the moderator analyses in a statistical meta-analysis (as we will discuss later, a statistical meta-analysis can be used within a quantitative strand of a segregated MMRS, see Chapter 6, or within a quantitative strand of a contingent MMRS, see Chapter 8). Review authors can use moderator analyses to test differences between subgroups and to test the influence of moderating variables on the overall effect. For instance, review authors can use moderator analyses to test formulated hypotheses such as the ones that follow: *Is the variation among the included primary studies associated with certain differences in participant characteristics? Is the variation among the included studies associated with certain differences in intervention characteristics?* Based on the descriptive data extraction, review authors can decide which variables they will include as possible predictors in their statistical meta-analysis.

Second, the descriptive data that are extracted from the primary studies can be of interest to the readers of the MMRS report. Many MMRS reports include a tabular overview of the primary studies included in the MMRS and their most important characteristics. This overview table allows the readers to get an overall idea of the most important characteristics of the primary studies included in the MMRS, and it simplifies the process of looking up the primary studies the readers are interested in (e.g., if a reader is only interested in those primary studies that were conducted on a certain subgroup of participants).

FOUR STEPS FOR EXTRACTING DESCRIPTIVE DATA

Most review authors who extract descriptive data from the primary studies included in their MMRS will use a four-step-process. First, they decide which descriptive data will be extracted and accordingly develop a preliminary data extraction form and coding guide. Second, they pilot this data extraction form and this coding guide. Third, after optimizing the data extraction form and the coding guide, at least two independent review authors from the review team use them to conduct the actual extraction of descriptive data from all the primary studies included in the MMRS. Fourth, the review authors who extracted

Figure 5.1   Descriptive Data Extraction Process

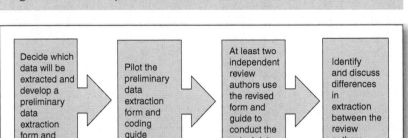

the descriptive data identify and discuss differences in extraction. Figure 5.1 presents an overview of this four-step process for descriptive data extraction. In the following sections, we will discuss each of these four steps in closer detail.

Step 1: Deciding Which Descriptive Data Will be Extracted and Developing the Descriptive Data Extraction Form and the Coding Guide

Depending on the topic and the aim of your literature review, different descriptive data characteristics might be relevant to extract from the primary studies included in your MMRS, such as characteristics relating to (1) the phenomenon or intervention of interest, (2) the population or participants studied, (3) the outcomes or evaluation measures used, (4) the geographical location or setting, (5) the primary studies themselves and the methods used, (6) the theoretical or disciplinary lens used, (7) the philosophical stance, (8) ethical issues, and (9) process and implementation characteristics. In the remainder of this section, we will discuss these nine descriptive data characteristics in closer detail.

First, you can extract data relating to the *phenomenon* or *intervention* that is being explored in each primary study. For instance, if you are conducting an MMRS on the effectiveness and applicability of various behavioral interventions for managing challenging behavior among persons with developmental disabilities, you can extract for each publication included in your MMRS which behavioral intervention or which combination of behavioral interventions was studied. Additional intervention characteristics that can be relevant to extract from the primary studies are, for instance, the length of the intervention (e.g., in hours, days, weeks, months, or years), the number of sessions or contact moments, and information on the person(s) who delivered the intervention (e.g., their age, gender, socioeconomic status, and ethnicity, as well as their qualifications, experience, and competence).

Second, you can extract descriptive characteristics relating to the *population* or *participants* included in each primary study. For example, you can extract the number of participants included in each study, as well as the participants' gender, age, and any other participant characteristic relevant for your MMRS. If you are, for instance, conducting an MMRS on persons with developmental disabilities, you could extract data on the developmental disability type for each participant and possible comorbidities. If you are, for instance, conducting an MMRS on high-school students, you could extract data on the grade level and the socioeconomic status of each student.

Third, you can extract descriptive characteristics relating to which *outcomes* or which *evaluation measures* were used in the primary studies. For example, if you are conducting an MMRS in the field of education, possible outcomes or evaluation measures are a standardized achievement test, another test measuring achievement (e.g., a teacher-developed achievement test or an achievement test from a textbook), class grades after homework, or students' study habits and skills (Cooper, 2010). If you are, for instance, conducting an MMRS in the health field, possible assessed outcomes are infection-related mortality, infection incidence, neutropenia incidence, neutropenia duration, treatment-related mortality, response, overall survival, event-free survival, progression-free survival, adverse events, or quality of life (http://chmg-old.cochrane.org/sites/chmg-old.cochrane.org/files/uploads/Template-Data%20Extraction-CHMG.pdf).

Fourth, it can be relevant to extract descriptive characteristics relating to the *geographical location* (e.g., country, state, and postal code) and *setting* for each included primary study. For example, if you are conducting an MMRS in the field of education, possible setting characteristics are the type of community where the study was conducted (e.g., urban, suburban, or rural), the type of the school where the study was conducted (e.g., public or private school), and the classroom types that were represented among the settings (e.g., regular or special education) (Cooper, 2010). If you are, for instance, conducting an

MMRS in the health field, possible setting characteristics are whether the primary study was conducted in an in-patient or out-patient setting, the hospital type (e.g., a single-center or a multicenter hospital or a community or an academic hospital), and the type of community where the study was conducted (e.g., urban, suburban, or rural).

Fifth, you can extract descriptive characteristics relating to characteristics of the *primary study* itself and the *methods* used. For example, you can extract information on the study design, on the recruitment and sampling strategy used, on the data collection methods used, and on the data analysis methods used. In addition, you can extract information relating to the *publication* itself, such as the publication year, the publication type (e.g., journal article, book or book chapter, doctoral dissertation, master thesis, private report, government report, or conference paper), whether it was a peer-reviewed publication, what type of organization produced the report (e.g., university, government entity, or contract research firm), and whether the research was funded (and, if yes, who was the funder) (Cooper, 2010).

Sixth, it can be relevant for your MMRS to extract information on the *theoretical or disciplinary lens* underpinning the primary studies. Some authors of primary studies explicitly mention a theoretical position or conceptual model that informed or guided their study in several research stages, such as the sampling stage, the data collection stage, and the data analysis and interpretation stage (Savin-Baden & Major, 2013). You can code for each primary study included in the MMRS whether such a framework was used, and if so, how this framework informed or guided the primary study.

Seventh, you can extract information relating to the *philosophical stance* of the primary study. A philosophical stance suggests a view of reality and knowledge that informs a researcher's perspectives, approaches, and methods, and that guides the researcher's actions and behaviors during the implementation of a study (Savin-Baden & Major, 2013). Examples of often used philosophical stances are (post)positivism, social constructionism, critical realism, and postmodernism.

Eighth, you can extract information on whether the primary study was approved by an ethics committee or institutional review board (IRB), whether and how the primary authors obtained informed consent from the participants, and how ethical issues were addressed in the primary studies (Schroter, Plowman, Hutchings, & Gonzalez, 2006).

Ninth, if your review project takes into account process and implementations issues, for example, in a qualitative strand of a segregated MMRS evaluating the applicability of an intervention (see Chapter 6), you can extract additional process and implementation characteristics from the primary studies. Authors such as Ray Pawson, Trisha Greenhalgh, Gill Harvey, and Kieran Walshe (2005) argued that complex social, health, and educational interventions and programs are not *magic bullets* that will always hit their target and that their effects are crucially dependent on context and implementation. Likewise, Karin Hannes (2014) argued that (a) programs or interventions may fail if one or more components are not delivered adequately to activate intervening variables, and (b) factors internal and external to the implementing environment play a powerful role in how providers deliver programs or interventions to reach their target group. We already mentioned some of these internal and external influencing factors in points one to eight, including (a) population or participant characteristics, such as the participants' age, gender, socioeconomic status, ethnicity, and risk status; (b) intervention/program characteristics, such as the level of detail that was provided on the intervention/program and on the steps to deliver the intervention/program in the field; (c) characteristics of the setting where the intervention/program was implemented; and (d) characteristics of the implementers of the intervention/program, such as their age, gender, socioeconomic status, and ethnicity, as well as their qualifications, experience, and competence (Cargo et al., 2015; Chen, 2005). Examples of additional process and implementation characteristics that you can include in the data extraction form are as follows:

- Characteristics of the organizations implementing the interventions/programs, such as their resources, provided training, quality of the provided materials, cultural sensitivity of the provided materials, and provided technical support
- Information on potential partnerships that may influence the intervention/program, such as the presence or absence of partnerships, and the consideration of community or institutional partnerships in decision making
- Intervention/program implementation characteristics, such as fidelity with the intervention/program, the dose delivered and received, recruitment and attrition characteristics, reach of the intervention/program, and the level of engagement from the providers and the participants (Cargo et al., 2015; Chen, 2005)

In addition to these nine groups of characteristics, some descriptive data extraction tables also include the primary studies' main results and the stated implications for policy, practice, and/or theory for each primary study.

Depending on the MMRS type and design, it is possible that you will extract different descriptive characteristics for different groups of studies included in your MMRS, and that you will present the descriptive data extracted for these separate groups of studies in separate tables in your MMRS report. For instance, if you are conducting a segregated MMRS design (see Chapter 2), it is possible that your report will include two descriptive data extraction tables: one for the qualitative primary studies that are included in the qualitative strand of the segregated MMRS, and one for the quantitative primary studies that are included in the quantitative strand. For both the qualitative and quantitative primary studies, it can, for instance, be relevant to extract data on the phenomenon or intervention under study, on sample and participant characteristics, on the outcome or evaluation measures used, on the geographical location and setting, on the design and methods used in the primary studies, and on process and implementation characteristics. For the qualitative primary studies, it can additionally be relevant to, for instance, extract data on the studies' theoretical background and on the philosophical stance used. For the quantitative primary studies, it can additionally be relevant to, for instance, extract data on allocation and randomization procedures. If you are conducting an integrated MMRS design (see Chapter 2), it is more likely that you will extract the same descriptive data characteristics for all the primary studies included in your MMRS. On the contrary, if you are conducting a contingent MMRS design (see Chapter 2), your descriptive data extraction will be separately conducted for each strand included in your MMRS.

After deciding on the descriptive data characteristics that you will extract from the primary studies, you can develop a preliminary version of the descriptive data extraction form. The data you will extract for a descriptive characteristic can be numerical, it can be a fixed response such as yes/no or a fixed response that should be picked from a list of provided categories (e.g., for the type of school where the primary study was conducted: public or private school), or it can be a free text box that has to be filled in (Centre for Reviews and Dissemination, 2009). Box 5.1 includes several examples of data extraction forms for various research domains.

The data extraction form is often accompanied by coding instructions. These coding instructions include guidelines on how the data extraction form

Box 5.1   Data Extraction Form Examples

Examples of data extraction forms in the field of health sciences:

- https://chmg.cochrane.org/sites/chmg.cochrane.org/files/uploads/Template-Data%20Extraction-CHMG.pdf
- Centre for Reviews and Dissemination (2009). *Systematic reviews. CRD's guidance for undertaking reviews in health care.* York, England: University of York Press. Retrieved from http://www.york.ac.uk/inst/crd/SysRev/!SSL!/WebHelp/1_3_UNDERTAKING_THE_REVIEW.htm
- Godfrey, C. M., & Harrison, M. B. (2012). *CAN-SYNTHESIZE. A quick reference resource to guide the use of the Joanna Briggs Institute methodology of synthesis* (Version 3.0). Adelaide, South Australia: Joanna Briggs Institute. Retrieved from http://joannabriggs.org/assets/docs/jbc/operations/can-synthesise/CAN_SYNTHESISE_Appendices-V3.pdf
- Noyes, J., & Lewin, S. (2011). Extracting qualitative evidence. In J. Noyes, A. Booth, K. Hannes, A. Harden, J. Harris, S. Lewin, & C. Lockwood (Eds.), *Supplementary guidance for inclusion of qualitative research in Cochrane systematic reviews of interventions. Version 1.* Cochrane Collaboration Qualitative Methods Group. Retrieved from http://cqrmg.cochrane.org/supplemental-handbook-guidance

Examples of data extraction forms in the field of educational sciences:

- Cooper, H. M. (2010). Chapter 4: Gathering information from studies. In H. M. Cooper, *Research synthesis and meta-analysis: A step-by-step approach* (4th ed., pp. 84–144). London, England: Sage Ltd.
- Wong, G. (2012). The Internet in medical education: A worked example of a realist review. In K. Hannes & C. Lockwood (Eds.), *Synthesizing qualitative research. Choosing the right approach* (pp. 83–112). Chichester, England: Wiley.

Example of a data extraction form in the field of social sciences:

- Petticrew, M., & Roberts, H. (2008). *Systematic reviews in the social sciences: A practical guide.* New York, NY: Wiley. doi:10.1002/9780470754887.app4. Retrieved from http://onlinelibrary.wiley.com/doi/10.1002/9780470754887.app4/pdf

has to be completed. In these coding instructions, you can make explicit which decision rules have to be applied for coding each descriptive characteristic. Good coding instructions can promote consistent completion of the data extraction form. The assembly of coding instructions is often called the **coding guide** or coding manual (see Cooper, 2010).

Step 2: Piloting the Extraction Form and the Coding Guide

We recommend piloting the data extraction form and the coding guide before you will use them for the actual data extraction. For the piloting exercise, at least two review authors independently look at a small set of retrieved publications (e.g., 10 publications) and use the form and the guide for extracting the necessary data from the publications. During this exercise, they can additionally note down any ambiguities or suggestions for improving the form and the guide. For instance, the coding instructions might be confusing for a certain characteristic, or the provided list of coding options for a certain characteristic might be incomplete because it does not cover all situations. Afterward, the two review authors should compare the data extracted from the publications. What is most important is the unambiguity of the coding form and of all the codes included in the form. The review authors should discuss any interpretational differences relating to the codes and the coding process. If there are inconsistencies in the extracted data and/or ambiguities in the form or in the coding instructions that accompany the form, the form and/or the guide should be revised. In case major changes were made to the form and/or the guide, we advise you to conduct a second pilot testing round, in which you use the adjusted extraction form and coding guide on a new set of retrieved publications (Higgins & Deeks, 2011).

Step 3: Conducting the Descriptive Data Extraction

After the descriptive data extraction form and the coding guide are finalized, they can be used to extract the descriptive data for all the studies included in the MMRS. The descriptive data extraction form can be filled in electronically or by hand. To increase the reliability of the MMRS, we recommend that at least two review authors from the MMRS team independently extract the data for all studies included. There are two important advantages of involving at least two independent review authors in the descriptive data extraction process: (1) Data extraction errors are minimized, and (2) potential biases being introduced to the data extraction process by the review authors are reduced (Higgins & Deeks, 2011). Furthermore, we recommend that the independent data extractors are from complementary disciplines or have complementary research skills, for example, a methodologist and a topic area specialist involved in the MMRS project (Higgins & Deeks, 2011).

A procedure that is sometimes also used in this stage, but that is less reliable than the procedure discussed earlier involving two independent review authors, is that one review author first conducts the descriptive data extraction for all studies included in the MMRS, and a second review author afterward checks the data extraction findings from the first review author for accuracy and completeness (Centre for Reviews and Dissemination, 2009).

Step 4: Identifying and Discussing Differences in Extraction

Finally, the data extraction findings by the independent review authors should be compared, and the review authors should discuss any differences and ambiguities relating to the extraction of the descriptive data. The MMRS protocol (see Chapter 2) should *a priori* mention the procedure or decision rule for identifying and resolving disagreements between the data extractors (Higgins & Deeks, 2011). Any disagreements should be noted and resolved by consensus among the data extractors or by arbitration by an additional independent review author (Centre for Reviews and Dissemination, 2009). The review authors will use the final data extraction findings they agree on for the MMRS report and for the remainder of the MMRS. It is possible to quantify the agreement on the descriptive data extraction, for example, using Cohen's kappa or the agreement percentage (see Chapter 3), and to include the final agreement score as a measure of reliability in the MMRS report, although this is not routinely done in MMRS and other literature reviews (Higgins & Deeks, 2011).

SYSTEMATIC AND TRANSPARENT DESCRIPTIVE DATA EXTRACTION PROCESS

The descriptive data extraction process should be systematic and transparent. A systematic data extraction process implies that you use a systematic and explicit methodology to extract the descriptive data from the primary studies included in the MMRS. You should describe in the MMRS report how the descriptive data extraction process was conducted. For instance, relating to the four steps presented in Figure 5.1, you should make explicit in the MMRS report what the descriptive data extraction form looked like, how this form was developed and piloted, who conducted the data extraction, and how the identified differences in extraction between the review authors were discussed and resolved. We want to remark that a systematic data extraction process is not by definition a linear process. For example, it is possible that during the data synthesis process (see Chapters 6, 7, and 8), you find out that the primary studies reveal descriptive characteristics you did not initially include in your extraction form, which turn out to be relevant to your MMRS after all. In that case, you should carefully re-read all the primary studies with this particular characteristic in mind, and extract data relating to this characteristic from all the primary studies included in your MMRS.

Transparency implies that it is clear to the reader of the MMRS report how exactly the descriptive data were extracted. Accordingly, we advise you to provide sufficient details on the descriptive data extraction process in your MMRS report. Transparency relates not only to how exactly the descriptive data extraction was conducted but also to the decisions made throughout the data extraction process and the rationale behind these decisions. Furthermore, we advise you to add the descriptive data extraction form and the coding guide you used for the descriptive data extraction as an appendix to the MMRS report to enhance transparency and to allow other review authors to replicate or update the descriptive data extraction process.

PRESENTING THE EXTRACTED DESCRIPTIVE DATA IN THE MMRS REPORT

After conducting these four steps, you can present the extracted descriptive data in the MMRS report. The overview of the extracted descriptive data is often presented in tabular format in the MMRS report. The descriptive data table allows the readers of the MMRS to get an overall idea of the most important characteristics of the primary studies included in the MMRS (e.g., in which countries has the program been studied and in which settings has the program been implemented and evaluated). It also allows the readers to look up the primary studies they find interesting. For instance, if a practitioner reads an MMRS on the effectiveness and applicability on an intervention that

Table 5.1 Example of a Table Presenting an Overview of the Primary Studies Included in the MMRS and Their Most Important Characteristics: Relatively Small Number of Included Studies

Author(s) and publication year	Participants	Intervention	Outcome measures	Location and setting	Study design	Sampling technique	Data collection methods	Data analysis methods	Results
Author(s) and publication year for Study 1	Participant characteristics	Details on the intervention used	Details on the outcome measures used	Details on where the intervention took place	Details on study design used	Sampling technique used	Data collection methods used	Data analysis methods used	Main results
...	...	...	...	...	...	...	...	...	...
...	...	...	...	...	...	...	...	...	...
...	...	...	...	...	...	...	...	...	...
Author(s) and publication year for Study N	Participant characteristics	Details on the intervention used	Details on the outcome measures used	Details on where the intervention took place	Details on study design used	Sampling technique used	Data collection methods used	Data analysis methods used	Main results

Table 5.2 Example of a Table Presenting an Overview of the Primary Studies Included in the MMRS and Their Most Important Characteristics: Large Number of Included Studies

Behavioral intervention	Study design	Primary studies[a]
Behavioral intervention A	Randomized controlled trial Prospective cohort study Retrospective cohort study Case-control study Cross sectional survey Case series	1–21 22–28 29–32 33–38 39–41 42–51
Behavioral intervention B	Randomized controlled trial Prospective cohort study Case-control study	52–65 66–70 71–73
Behavioral intervention C	Randomized controlled trial Retrospective cohort study Cross sectional survey Case series	74–84 85–94 95–101 102–108
Behavioral intervention D	Prospective cohort study Retrospective cohort study Case series	109–116 117–123 124–126
…	…	…
Behavioral intervention N	…	…

[a] The primary studies included in the MMRS appear numbered in the appendix of the MMRS report. The numbers included in the last column refer to the numbered primary studies.

is used for managing the challenging behavior of persons with developmental disabilities, but this practitioner only works with persons with autism, the practitioner can—using this table—solely look up the articles included in this MMRS that concern persons with autism.

When the number of studies included in the MMRS is relatively small (e.g., up to 40 included studies), it is possible to present the main characteristics for all included studies in tabular format in the MMRS report. Often, each row of this table represents one included study, and the columns represent the studies' characteristics most relevant to the MMRS. Table 5.1 shows an example of such a table.

When a larger amount of studies is included in the MMRS, the table (similar to Table 5.1, but containing a larger number of rows) can be presented as an appendix or online annex to the MMRS report. Another possibility in this case is to group the included studies according to the most relevant characteristic(s). This implies that each row of this table no longer represents one included study but a relevant study characteristic. Table 5.2 shows an example of such a table.

CHALLENGES OF DESCRIPTIVE DATA EXTRACTION FOR MMRS LITERATURE REVIEWS

Two important challenges for the descriptive data extraction process are incomplete reporting and incorrect reporting of the descriptive characteristics in the primary studies.

Incomplete reporting of the descriptive characteristics refers to the "blanks" in the descriptive data table generated by the MMRS authors (see Table 5.1 for an example). It is not uncommon that review authors intend to extract descriptive data that are not reported in every primary study included in the MMRS. For instance, for the qualitative strand of their segregated MMRS, review authors might want to extract data on the theoretical background and the philosophical stance for each included primary study. However, some of the primary authors might not have mentioned the study's theoretical background or the authors' philosophical stance. A first way to deal with this issue is to leave these cells in the descriptive data table in the MMRS report blank. A second way to deal with this issue is to look for other publications on the same study and to see whether the missing data are available in these publications. When we discussed the concept *multiple publication bias* in Chapter 3, we said that certain studies were repeatedly reported in several publications. It is, for instance, possible that a publication included in an MMRS is a journal article but that the accompanying *Author Note* says that this study was conducted as a doctoral dissertation (Cooper, 2010). In that case, it is likely that the doctoral dissertation contains more detailed information than the journal article. A third way to deal with this issue is to try to contact the authors of all the primary studies for which descriptive data are missing to try to fill in the blanks.

Incorrect reporting of the descriptive characteristics refers to errors and inconsistencies in the primary reports. An example is an empirical study on a group of participants for which the average age is reported more than once in the research report (e.g., in a table as well as in the text), but the reported average ages are different. In that case, it is likely that the authors of the primary study made a mistake. If you are confronted with an issue like this, we advise you to try to contact the authors and ask for clarification. If you are not able to contact the authors, you can decide to leave this cell in the descriptive data table blank.

Summary Points

- Review authors extract descriptive data from the primary studies included in their MMRS.
- Descriptive data refer to important characteristics of the primary studies included in the MMRS, such as characteristics relating to the phenomenon or intervention of interest, the population or participants studied, the outcomes or evaluation measures used, the geographical location or setting, the primary studies themselves and the methods used, the theoretical or disciplinary lens used, the philosophical stance, ethical issues, and process and implementation characteristics.
- The descriptive data extraction process consists of four steps: (1) deciding which data will be extracted and developing a preliminary data extraction form and coding guide, (2) piloting the form and the guide, (3) conducting the data extraction, and (4) identifying and discussing differences in extraction between review authors.
- We recommend that at least two independent review authors extract the data using a data extraction form and a coding guide and that they afterward identify and discuss differences in the data extraction findings.
- The descriptive data extraction process should be as systematic and transparent as possible.
- The extracted descriptive data are often reported in tabular format in the MMRS report.

Questions for Thought

- Which descriptive data will you extract from the primary studies included in your MMRS?
- How will you conduct the descriptive data extraction?
- How will you present the extracted descriptive data to your readers?

Exercises

- First, think about which descriptive data are relevant to be extracted from the primary studies included in your MMRS, and accordingly develop a preliminary data extraction form and coding guide.
- Second, pilot this preliminary data extraction form and coding guide. Have at least two review authors independently look at a small set of the publications retrieved for your MMRS (e.g., 10 publications), and let them use the form and coding guide to extract the data. Afterward, compare the extracted data and discuss any interpretational differences between the data extractors relating to the codes and the coding process. Revise the data extraction form and/or the coding guide if there are any inconsistencies and/or ambiguities. In case major changes were made to the extraction form and/or the coding guide, let the review authors independently conduct a second pilot testing round, in which they use the adjusted extraction form and coding guide on a new set of retrieved publications.
- Third, after optimizing the data extraction form and the coding guide, have at least two review authors independently conduct the *actual* descriptive data extraction for *all* the primary studies included in the MMRS.
- Fourth, the review authors who conducted the data extraction should discuss the extracted descriptive data for all included studies, and identify and resolve any extraction disagreements. Finally, they should report on the final descriptive data extraction findings.

Suggestions for Further Reading

Cooper, H. M. (2010). Gathering information from studies. In H. M. Cooper (Ed.), *Research synthesis and meta-analysis: A step-by-step approach* (4th ed., pp. 84–144). London, England: Sage.

Higgins, J. P. T., & Deeks, J. J. (2011). Chapter 7: Selecting studies and collecting data. In J. P. T. Higgins & S. Green (Eds.), *Cochrane handbook for systematic reviews of interventions*. Version 5.1.0 (updated March 2011). Retrieved from http://www.cochrane-handbook.org

Noyes, J., & Lewin, S. (2011). Extracting qualitative evidence. In J. Noyes, A. Booth, K. Hannes, A. Harden, J. Harris, S. Lewin, & C. Lockwood (Eds.),

Supplementary guidance for inclusion of qualitative research in Cochrane systematic reviews of interventions. Version 1. Retrieved from http://cqrmg.cochrane. org/supplemental-handbook-guidance

References

Cargo, M., Stankov, I., Thomas, J., Rogers, P., Saini, M., Mayo-Wilson, E., & Hannes, K. (2015). Checklist to assess implementation in systematic reviews of complex interventions (ChIMP): Development and inter-rater reliability. *BMC Medical Research Methodology.* doi: 10.1186/s12874-015-0037-7

Centre for Reviews and Dissemination. (2009). *Systematic reviews: CRD's guidance for undertaking reviews in health care.* York, England: University of York Press.

Chen, H.-T. (2005). *Practical program evaluation: Assessing and improving planning, implementation and effectiveness.* Thousand Oaks, CA: Sage.

Cooper, H. M. (2010). Gathering information from studies. In H. M. Cooper (Ed.), *Research synthesis and meta-analysis: A step-by-step approach* (4th ed., pp. 84–144). London, England: Sage.

Hannes, K. (2014). *Evaluating the right program in the wrong circumstances: Prevention strategies for authors of systematic reviews.* Madrid, Spain: International Nursing Research Conference.

Higgins, J. P. T., & Deeks, J. J. (2011). Chapter 7: Selecting studies and collecting data. In J. P. T. Higgins & S. Green (Eds.), *Cochrane handbook for systematic reviews of interventions Version 5.1.0* (updated March 2011). Retrieved from http://www .cochrane-handbook.org

Pawson, R., Greenhalgh, T., Harvey, G., & Walshe, K. (2005). Realist review: A new method of systematic review designed for complex policy interventions. *Journal of Health Services Research & Policy, 10*(suppl 1), 21–34. doi:10.1258/ 1355819054308530

Savin-Baden, M., & Major, C. (2013). *Qualitative research: The essential guide to theory and practice.* London, England: Routledge.

Schroter, S., Plowman, R., Hutchings, A., & Gonzalez, A. (2006). Reporting ethics committee approval and patient consent by study design in five general medical journals. *Journal of Medical Ethics, 32,* 718–723. doi:10.1136/jme.2005.015115

✵ 6 ✵

DATA SYNTHESIS FOR SEGREGATED MMRS LITERATURE REVIEWS

━━━━━━━━━━━━━━━ ❧ ━━━━━━━━━━━━━━━

Chapter Outline

For MMRS following the segregated design, the data synthesis stage involves the separate use of qualitative and quantitative synthesis approaches for synthesizing the corresponding qualitative and quantitative primary data included in the MMRS. In this chapter, we first discuss four qualitative synthesis approaches that can be used in the qualitative strand of a segregated MMRS for synthesizing the included qualitative primary data: formal grounded theory, meta-ethnography, thematic synthesis, and meta-aggregation. Second, for the quantitative strand of a segregated MMRS, the included quantitative primary data are often synthesized by using statistical meta-analytical techniques. In case statistical meta-analysis is impossible or undesirable, you can synthesize the quantitative data by conducting a vote counting synthesis or by presenting a narrative summary of the data. In the second part of this chapter, we discuss how you can conduct a statistical meta-analysis, a vote counting synthesis, and a narrative summary of the quantitative data. Finally, we discuss how the findings of the qualitative and the quantitative strands can be brought together in a segregated MMRS literature review.

━━━━━━━━━━━━━━━ ❧ ━━━━━━━━━━━━━━━

DATA SYNTHESIS FOR SEGREGATED, INTEGRATED, AND CONTINGENT MMRS

The **data synthesis** stage of an MMRS is the stage where the data from the primary studies are summarized, aggregated, or synthesized. In Chapter 2, three MMRS design types were discussed: segregated, integrated, and contingent (Sandelowski, Voils, & Barroso, 2006). Depending on the design type that was selected for the MMRS, the review objectives, and the review questions that were posed, various data synthesis approaches can be used. In this chapter, we will discuss possible data synthesis approaches for segregated MMRS. In Chapter 7, we will discuss possible data synthesis approaches for integrated MMRS. In Chapter 8, we will discuss data synthesis for contingent MMRS.

POSSIBLE DATA SYNTHESIS APPROACHES FOR SEGREGATED MMRS

As we discussed in Chapter 2, the segregated MMRS design is based on the assumptions that (a) qualitative and quantitative studies are fundamentally different entities and, therefore, should be treated separately; (b) qualitative and quantitative studies can readily be distinguished from each other; (c) the differences between qualitative and quantitative studies warrant separate analyses and syntheses of their findings; (d) syntheses of qualitative findings require methods developed just for synthesizing qualitative findings; and (e) syntheses of quantitative findings require methods developed just for synthesizing quantitative findings (Sandelowski et al., 2006, p. 32). In this description of segregated MMRS, Margarete Sandelowski and colleagues (2006) only mention that qualitative and quantitative primary-level studies can be synthesized within a segregated MMRS. However, it is also possible to include qualitative and quantitative data that are reported in mixed primary-level studies within a segregated MMRS. Within the quantitative strand of a segregated MMRS, you can synthesize quantitative data from quantitative primary-level studies and quantitative data from mixed primary-level studies. Similarly, within the qualitative strand of a segregated MMRS, you can synthesize qualitative data from qualitative primary-level studies and qualitative data from mixed primary-level studies. For an MMRS following the segregated design, the data synthesis stage involves the separate use of qualitative and quantitative synthesis approaches for, respectively, synthesizing the qualitative and quantitative primary data included in the MMRS.

Throughout this chapter, we will discuss several qualitative and quantitative synthesis approaches that can be used for the separate strands included in segregated MMRS. In Figure 6.1, we present an overview of the most often used qualitative and quantitative synthesis approaches within segregated MMRS literature reviews. These data synthesis approaches will be discussed in more detail in this chapter. We want to stress that this list of synthesis approaches is not exhaustive.

SYNTHESIS APPROACHES FOR THE QUALITATIVE STRAND OF A SEGREGATED MMRS

Various qualitative synthesis approaches can be used in the qualitative strand of a segregated MMRS for synthesizing the qualitative primary data included in the review, such as formal grounded theory, meta-ethnography, thematic synthesis, and meta-aggregation (Barnett-Page & Thomas, 2009; Dixon-Woods, Agarwal, Jones, Young, & Sutton, 2005; Hannes & Lockwood, 2012; Hannes & Macaitis, 2012; Ring, Jepson, & Ritchie, 2011). These qualitative synthesis approaches serve various review goals (see Figure 6.1). For instance, if you want to generate theory, you can select the formal grounded theory approach or the meta-ethnographical approach. You can use the formal grounded theory approach if you want to produce theories that are based on phenomena involving processes of contextualized understanding and action (Eaves, 2001; Kearney, 1998, 2001). You can select the meta-ethnographical approach if you intend to bring together qualitative primary-level findings into an interpretative explanation that is greater than the sum of the parts (Britten et al., 2002; Noblit & Hare, 1988). However, if you just want to describe the themes in the qualitative primary-level data you collected, you can use the thematic synthesis approach (Thomas & Harden, 2008). In contrast, if you want to generate practical and usable "lines of action" (i.e., recommendations for policy and practice), we recommend you use the meta-aggregative approach developed by the Joanna Briggs Institute (Hannes & Lockwood, 2011). In the remainder of this section, we will discuss these four qualitative synthesis approaches in closer detail.

Figure 6.1 Data Synthesis for Segregated MMRS Literature Reviews

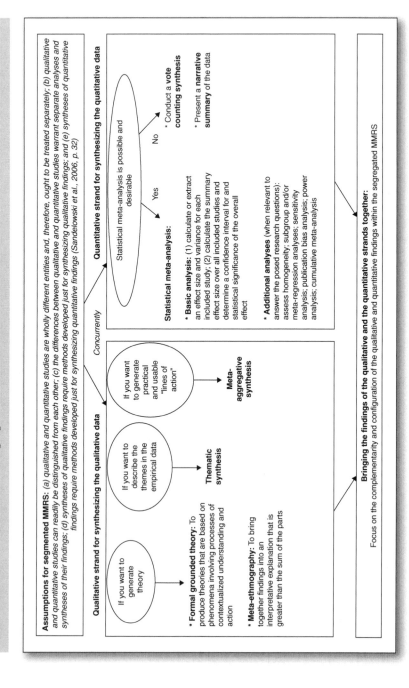

Assumptions for segmented MMRS: *(a) qualitative and quantitative studies are wholly different entities and, therefore, ought to be treated separately; (b) qualitative and quantitative studies can readily be distinguished from each other; (c) the differences between qualitative and quantitative studies warrant separate analyses and syntheses of their findings; (d) syntheses of qualitative findings require methods developed just for synthesizing qualitative findings; and (e) syntheses of quantitative findings require methods developed just for synthesizing quantitative findings (Sandelowski et al., 2006, p. 32)*

Qualitative strand for synthesizing the qualitative data   *Concurrently*   **Quantitative strand for synthesizing the quatitative data**

If you want to generate theory

* **Formal grounded theory:** To produce theories that are based on phenomena involving processes of contextualized understanding and action

* **Meta-ethnography:** To bring together findings into an interpretative explanation that is greater than the sum of the parts

If you want to describe the themes in the empirical data

Thematic synthesis

If you want to generate practical and usable "lines of action"

Meta-aggregative synthesis

Statistical meta-analysis is possible and desirable

Yes

No

Statistical meta-analysis:

* **Basic analysis:** (1) calculate or extract an effect size and variance for each included study; (2) calculate the summary effect size over all included studies and determine a confidence interval for and statistical significance of the overall effect

* **Additional analyses** (when relevant to answer the posed research questions): assess homogeneity; subgroup and/or meta-regression analyses; sensitivity analysis; publication bias analysis; power analysis; cumulative meta-analysis

* Conduct a **vote counting synthesis**

* Present a **narrative summary** of the data

Bringing the findings of the qualitative and the quantitative strands together:
Focus on the complementarity and configuration of the qualitative and quantitative findings within the segregated MMRS

Formal Grounded Theory

Grounded theory is an approach used for analyzing qualitative data within a *primary study*. The purpose of the grounded theory approach, originally developed by Barney Glaser and Anselm Strauss (1967), was to generate a new theory from empirical data to explain a phenomenon of interest by using an inductive analysis called **constant comparison of data**. The essentials of the grounded theory approach are theoretical sampling, concurrent data collection and data analysis phases, an inductive approach to analysis, the use of constant comparative analysis, the premise that theory can emerge from the data, and the continuation of the processes of data collection and data analysis until theoretical saturation is reached. Based on the purposes, methods, and assumptions of the grounded theory approach for analyzing qualitative data within a primary study, review authors such as Yvonne Eaves (2001) and Margaret Kearney (1998, 2001) adapted the grounded theory approach to be used at the synthesis level. Similar to the basic grounded theory approach applied at the primary study level, the **formal grounded theory** approach applied at the *synthesis level* uses theoretical sampling, is aimed at theory building, uses the inductive constant comparative method for synthesizing the included data, and involves continuation of data collection and data analysis until theoretical saturation is reached.

In case you aim to generate theory related to your phenomenon of interest (i.e., generalizable explanations for the phenomenon of interest) based on the qualitative primary data included in your MMRS, you might consider the formal grounded theory approach. A merit of selecting the formal grounded theory approach is that many qualitative researchers are already familiar with the grounded theory approach for analyzing qualitative data within a primary study, and that the primary- and the synthesis-level approaches share the same purposes, methods, and assumptions. This might facilitate your literature review process in case you are already familiar with the grounded theory approach. It might also facilitate the understanding of the synthesis's methods and findings by the audience that is probably already familiar with the grounded theory approach. The main challenges of the formal grounded theory approach are the difficulty to report transparently on the process of how the theory exactly emerged from the data and the difficulty to come up with an end product that truly rises to the level of theory.

An empirical example of formal grounded theory is the study of Kearney (2001). In Practical Tip 6.1, we describe how you can conduct formal grounded theory.

Practical Tip 6.1: How to Conduct Formal Grounded Theory

Aim: Let's assume that you are interested in positive behavioral support that is used with persons with intellectual disabilities. Your ultimate goal for the qualitative strand of your segregated MMRS is to develop a theory on how positive behavioral support works for and with persons with intellectual disabilities.

Synthesis: Within the formal grounded theory approach, you use the constant comparative method to synthesize the data. You synthesize the data by using the following three grounded theory coding techniques:

- **Open coding**: Immerse yourself in the data; read the data line by line, and meanwhile write memos about the conceptual and theoretical ideas that emerge; identify important concepts across the included studies during this process; describe the properties and dimensions that relate to each concept; and afterward cluster these concepts into categories.

- **Axial coding**: Examine and describe the nature of the categories, the relation between the categories and their subcategories, and the relationships between the categories; afterward go again through the entire data set and test the identified relationships by comparing them anew to the empirical data.

- **Selective coding**: Integrate all the empirical data by a central theory that links all identified categories and the relationships between the categories; afterward test the appropriateness of this theory by going to the entire data set once more; keep on adjusting and fine-tuning the central theory until it fits the data (Kearney, 2001; Walker & Myrick, 2006).

We recommend you write memos during the entire data synthesis process and explicitly link your memos to the included primary studies. This will help you keep track of what you did (e.g., which concepts you clustered into one category) and why you did what you did (e.g., your arguments for clustering these concepts into this one category). It will also help you to ground your theory carefully in the included primary studies.

Meta-Ethnography

George Noblit and R. Dwight Hare (1988) originally proposed the **meta-ethnographical approach** for synthesizing qualitative primary-level evidence. The purpose of a meta-ethnographical synthesis is to bring together qualitative primary-level evidence so that it can form a *whole*: a *whole* that adds something *new* to the primary studies included in the synthesis and a *whole* that is greater than the sum of its parts. Accordingly, the purpose of a meta-ethnographical synthesis is not aggregation or integration, but it is *creation* and *comparative understanding*.

In their 1988 book, Noblit and Hare outlined seven phases for a meta-ethnographical synthesis, which overlap and repeat as the synthesis proceeds: (1) identifying the intellectual interest that might inform the literature review; (2) deciding what primary studies are relevant to the initial topic of interest; (3) repeatedly and carefully reading the retrieved primary studies; (4) determining how the primary studies are related to one another (i.e., reciprocal, refutational, or line-of-argument relationship), creating a list of the key metaphors, phrases, ideas, and concepts (and their relations) used in the primary studies, and juxtaposing them; (5) translating the primary studies into one another by maintaining the central metaphors and concepts of each primary study *in their relationship to other* central metaphors and concepts; (6) synthesizing these translations by creating a *whole* that is something more than the included studies alone imply; and (7) expressing the synthesis and rendering the translations in the audience's particular language (Noblit & Hare, 1988, pp. 26–29).

In regard to the fourth phase, Noblit and Hare (1988) said that for the purposes of conducting a meta-ethnography, the key assumption is one of the three following possibilities: (1) The primary studies are directly comparable as *reciprocal* translations; (2) the primary studies stand in relative opposition to one another and are essentially *refutational*; or (3) the primary studies taken together represent a *line-of-argument* rather than a reciprocal or refutational translation (p. 36). You can conduct a **reciprocal meta-ethnographical synthesis** in case the key metaphors, themes, and concepts from the individual primary studies are directly comparable with one another. In that case, these key metaphors, themes, and concepts can be translated into one another and can evolve into overarching concepts or metaphors. Alternatively, you can conduct a **refutational meta-ethnographical synthesis** in case there are important contradictions between the included primary studies, and when you aim to explore and explain these contradictions. Finally, you can conduct a **line-of-argument meta-ethnographical synthesis** in case the included primary studies are neither directly comparable as in a reciprocal meta-ethnographical synthesis nor contradictory as in a refutational meta-ethnographical synthesis but rather represent different arguments or different parts of the puzzle that can be lined up. A line-of-argument meta-ethnographical synthesis aims at creating a picture of the *whole* phenomenon of interest from studies of its parts. Noblit and Hare (1988) devoted a complete chapter to each of the three types of meta-ethnographical syntheses in their handbook.

A meta-ethnographical synthesis is complete when the assumptions have been checked (i.e., reciprocal, refutational, and line-of-argument), the appropriate translations have been made, a text has been created that reveals the process, and the synthesis results have been reported in a form that is appropriate to the audience (Noblit & Hare, 1988, p. 36). Noblit and Hare (1988) mentioned the possibility of a *second level of synthesis* in their book, but they did not further develop this idea. However, in recently conducted meta-ethnographical syntheses, review authors often identify key concepts or **first-order constructs**; then, based on the first-order constructs, they derive **second-order interpretations**; and finally, based on the first-order constructs and second-order interpretations, the review authors construct **third-order interpretations** (Britten et al., 2002). The advantages of meta-ethnography are its systematic approach combined with the potential for preserving the interpretive properties of the primary data (Dixon-Woods et al., 2005). The challenge for meta-ethnography is that it is a very demanding and laborious synthesis approach (Dixon-Woods et al., 2005).

An empirical example of a more recently conducted meta-ethnographical synthesis is the study of Nicky Britten and colleagues (2002). In Practical Tip 6.2, we describe how you can conduct a meta-ethnographical synthesis.

Thematic Synthesis

The thematic synthesis approach was developed based on the thematic analysis approach. **Thematic analysis** is aimed at identifying themes and analyzing empirical data using thematic headings within a *primary study*. At the *synthesis level*, James Thomas and Angela Harden (2008) outlined how **thematic synthesis** can be used to bring together and integrate the findings of several primary-level studies. Thematic synthesis involves the identification

Practical Tip 6.2: How to Conduct a Meta-Ethnographical Synthesis

Aim: Let's say you are interested in the responses of professional caretakers to the challenging behavior of clients with intellectual disabilities for the qualitative strand of your segregated MMRS. Based on your scoping review (see Chapter 2), you know that several factors have been identified in empirical research that each may contribute to the responses of professional caretakers to this challenging behavior. With your synthesis, you aim to bring together the findings of these primary studies into an interpretative explanation that is greater than the sum of the parts. You want to study what the contributing factors are and how these factors may influence one another.

Synthesis: You apply Noblit and Hare's (1988) seven-step process for conducting a meta-ethnography:

- First, you identify the topic and purpose of your study (see Chapter 2).
- Second, you decide on the inclusion and exclusion criteria, and you search for relevant studies to be included in your review (see Chapter 3). Afterward, you critically appraise the methodological quality of the studies (see Chapter 4).
- Third, you carefully read the retrieved studies, mark things that seem relevant to you in the papers, and jot down some initial notes in the margins of the papers.
- Fourth, you study how the included primary studies relate to each other and whether they are in a reciprocal, refutational, or line-of-argument relationship to each other. You determine that the studies you retrieved are in a line-of-argument relationship to each other. Accordingly, you decide to read carefully the chapter of Noblit and Hare's (1988) handbook that is devoted to line-of-argument meta-ethnographical syntheses. The following question will guide your line-of-argument meta-ethnographical synthesis: *What can I say about the whole phenomenon of responses of professional caretakers*

(Continued)

(Continued)

> to the challenging behavior of clients with intellectual disabilities based on the retrieved studies that each discuss one of a few factors that have been identified to contribute to the responses of professional caretakers to this challenging behavior? Afterward, you read again all the included papers and make a list of the factors that are discussed in the papers, as well as the key metaphors, phrases, ideas, and concepts that are used by the primary authors to describe your phenomenon of interest and the factors that contribute to this phenomenon.

- Fifth, you translate the retrieved studies into each other, and you examine whether and how they truly make up one line of argument. Translating the retrieved studies into each other implies that you compare the metaphors, concepts, and themes that are used in each of the retrieved studies with the metaphors, concepts, and themes that are used in all the other retrieved studies, and that you examine which metaphors, concepts, and themes are similar or related.

- Sixth, you synthesize the translations you made between the included studies and the factors described in these studies by creating a whole that is something more than the included studies alone imply. You can do that by developing a holistic scheme that integrates all the factors described in the primary studies. This scheme describes which factors contribute to the responses of professional caretakers to the challenging behavior of their clients with intellectual disabilities and how these factors influence one another.

- Seventh, you describe the line-of-argument meta-ethnographical synthesis you conducted in your MMRS report, and you describe the holistic scheme resulting from this synthesis. You describe the process and the findings in a way that is appropriate for the targeted audience (see Chapter 9).

of prominent or recurrent themes and the summarization of the findings of the included primary-level studies under thematic headings (Dixon-Woods et al., 2005). Thomas and Harden (2008) proposed a three-staged approach for thematic synthesis: (1) coding of text *line by line*, (2) development of *descriptive themes*, and (3) generation of *analytical themes*. The synthesis remains close to the data reported in the retrieved primary studies in stages 1 and 2, and it aims to *go beyond* the retrieved primary studies to generate new constructs, explanations, or hypotheses in stage 3.

The thematic synthesis approach is based on the strategies used in a primary-level thematic analysis, but it also combines and adapts principles and techniques from both formal grounded theory and meta-ethnography at the synthesis level. For instance, the analytical themes from the thematic synthesis approach are comparable with the *third-order interpretations* from the later adaptations of meta-ethnography, and the development of descriptive and analytical themes invoke *reciprocal translations* just like in Noblit and Hare's (1988) reciprocal meta-ethnographical synthesis (Barnett-Page & Thomas, 2009). Furthermore, coding of text line by line is also done in formal grounded theory (see the *open coding* stage in Practical Tip 6.1). Although both thematic synthesis and formal grounded theory share the line-by-line coding mechanism, the line-by-line coding within thematic synthesis does not involve the constant comparison of the data, which is central to formal grounded theory.

The advantages of the thematic synthesis approach are that it allows identification of prominent themes and that it prescribes organized and structured ways of dealing with the included primary-level data under these themes (Dixon-Woods et al., 2005). A first pitfall of the thematic synthesis approach is that it remains unclear whether thematic synthesis is a *bottom-up*, data-driven approach (that is driven by the themes identified in the included primary studies themselves) or a *top-down*, theory-driven approach (that is oriented to evaluation of particular themes through interrogation of the literature), which results in a lack of transparency (Dixon-Woods et al., 2005). A second pitfall of the thematic synthesis approach is that there is lack of clarity on the extent to which thematic analyses should be descriptive or interpretive, that is, whether the structure of the synthesis should reflect the *frequency* with which particular themes are reported or whether the synthesis should be weighted toward themes that seem to have a *high level of explanatory value* (Dixon-Woods et al., 2005).

An empirical example of a thematic synthesis is the study of Thomas and Harden (2008). In Practical Tip 6.3, we describe how you can conduct a thematic synthesis.

Meta-Aggregative Synthesis

The **meta-aggregative approach** was developed by the Joanna Briggs Institute (JBI) and is largely inspired by the philosophy of pragmatism.

Practical Tip 6.3: How to Conduct a Thematic Synthesis

Aim: Let's say you are interested in how professional caretakers experience the challenging behavior of their clients with intellectual disabilities for the qualitative strand of your segregated MMRS. You want to identify recurring themes across their experiences and analyze the primary studies published on this topic using thematic headings.

Synthesis: Thematic synthesis includes three stages:

- **Line-by-line coding** or **free coding:** First, you carefully read the *Results/Findings* sections of the included primary studies. After reading the studies once, you read them a second time, but during this reading, you add codes in the margins. You conduct this coding line by line. This implies that you do not code paragraphs or sections but words, subphrases, or phrases. This coding is called line-by-line coding or free coding. It is possible to use several codes for one phrase or subphrase. Your goal for this stage is to apply one or more codes for every phrase or subphrase in the *Results/Findings* sections of the included primary studies. As a check, you can go near the end of this stage through all the *Results/Findings* sections and see whether you forgot to code certain fragments.

  Afterward, we advise you to list all the codes you assigned and gather all the phrases and subphrases that you assigned to each code. Doing this can help you to examine your codes critically and alter them when necessary. Based on this list, you may, for instance, decide to merge two of your initial codes together because they actually mean the same thing. Or, based on this list, you may decide to insert subcategories for a certain category that actually seems to cover different pieces of information or different ideas.

- **Descriptive themes:** Second, you organize the free codes from the first stage into descriptive themes. You can do this by examining similarities and differences between your free codes. By using the descriptive themes, you gather free codes that relate to the same topic, concept, metaphor, or idea. Keep track of which free codes were grouped into which descriptive theme, as well as your reasons for doing so.

- **Analytical themes:** Third, you develop analytical themes to cluster your descriptive themes. In the first two stages, you stayed close to the findings of the primary studies. However, in this third stage, you may *go beyond* the findings of the primary studies and generate additional concepts and themes that help you to grasp your phenomenon of interest. The analytical themes may be more abstract than the descriptive themes from the second stage. Near the end of the synthesis process, we recommend you take a step back and critically check whether your analytical themes enable you to describe and/or explain all your descriptive themes, and whether they enable you to answer your review question(s).

Review authors mainly choose this approach when they want to generate practical and usable *lines of action* (i.e., recommendations for policy and practice) as outcomes of the synthesis within the qualitative strand of their segregated MMRS. The meta-aggregative approach mirrors the linear, transparent Cochrane and Campbell synthesis procedure; however, it remains sensitive to the complexity of interpretive and critical understandings of the phenomenon of interest (Hannes & Lockwood, 2011). The JBI developed a tool that can assist review authors throughout the entire meta-aggregative synthesis process: the Qualitative Assessment and Review Instrument (QARI; see Pearson, 2004, and http://qari.joannabriggs.edu.au/).

A meta-aggregative synthesis involves three stages: (1) extracting qualitative research findings from the primary studies and rating these findings according to their credibility based on supporting illustrations for each finding (called *level 1 findings*); (2) categorizing the level 1 findings on the basis of similarity in meaning (called *level 2 categories*); and (3) conducting a meta-synthesis on the level 2 categories, aiming to produce lines of action that can be used as a basis for evidence-based practice or informing policy decisions (Munn, Tufanaru, & Aromataris, 2013).

For the first stage, you start with extracting qualitative empirical findings from the primary studies. Within the meta-aggregative approach, a finding can be a theme, metaphor, or category (Hannes & Lockwood, 2011). Afterward, you have to rate the extracted findings according to their credibility. You can conduct the credibility rating based on whether you find supporting illustrations for each empirical finding. The three levels of credibility that are used to rate the extracted findings within the meta-aggregative synthesis approach are as follows:

(a) **Unequivocal**: The evidence is beyond reasonable doubt and includes findings that are factual, directly reported/observed, and not open to challenge.

(b) **Credible**: The evidence, although interpretative, is plausible in light of the data and theoretical framework. Conclusions can be logically inferred from the data, but because the findings are essentially interpretative, these conclusions are open to challenge.

(c) **Not supported**: Findings are not supported by the data, and none of the other level descriptors apply. (Pearson, 2004, p. 52)

In regard to the second stage, the similarity of the level 1 findings may be conceptual (e.g., when a particular theme or metaphor is identified across multiple papers) or descriptive (e.g., when the terminology associated with a theme or metaphor is consistent across papers) (Hannes & Lockwood, 2011). The move from *level 1 findings* to *level 2 categories* in this second stage shows similarities with the *constant comparison* method from formal grounded theory.

The third stage of the meta-aggregative synthesis truly sets the approach apart from other qualitative synthesis approaches. The meta-aggregative approach explicitly aims to move *beyond* the production of theory and (re-) interpretation of primary-level evidence to produce statements in the form of practical and usable "lines of action" as the outcomes of the synthesis (Hannes & Lockwood, 2011). With these lines of action, you intend to inform, guide, and inspire practice and policy.

A first advantage of the meta-aggregative approach is that it directly results in practicable and usable implications or lines of action for policy and practice. A second benefit of the meta-aggregative approach is that it is a linear, fairly straightforward synthesis approach that can be conducted in a relatively short period of time (e.g., a few months). A third benefit of the meta-aggregative approach is the quality control that is conducted at the findings level, by means of the levels of evidence (i.e., unequivocal, credible, and unsupported) that are assigned to all the empirical findings extracted from the primary-level publications. An important pitfall of the meta-aggregative approach, which is related to this third benefit, is that "unsupported statements" are often excluded from the synthesis (see Hannes, Von Arx, Christiaens, Heyvaert, & Petry, 2012, for an example). The synthesis can lose substantive richness by discarding all the empirical findings for which no supporting data (e.g., experiences, perspectives, and quotes from the participants) are reported in the primary-level publications. Moreover, it is possible that the primary-level authors *did* collect supporting data for the findings they reported in their publication but that they *cannot* report on all the supporting data in their publication because of practical reasons, such as page or word count limitations set by the journal their article is published in.

An empirical example of a meta-aggregative synthesis is the study of Karin Hannes and Alan Pearson (2012). In Practical Tip 6.4, we describe how you can conduct a meta-aggregative synthesis.

Practical Tip 6.4: How to Conduct a Meta-Aggregative Synthesis

Aim: Let's say you are interested in the feasibility of various interventions for managing challenging behavior of persons with intellectual disabilities for the qualitative strand of your segregated MMRS. You consider interventions for managing challenging behavior of persons with intellectual disabilities as a complex phenomenon, and you acknowledge that several factors will contribute to the feasibility of these interventions. With your review, you want to generate practical and usable lines of action that can serve as recommendations for policy and practice.

Synthesis: The meta-aggregative synthesis process consists of three stages:

- **Level 1 findings:** First, you extract empirical qualitative findings from the primary studies and judge which findings were *unequivocal, credible,* and *not supported* (Pearson, 2004; see definitions provided earlier). As such, you judge the credibility of each of these findings. You can as a check go through all the *Results/Findings* sections of the included primary studies to make sure that you did not forget to extract certain empirical findings.

- **Level 2 categories:** Second, you aggregate the empirical findings into categories. You can do this by examining similarities and differences between the empirical findings. You can use a category to group empirical findings that relate to the same topic or idea. We advise you to develop a hierarchical tree structure for each category that shows which empirical findings were grouped into which category (see Figure 6.2).

(Continued)

- **Synthesized findings and lines of action:** Third, you aggregate the categories into syntheses or synthesized findings. Parallel to the second stage, we advise you to develop a hierarchical tree structure for each synthesis that shows which categories were grouped into which synthesis (see Figure 6.2). Often, the meta-aggregative approach results in a small number of syntheses. The syntheses are formulated as practical and usable lines of action that can serve as recommendations for policy and practice. Finally, you can develop one overall hierarchical tree structure that shows (a) which syntheses were the result of your analysis process, (b) which categories were grouped under which synthesis, (c) which empirical findings were grouped under which category, and (d) what the level of credibility was for each empirical finding. Often, the overall hierarchical tree structure is included as a figure is the final report (see Chapter 9). In Figure 6.2, we show what such as an overall hierarchical tree structure might look like.

SYNTHESIS APPROACHES FOR THE QUANTITATIVE STRAND OF A SEGREGATED MMRS

For the quantitative strand of a segregated MMRS, the included quantitative primary data are often synthesized by using statistical meta-analytical techniques. In case statistical meta-analysis is impossible or undesirable, you can synthesize the quantitative data by conducting a vote counting synthesis or by presenting a narrative summary of the data. In the remainder of this section, we will consecutively discuss how you can conduct a statistical meta-analysis, a vote counting synthesis, and a narrative summary of the quantitative data within the quantitative strand of a segregated MMRS.

Statistical Meta-Analysis

The main question addressed by review authors who use statistical meta-analysis for synthesizing the quantitative primary data within the quantitative strand of a segregated MMRS is as follows: *What is the average effect of X*

Figure 6.2 Hierarchical Tree Structure for a Meta-Aggregative Synthesis

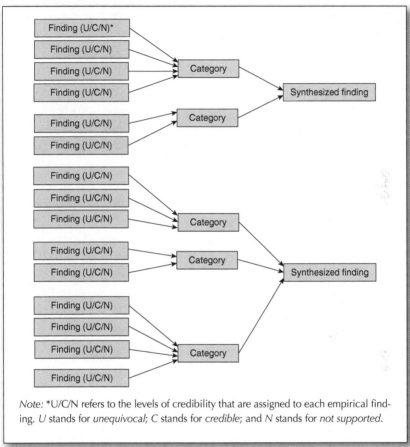

Note: *U/C/N refers to the levels of credibility that are assigned to each empirical finding. *U* stands for *unequivocal*; *C* stands for *credible*; and *N* stands for *not supported*.

(i.e., the intervention or program of interest)? Meta-analysis involves the statistical analysis of the intervention or program effects across the independent primary studies included in the analysis. The data that are the input of the meta-analysis are the estimates of the intervention or program effects and their variances, which are described in the primary reports.

In case you intend to use meta-analytical techniques for synthesizing the quantitative primary data within the quantitative strand of your segregated MMRS, you should consider two important issues. A first important issue is whether (the results of) the included primary studies are similar enough to be combined. You should consider whether similar interventions and treatment conditions, similar comparative conditions, similar participants, similar settings, and similar outcomes are studied across the primary studies that you intend to include in your meta-analysis, and whether similar methodological designs are used within these primary studies.

Second, the **data type** of the outcome measures of the included studies should be considered (e.g., binary data or continuous data) and the necessary data should be available or obtainable from the primary reports that will be included in the meta-analysis. For example, if you want to analyze a continuous outcome, it is necessary that the included studies all report on means and standard deviations. If the results are not reported in this format by the authors of the primary reports, the means and standard deviations can often be derived from the data that are provided in the primary reports (Ryan, 2013). In case the data described in the primary reports are continuous, the standardized mean difference can be used as a measure of effect size. Another common example is that the data described in the primary reports are binary data, and in that case, odds ratios can be calculated as effect sizes. Michael Borenstein, Larry Hedges, Julian Higgins, and Hannah Rothstein (2009) distinguish among three groups of **effect size measures** that are used within the context of statistical meta-analyses: (a) effect sizes based on means, (b) effect sizes based on binary data, and (c) effect sizes based on correlational data. Examples of effect sizes based on means are raw (unstandardized) mean differences, standardized mean differences (such as Cohen's *d* and Hedges's *g*), and response ratios. Examples of effect sizes based on binary data are risk ratios, odds ratios, and risk differences. When the primary studies report data as correlations, the correlation coefficient can be used as the effect size (Borenstein et al., 2009). To conduct a statistical meta-analysis, you start with extracting the relevant effect sizes based on means, binary data, or correlational data from the primary reports. It is possible to convert effect sizes into one common effect size measure to combine studies reporting on various data types in one meta-analysis (Borenstein et al., 2009; Rosenthal, 1994).

A meta-analysis consists of at least two consecutive steps: (1) calculating or extracting an **effect size** and variance for each included primary study, and (2) calculating the **summary effect size** over all included studies and determining a confidence interval for, and statistical significance of, the overall effect. Possible additions to these two basic steps are assessing homogeneity, identifying sources of heterogeneity by using subgroup and/or meta-regression analyses, conducting sensitivity analysis, assessing publication bias, conducting power analysis, and cumulative meta-analysis.

Based on your assumptions relating to the included studies, you can conduct a fixed or random effects meta-analysis. **Fixed effect meta-analyses** build on the assumption that there is one true effect size that underlies all the included studies, whereas **random effects meta-analyses** build on the assumption that the true effect could vary across the included studies (see Borenstein et al., 2009; Van den Noortgate & Onghena, 2003). The differences between meta-analyses using fixed and random effects models is further explained in Practical Tip 6.5. For more information on meta-analytical techniques that can be used for synthesizing quantitative primary-level evidence, we refer to the handbooks of Michael Borenstein et al. (2009), Harris Cooper (2010), and Harris Cooper, Larry Hedges, and Jeff Valentine (2009).

An empirical example of a statistical meta-analysis is the study of Liesl Geeraert, Wim Van den Noortgate, Hans Grietens, and Patrick Onghena (2004). In Practical Tip 6.5, we describe how you can conduct a basic statistical meta-analysis by using a statistical software program.

Practical Tip 6.5: How to Conduct a Statistical Meta-Analysis

Aim: Let's say you are interested in the effects of a new reading program (*program N*) on the reading skills of 10-year-old children. More specifically, for the quantitative strand of your segregated MMRS, you want to meta-analyze empirical quantitative studies that compared 10-year-old children attending classes where this new reading program (*program N*) was implemented with 10-year-old children attending classes where an old reading program (more specifically, *program O*) was still in use. You searched for primary quantitative studies in which the comparison between *program N* and *program O* was assessed by using the standardized reading test R. You decide to use the software program *Comprehensive Meta-Analysis Version 2.0* (CMA; http://www.meta-analysis.com) for conducting your statistical meta-analysis.

(Continued)

(Continued)

Inclusion criteria relating to the format of the data: You decided to apply the following inclusion criteria relating to the format of the data reported in the primary studies (see Chapter 3):

- The data are continuous. The mean effects for both the intervention group (i.e., *program N*) and the control group (i.e., *program O*) are reported for each primary study.
- The studies concern unmatched groups. For each primary study, postdata only are reported for both the intervention group and the control group.
- For each primary study, the mean, standard deviation, and sample size are reported for both the intervention group and the control group.

Data extraction: You found 10 primary studies that answered to your inclusion criteria (see Chapter 3). After critically appraising the primary studies (see Chapter 4), you extracted the following data from them:

- *Descriptive data:* author(s) and publication year
- *Analytical data:* mean, standard deviation, and sample size for both the intervention group (IG) and the control group (CG)

The analytical data you extracted are shown in Table 6.1.

Statistical meta-analysis: Now you can conduct the statistical meta-analysis within the quantitative strand of your segregated MMRS. We will demonstrate how you can perform a meta-analysis using fixed and random effects models, and we will discuss what the differences are between both models.

You open CMA, and you enter your data in the second to the eighth columns (see Figure 6.3). In these columns, you enter the study name, IG mean, IG standard deviation, IG sample size, CG mean, CG standard deviation, and CG sample size information that you extracted from the 10 primary studies (see Table 6.1). In the ninth column, labeled *Effect direction*, you select *Auto* from the drop-down box (see Figure 6.3). *Auto* implies that CMA will compute the mean difference as *Treated minus Control*. In other words,

Table 6.1   Extracted Analytical Data

Study	IG	IG	IG	CG	CG	CG
Name	Mean	Standard deviation	Sample size	Mean	Standard deviation	Sample size
Study A	413	91	107	366	97	98
Study B	418	89	99	346	95	96
Study C	438	82	217	413	86	204
Study D	447	94	211	403	93	195
Study E	479	83	202	401	102	227
Study F	482	85	103	411	112	123
Study G	517	103	414	492	95	423
Study H	531	99	55	511	111	56
Study I	537	76	333	487	88	324
Study J	551	111	53	505	108	61

Figure 6.3   Data and Effect Sizes in CMA

	Study name	Intervention Mean	Intervention Std-Dev	Intervention Sample size	Control Mean	Control Std-Dev	Control Sample size	Effect direction	Std diff in means	Std Err	Hedges's g	Std Err	Difference in means
1	Study A	413.000	91.000	107	366.000	97.000	98	Auto	0.500	0.142	0.499	0.141	47.000
2	Study B	418.000	89.000	99	346.000	95.000	96	Auto	0.783	0.149	0.780	0.148	72.000
3	Study C	438.000	82.000	217	413.000	86.000	204	Auto	0.298	0.098	0.297	0.098	25.000
4	Study D	447.000	94.000	211	403.000	93.000	195	Auto	0.470	0.101	0.470	0.101	44.000
5	Study E	479.000	83.000	202	401.000	102.000	227	Auto	0.834	0.101	0.832	0.101	78.000
6	Study F	482.000	85.000	103	411.000	112.000	123	Auto	0.706	0.138	0.703	0.137	71.000
7	Study G	517.000	103.000	414	492.000	95.000	423	Auto	0.252	0.069	0.252	0.069	25.000
8	Study H	531.000	99.000	55	511.000	111.000	56	Auto	0.190	0.190	0.189	0.189	20.000
9	Study I	537.000	76.000	333	487.000	88.000	324	Auto	0.609	0.080	0.608	0.080	50.000
10	Study J	551.000	111.000	53	505.000	108.000	61	Auto	0.420	0.190	0.418	0.189	46.000

you expect that the participants from the IG will have higher reading scores compared with the participants from the CG.

After entering the data in these columns, CMA will automatically compute the effect size for each primary study. The effect sizes are displayed in the gray columns in Figure 6.3. You elected to enter means and standard deviations (see "Inclusion criteria relating to

(Continued)

(Continued)

the format of the data"). CMA initially displays columns for three indices of effect size: the standardized mean difference (Cohen's d), the bias-corrected standardized mean difference (Hedges's g), and the raw mean difference (see Figure 6.3). You decide to set the default index to Hedges's g. This implies that CMA will use Hedges's g for running the analyses.

Forest plot: Next, you let CMA conduct the statistical meta-analysis. As a default, CMA will display the results under the fixed effect model. First, CMA will show you a forest plot for your data (see Figure 6.4). A forest plot can help you to gain insight into the studies and the combined effect. Figure 6.4 shows the forest plot for the fixed effect model. When looking at Figure 6.4, you first of all see that all the effects sizes are positive, and that they range from 0.189 to 0.832. Second, based on this forest plot, you can also get an idea of the precision of the primary studies included in your meta-analysis. By inspecting the lengths of the horizontal lines that are depicted for each primary study (these lines represent the 95% confidence intervals), you see that some of the studies are clearly more precise than others. For instance, you see that study G, with a smaller 95% confidence interval, is more precise than study H. Third, you see that the combined effect over the 10 included studies is 0.485 with a 95% confidence interval ranging from 0.418 to 0.551.

Figure 6.4 presents the forest plot for the fixed effect model. You might wonder what the forest plot for your data would look

Figure 6.4   Forest Plot for the Fixed Effect Model

Model	Study name	Statistics for each study							Hedges's g and 95% CI				
		Hedges's g	Standard error	Variance	Lower limit	Upper limit	Z-Value	p-Value	-1,00	-0,50	0,00	0,50	
	Study A	0,499	0,141	0,020	0,221	0,776	3,525	0,000					
	Study B	0,780	0,148	0,022	0,489	1,070	5,266	0,000					
	Study C	0,297	0,098	0,010	0,105	0,489	3,036	0,002					
	Study D	0,470	0,101	0,010	0,273	0,667	4,672	0,000					
	Study E	0,832	0,101	0,010	0,635	1,030	8,270	0,000					
	Study F	0,703	0,137	0,019	0,435	0,972	5,128	0,000					
	Study G	0,252	0,069	0,005	0,116	0,388	3,637	0,000					
	Study H	0,189	0,189	0,036	-0,182	0,559	0,999	0,318					
	Study I	0,608	0,080	0,006	0,452	0,764	7,626	0,000					
	Study J	0,418	0,189	0,036	0,048	0,787	2,215	0,027					
Fixed		0,485	0,034	0,001	0,418	0,551	14,312	0,000					

like under the random effects model. Figure 6.5 illustrates this. The first (i.e., the effects sizes calculated for the 10 individual studies) and the second (i.e., the 95% confidence intervals for each of the 10 studies) features are the same for Figure 6.4 and Figure 6.5 because these two features belong to the primary studies that were included in the meta-analysis, not to the model used to combine the studies (i.e., fixed or random effects model). The third feature is different for the fixed and random effects models because this feature refers to the combined effect over the 10 included studies. For the fixed effect model, the combined effect was 0.485, with a 95% confidence interval ranging from 0.418 to 0.551 (see Figure 6.4). However, for the random effects model, the combined effect was 0.508, with a 95% confidence interval ranging from 0.363 to 0.653 (see Figure 6.5). In comparing the two, you see that the combined effect is higher under the random effects model than under the fixed effect model. The 95% confidence interval is broader under the random effects model than under the fixed effect model.

Weights assigned to the included studies: One of the major differences between the fixed and the random effects models are the weights assigned to the included studies. You can ask CMA to display these weights under the fixed and the random effects models. This is shown in Figures 6.6 and 6.7, respectively. For both figures, the weights assigned to the included primary studies sum up to 100%.

In Figures 6.6 and 6.7, you see in the last column the weights for both the fixed and random effects models. In comparing these

Figure 6.5 Forest Plot for the Random Effects Model

Model	Study name	Statistics for each study							Hedges's g and 95% CI			
		Hedges's g	Standard error	Variance	Lower limit	Upper limit	Z-Value	p-Value	-1.00	-0.50	0.00	0.50
	Study A	0.499	0.141	0.020	0.221	0.776	3.525	0.000				
	Study B	0.780	0.148	0.022	0.489	1.070	5.266	0.000				
	Study C	0.297	0.098	0.010	0.105	0.489	3.036	0.002				
	Study D	0.470	0.101	0.010	0.273	0.667	4.672	0.000				
	Study E	0.832	0.101	0.010	0.635	1.030	8.270	0.000				
	Study F	0.703	0.137	0.019	0.435	0.972	5.128	0.000				
	Study G	0.252	0.069	0.005	0.116	0.388	3.637	0.000				
	Study H	0.189	0.189	0.036	-0.182	0.559	0.999	0.318				
	Study I	0.608	0.080	0.006	0.452	0.764	7.626	0.000				
	Study J	0.418	0.189	0.036	0.048	0.787	2.215	0.027				
Random		0.508	0.074	0.005	0.363	0.653	6.875	0.000				

(Continued)

(Continued)

two figures, you see the impact of the model on the weights assigned to the 10 studies. For instance, study G, the study with the largest sample size ($N = 414$ for the treated group and $N = 423$ for the control group) is assigned 23.84% of the weight under the fixed effect model but only 12.42% of the weight under the random effects model. Under the fixed effect model, you assume that all 10 primary studies are estimating the same value and that Study G yields a better estimate than the other primary studies, so you take advantage of that. Under the random effects model, you assume that each primary study is estimating a unique effect. Study G yields a precise estimate of its population, but that population is only one of many, and you do not want it to dominate the analysis. Therefore, Study G is assigned 12.42% of the total weight under the random effects model. This weight is higher than the weights assigned to the other studies included

Figure 6.6 Forest Plot and Study Weights for the Fixed Effect Model

Model	Study name	Hedges's g	Standard error	Variance	Lower limit	Upper limit	Z-Value	p-Value	Hedges's g and 95% CI	Weight Relative
	Study A	0.499	0.141	0.020	0.221	0.776	3.525	0.000		5.73
	Study B	0.780	0.148	0.022	0.489	1.070	5.266	0.000		5.23
	Study C	0.297	0.098	0.010	0.105	0.489	3.036	0.002		11.97
	Study D	0.470	0.101	0.010	0.273	0.667	4.672	0.000		11.35
	Study E	0.832	0.101	0.010	0.635	1.030	8.270	0.000		11.32
	Study F	0.703	0.137	0.019	0.435	0.972	5.128	0.000		6.09
	Study G	0.252	0.069	0.005	0.116	0.388	3.637	0.000		23.84
	Study H	0.189	0.189	0.036	-0.182	0.559	0.999	0.318		3.21
	Study I	0.608	0.080	0.006	0.452	0.764	7.626	0.000		18.04
	Study J	0.418	0.189	0.036	0.049	0.787	2.215	0.027		3.22
Fixed		0.485	0.034	0.001	0.418	0.551	14.312	0.000		

Figure 6.7 Forest Plot and Study Weights for the Random Effects Model

Model	Study name	Hedges's g	Standard error	Variance	Lower limit	Upper limit	Z-Value	p-Value	Hedges's g and 95% CI	Weight (F Relative
	Study A	0.499	0.141	0.020	0.221	0.776	3.525	0.000		8.23
	Study B	0.780	0.148	0.022	0.489	1.070	5.266	0.000		8.94
	Study C	0.297	0.099	0.010	0.105	0.489	3.036	0.002		11.21
	Study D	0.470	0.101	0.010	0.273	0.667	4.672	0.000		11.09
	Study E	0.832	0.101	0.010	0.635	1.030	8.270	0.000		11.08
	Study F	0.703	0.137	0.019	0.435	0.972	5.128	0.000		9.42
	Study G	0.252	0.069	0.005	0.116	0.388	3.637	0.000		12.42
	Study H	0.189	0.189	0.036	-0.182	0.559	0.999	0.318		7.30
	Study I	0.608	0.080	0.006	0.452	0.764	7.626	0.000		12.00
	Study J	0.418	0.189	0.036	0.049	0.787	2.215	0.027		7.31
Random		0.508	0.074	0.005	0.363	0.653	6.875	0.000		

in your meta-analysis. However, this weight is not as dominant as the weight that was given to Study G under the fixed effect model.

Whether you select the fixed or random effects model for conducting your meta-analysis has important implications for the combined effect and for the confidence interval. First, we will discuss the impact of the model on the combined effect. In Figures 6.6 and 6.7, you see that Study G has a low effect size (i.e., Hedges's $g = 0.252$). Under the fixed effect model, where Study G dominates the weights, it pulls the effect size down to 0.485. Under the random effects model, it still pulls the effect size down but only to 0.508.

Second, we will discuss the impact of the model on the confidence interval. Under the fixed effect model, the standard error is 0.034. Under the random effects model, the standard error is 0.074. The standard error influences the width of the confidence interval. Accordingly, the 95% confidence interval is broader under the random effects model than under the fixed effect model.

Overall effect size, 95% confidence interval, and test of the null hypothesis: Next, the CMA output shows the overall effect size, 95% confidence interval, and the test of the null hypothesis (see Table 6.2). The point estimate, standard error, variance, and confidence interval for the overall effect size under the fixed and random effects models are the same values that were shown in the forest plots (i.e., Figures 6.4 and 6.5).

CMA also shows the test of the null hypothesis under the fixed and the random effects models (see Table 6.2). The test of the null hypothesis is different for both models. Under the fixed effect model, the null hypothesis is that the common effect is zero. Under the random effects model, the null hypothesis is that the mean of the true effects is zero. For both the fixed and random effects models, the null hypothesis is tested by the Z value, which is computed as Hedges's g divided by the standard error. For the fixed effect model, this means that $Z = 0.485 / 0.034 = 14.312$. For the random effects model, this means that $Z = 0.508 / 0.074 = 6.875$. For both the fixed and random effects models, the two-tailed p value is $< .001$, implying that you can reject the null hypothesis.

(Continued)

(Continued)

Table 6.2 Overall Effect Size, 95% Confidence Interval, and Test of the Null Hypothesis

| Model | Number of studies | Overall effect size and 95% confidence interval | | | | | Test of the null hypothesis | |
		Point estimate	Standard error	Variance	Lower limit	Upper limit	Z value	p value
Fixed	10	0.485	0.034	0.001	0.418	0.551	14.312	<.001
Random	10	0.508	0.074	0.005	0.363	0.653	6.875	<.001

The techniques that are described and illustrated in Practical Tip 6.5 can be used for synthesizing various quantitative primary studies, such as group-experimental studies, single-case experimental studies, quasi-experimental studies, and nonexperimental quantitative studies. Diverse quantitative primary studies using different designs can also be combined into one quantitative strand of a segregated MMRS. For instance, Van den Noortgate and Onghena (2008) described how single-case experimental studies and group-experimental studies can be combined within a single meta-analysis.

Conditions under which it is impossible or undesirable to conduct a statistical meta-analysis. Under certain conditions, it is impossible or undesirable to conduct a statistical meta-analysis to synthesize the quantitative data within the quantitative strand of a segregated MMRS. A first possible reason is that the number of primary studies that is retrieved to be included in the quantitative strand is too small, or that the number of similar primary studies that can be synthesized within the subgroups is too small. In case you plan to use more complex statistical models in the meta-analysis, you will need a larger number of primary studies. For instance, in case you intend to use complex multilevel regression models for the meta-analysis within the quantitative strand of your segregated MMRS, you should include at least 10 primary studies. You can use fixed or random effects power analysis to examine prospectively how many primary studies you need to include in the meta-analysis (see Valentine, Pigott, & Rothstein, 2010).

Second, as we discussed earlier, the primary studies should be similar enough to be combined within a single meta-analysis. In case you intend to conduct a statistical meta-analysis, you should first consider whether similar interventions and treatment conditions, similar comparative conditions, similar participants, similar settings, and similar outcomes are studied across the primary studies that you intend to include in the meta-analysis, and whether similar methodological designs are used within these primary studies. As argued by Jonathan Deeks, Julian Higgins, and Douglas Altman (2011), decisions concerning what should and should not be combined are inevitably subjective, and are not amenable to statistical solutions but require discussion and clinical judgment. For instance, it is possible that the primary studies you retrieved for the quantitative strand of your segregated MMRS describe various comparisons of different treatment conditions with different comparative conditions. In that case, you may need to examine each combination of treatment and comparative conditions separately, that is, in a separate meta-analysis (Deeks et al., 2011). If you ignore this issue, and combine dissimilar primary studies within a single meta-analysis, you fall into the *combining-apples-and-oranges* trap.

Third, in case the methodological quality of the primary studies you intended to include in the statistical meta-analysis is very low (see Chapter 4), you may decide that it is undesirable to synthesize the data by means of conducting a meta-analysis. If you ignore this issue, and combine primary studies with a very low methodological quality within a meta-analysis, you fall into the *garbage-in–garbage-out* trap.

Fourth, in case there is serious publication and/or reporting bias (see Chapter 3), it is undesirable to conduct a statistical meta-analysis.

Fifth, it is possible that the primary studies you retrieved for the quantitative strand of your segregated MMRS do not contain the information necessary for conducting a statistical meta-analysis. For instance, for the example we presented in Practical Tip 6.5, we extracted the mean intervention effect, standard deviation, and sample size for both the intervention group and the control group for every primary study included in our meta-analysis (see table 6.1). In case the necessary information is not reported in one or more of the retrieved primary studies, you can try to contact the authors of these primary studies and ask them to send you the data you need to conduct your meta-analysis. In case you are not able to contact the authors, you can decide to consider another approach for synthesizing the quantitative data within the quantitative strand of your segregated MMRS.

In case statistical meta-analysis is impossible or undesirable, you can synthesize the quantitative data within the quantitative strand of your segregated MMRS by conducting a vote counting synthesis or by presenting a narrative summary of the data (McKenzie, 2014). We will discuss these two approaches in the following two sections.

Vote Counting

A first alternative option to statistical meta-analysis is to synthesize the quantitative data by conducting a vote counting synthesis (see Figure 6.1). **Vote counting** can be an attractive alternative procedure for synthesizing the quantitative data within the quantitative strand of a segregated MMRS for several reasons. First, it is a relatively easy procedure. Second, it allows merging different outcomes described in the primary studies, as long as the outcomes refer to the same underlying phenomenon. Third, only a minimal amount of data from each primary study has to be included in the vote counting synthesis.

The vote counting approach consists of two steps. First, the findings of the included studies are sorted into the categories *yielding significantly positive results*, *yielding significantly negative results*, and *yielding nonsignificant results*. Second, after each study included in the quantitative strand of the segregated MMRS has cast a vote relating to these three categories, the votes are counted. In regard to the second step, there are two common variants of the vote counting approach. The first variant is that you determine in which of the three categories most of the primary studies fall based on the counting results. You can declare this category to be the "winning category." This category is the largest and, thus, provides the most convincing evidence according to the vote counting approach. The second variant is that you decide only to formulate a definite conclusion if the ratio of votes to the total number of primary studies is over a predetermined cut-off value (Mohagheghi & Conradi, 2006).

Important critiques have been raised against vote counting used for synthesizing the findings of quantitative primary studies. A first critique is that the vote counting approach gives one vote to each primary study that is included in the synthesis, regardless of the sample size of the primary study or the statistical precision with which the outcome was determined (Koricheva & Gurevitch, 2013). A second critique that has been raised against vote counting is that it treats p values that are larger than the significance level as evidence that an effect is absent, whereas in fact, small, moderate, or even large effect sizes may yield a large p value due to inadequate statistical power (Borenstein et al., 2009). In Practical Tip 6.6, we describe how you can use the vote counting approach for synthesizing the retrieved quantitative data within the quantitative strand of a segregated MMRS.

Narrative Summary

In case statistical meta-analysis is impossible or undesirable, a second option you have is to synthesize the quantitative data by presenting a narrative summary of the data (see Figure 6.1). The **narrative summary** approach can be used to summarize in words the evidence coming from the quantitative data included in the MMRS. The advantages of the narrative summary approach

Practical Tip 6.6: How to Conduct a Vote Counting Synthesis Within the Quantitative Strand of a Segregated MMRS

Aim: Let's say you are interested in the effects of a new reading program (*program N*) on the reading skills of 10-year-old children. More specifically, for the quantitative strand of your segregated MMRS, you want to meta-analyze empirical quantitative studies that compared 10-year-old children attending classes where this new reading program (*program N*) was implemented with 10-year-old children attending classes where an old reading program (more specifically, *program O*) was still in use. You retrieved 25 empirical quantitative studies that answered these inclusion criteria. However, the outcomes measured in these 25 studies are not the same. Some studies used standardized reading tests as outcome measures, other studies used teacher-developed reading tests as outcome measures, and still other studies used reading tests from textbook chapters as outcome measures. Because the outcomes are not directly comparable, you decide not to combine the data from these 25 studies by using statistical meta-analytical techniques. Instead, you decide to conduct a vote counting synthesis within the quantitative strand of your segregated MMRS to summarize the evidence coming from these 25 quantitative studies.

Synthesis: First, you sort the findings of the 25 studies into the categories (1) *yielding significantly positive results*, (2) *yielding significantly negative results*, and (3) *yielding nonsignificant results*:

- The studies you assign to the first category show significant evidence of the effectiveness of *program N*. For these studies, *program N* resulted in significantly better reading outcomes compared with *program O*.

- The studies you assign to the second category show significant evidence of the effectiveness of *program O*. For these studies, *program O* resulted in significantly better reading outcomes compared with *program N*.

- The studies you assign to the third category are studies that showed nonsignificant results.

Second, you can count the number of primary studies that you allocated to each of these three categories. In regard to the second step, there are two common variants of the vote counting approach. The first variant is that you determine in which of the three categories most of the quantitative studies fall based on your counting results. You can declare this category to be the "winning category." This category is the largest and, thus, provides the most convincing evidence according to the vote counting approach.

The second variant is that you *a priori* decided only to formulate a definite conclusion if the ratio of votes to the total number of studies is over a predetermined cut-off value (Mohagheghi & Conradi, 2006). For instance, you might have decided based on the results of your scoping review (see Chapter 2) that you would only conclude that *program N* is clearly more effective than *program O* when the ratio of *yielding significantly positive results for program N* votes to the total number of studies would be greater than 75%.

Practical Tip 6.7: How to Conduct a Narrative Summary Within the Quantitative Strand of a Segregated MMRS

Aim: Let's say you are interested in the effects of a new reading program (*program N*) on the reading skills of 10-year-old children. For the quantitative strand of your segregated MMRS, you found 20 empirical quantitative publications in which *program N* was studied among 10-year-old children by using the standardized reading test *R* as the outcome measure. However, the comparative intervention that was studied among these 20 empirical quantitative publications differed: In 6 publications, *program N* was compared with *program A*; in 5 publications, *program N* was compared with *program B*; in 4 publications, *program N* was compared with *program C*; in 3 publications, *program N* was compared with *program D*; and in 2 publications, *program N* was compared with *program E*. Based on your reading of the 20 publications and your knowledge of *programs A, B, C, D,* and *E*, you decide that the comparative interventions (i.e., *programs A, B, C, D,* and *E*) are not similar enough to allow combining the data from these 20 quantitative

(Continued)

(Continued)

publications into a single statistical meta-analysis. Instead, you decide to summarize narratively the evidence coming from these 20 publications.

Synthesis: You can summarize the empirical evidence described in the 20 quantitative primary studies you retrieved by conducting the following steps:

- First, you group the publications that concern the same comparative intervention. This means that you will have five groups of publications:
  - Group *A* including the 6 publications on the comparison between *programs N* and *A*
  - Group *B* including the 5 publications on the comparison between *programs N* and *B*
  - Group *C* including the 4 publications on the comparison between *programs N* and *C*
  - Group *D* including the 3 publications on the comparison between *programs N* and *D*
  - Group *E* including the 2 publications on the comparison between *programs N* and *E*
- Second, for each of the five groups, you narratively summarize the empirical evidence that is described in the retrieved quantitative publications. The *Results* section for the quantitative strand of your segregated MMRS might consist of five subsections, with the headings *Studies comparing programs N and A, Studies comparing programs N and B, Studies comparing programs N and C, Studies comparing programs N and D,* and *Studies comparing programs N and E.*

are that it is easy to conduct for (novice) review authors and that it is easy to understand for the readers of the MMRS. The approach simply involves narrative description and summary of the findings reported in the primary-level publications. A critique raised against the narrative summary approach is that it is a largely informal approach that lacks transparency on the process of how to synthesize the included data (Dixon-Woods et al., 2005). In Practical Tip 6.7, we describe how you can use the narrative summary approach for synthesizing the retrieved quantitative data within the quantitative strand of a segregated MMRS.

BRINGING THE FINDINGS OF THE QUALITATIVE AND THE QUANTITATIVE STRANDS TOGETHER

In this chapter, we discussed how the data synthesis stage for a segregated MMRS involves the separate use of qualitative and quantitative synthesis approaches for, respectively, synthesizing the qualitative and quantitative primary data included in the MMRS. Throughout the chapter, we discussed several qualitative and quantitative synthesis approaches that you can use for the separate strands within your segregated MMRS. When you report on your segregated MMRS, you will first separately describe and discuss your qualitative and quantitative findings.

After each set of qualitative and quantitative findings (in the common domain of research) has been separately synthesized by means of qualitative and quantitative synthesis approaches, respectively, you can synthesize the findings of these separate syntheses, for instance, into a set of conclusions, theoretical framework, or path analysis in the *Discussion* section of your MMRS report (Sandelowski et al., 2006). In this *Discussion* section, you can focus on the complementarity and configuration of the qualitative and quantitative findings within your segregated MMRS.

The **complementarity** of findings refers to the fact that because the qualitative and quantitative research findings addressed different aspects or dimensions of your phenomenon of interest (see the assumptions of the segregated design we discussed in the beginning of this chapter), they can neither confirm nor refute, but only complement, each other (Sandelowski et al., 2006). In the *Discussion* section of your MMRS report, you can relate the qualitative and quantitative research findings to each other, as well as discuss how they complement each other.

According to Sandelowski et al. (2006), the **configuration** of findings refers to the arrangement of these complementary findings into a line of argument (see Noblit & Hare, 1988), into a theory that posits relationships among concepts, or into a narrative that posits a temporal ordering of events (Greenhalgh et al., 2005; Pound et al., 2005). Because the qualitative and quantitative research findings in a segregated MMRS could not address the same aspects or dimensions of the phenomenon of interest, you cannot reduce or translate these findings to one another (analogous to the reciprocal meta-ethnographical synthesis we discussed previously in this chapter). However, you *can* organize the qualitative and quantitative research findings into a coherent whole (analogous to the line-of-argument meta-ethnographical synthesis we discussed previously in this chapter) in the *Discussion* section of your MMRS report.

We give two brief examples of how you can focus on the complementarity and configuration of the qualitative and quantitative findings of your segregated MMRS. A first example is that you position the findings of the qualitative strand of your MMRS as antecedent, mediating, or moderating variables that might explain or delineate the conditions for the occurrence of events that are depicted in the quantitative strand (Sandelowski et al., 2006). Based on the quantitative strand of your segregated MMRS, you may, for instance, have generated knowledge on causal observations, and based on the qualitative strand, you may have generated knowledge on causal explanations. After separately discussing the findings of both strands of your segregated MMRS, you may in the *Discussion* section of your MMRS report link these causal explanations (from the qualitative strand) to the causal observations (from the quantitative strand) as complementary findings. A second example is that you use the findings generated in the quantitative strand of your MMRS to make more explicit comparisons between groups that were only implied in the findings of the qualitative strand in the *Discussion* section of your MMRS report (Sandelowski et al., 2006).

Summary Points

- For segregated MMRS literature reviews, qualitative and quantitative synthesis approaches are used separately for, respectively, synthesizing the qualitative and quantitative primary data included in the MMRS.
- Qualitative approaches for synthesizing qualitative primary data are formal grounded theory, meta-ethnography, thematic synthesis, and meta-aggregative synthesis.
- When synthesizing quantitative primary data by using statistical meta-analytical techniques, you first calculate or extract an effect size and

variance for each included study. Afterward you calculate the summary effect size over all included studies and determine a confidence interval for, and statistical significance of, the overall effect. Possible additions to these two steps are assessing homogeneity, identifying sources of heterogeneity by using subgroup and/or meta-regression analyses, conducting sensitivity analysis, assessing publication bias, conducting power analysis, and cumulative meta-analysis.

- In case statistical meta-analysis of the quantitative data is impossible or undesirable, you can synthesize the quantitative data by conducting a vote counting synthesis or by presenting a narrative summary of the data.
- After separately synthesizing the sets of qualitative and quantitative data by means of qualitative and quantitative synthesis approaches, respectively, you can synthesize these separate syntheses in the *Discussion* section of your MMRS report.

Questions for Thought

- Which qualitative synthesis approach will you use for synthesizing the qualitative primary data included in the qualitative strand of your segregated MMRS? Why? What will the synthesis for the qualitative strand of your segregated MMRS look like?
- Which quantitative synthesis approach will you use for synthesizing the quantitative primary data included in the quantitative strand of your segregated MMRS? Why? What will the synthesis for the quantitative strand of your segregated MMRS look like?
- How will you synthesize the findings of the separate qualitative and quantitative syntheses within your segregated MMRS? Is there a complementarity relationship between the findings from the qualitative strand and the findings from the quantitative strand of your segregated MMRS?

Suggestions for Further Reading on Formal Grounded Theory

Eaves, Y. D. (2001). A synthesis technique for grounded theory data analysis. *Journal of Advanced Nursing, 35*, 654–663. doi:10.1046/j.1365-2648.2001.01897

Kearney, M. H. (1998). Truthful self-nurturing: A grounded formal theory of women's addiction recovery. *Qualitative Health Research, 8*, 495–512. doi:10.1177/104973239800800405

Kearney, M. H. (2001). Enduring love: A grounded formal theory of women's experience of domestic violence. *Research in Nursing & Health, 24*, 270–282. doi:10.1002/nur.1029

Suggestions for Further Reading on Meta-Ethnography

Britten, N., Campbell, R., Pope, C., Donovan, J., Morgan, M., & Pill, R. (2002). Using meta ethnography to synthesise qualitative research: A worked example. *Journal of Health Services Research & Policy, 7*, 209–215. doi:10.1258/135581902320432732

Noblit, G. W., & Hare, R. D. (1988). *Meta-ethnography: Synthesising qualitative studies*. London, England: Sage.

Suggestion for Further Reading on Thematic Synthesis

Thomas, J., & Harden, A. (2008). Methods for the thematic synthesis of qualitative research in systematic reviews. *BMC Medical Research Methodology, 8*, 45. doi:10.1186/1471-2288-8-45

Suggestions for Further Reading on Meta-Aggregative Synthesis

Hannes, K., & Lockwood, C. (2011). Pragmatism as the philosophical foundation for the Joanna Briggs meta-aggregative approach to qualitative evidence synthesis. *Journal of Advanced Nursing, 67*, 1632–1642. doi:10.1111/j.1365-2648.2011.05636

Pearson, A. (2004). Balancing the evidence: Incorporating the synthesis of qualitative data into systematic reviews. *Joanna Briggs Institute Reports, 2*, 45–64. doi:10.1111/j.1479-6988.2004.00008.x

Suggestions for Further Reading on Statistical Meta-Analysis

Borenstein, M., Hedges, L. V., Higgins, J., & Rothstein, H. (2009). *Introduction to meta-analysis*. Chichester, England: Wiley.

Cooper, H. M. (2010). *Research synthesis and meta-analysis: A step-by-step approach* (4th ed.). London, England: Sage.

Cooper, H. M., Hedges, L. V., & Valentine, J. C. (Eds.). (2009). *The handbook of research synthesis and meta-analysis* (2nd ed.). New York, NY: Russell Sage Foundation.

McKenzie, J. (2014). *In lieu of meta-analysis: Methods for summary and synthesis.* Retrieved from http://methods.cochrane.org/sites/methods.cochrane.org/files/Mckenzie.pdf

References

Barnett-Page, E., & Thomas, J. (2009). Methods for the synthesis of qualitative research: A critical review. *BMC Medical Research Methodology*, *9*, 59. doi:10.1186/1471-2288-9-59

Borenstein, M., Hedges, L. V., Higgins, J., & Rothstein, H. (2009). *Introduction to meta-analysis*. Chichester, England: Wiley.

Britten, N., Campbell, R., Pope, C., Donovan, J., Morgan, M., & Pill, R. (2002). Using meta ethnography to synthesise qualitative research: A worked example. *Journal of Health Services Research & Policy*, *7*, 209–215. doi:10.1258/135581902320432732

Cooper, H. M. (2010). *Research synthesis and meta-analysis: A step-by-step approach* (4th ed.). London, England: Sage.

Cooper, H. M., Hedges, L. V., & Valentine, J. C. (Eds.). (2009). *The handbook of research synthesis and meta-analysis* (2nd ed.). New York, NY: Russell Sage Foundation.

Deeks, J. J., Higgins, J. P. T., & Altman, D. G. (2011). Chapter 9: Analysing data and undertaking meta-analyses. In J. P. T. Higgins & S. Green (Eds.), *Cochrane handbook for systematic reviews of interventions Version 5.1.0* (updated March 2011). Retrieved from http://www.cochrane-handbook.org

Dixon-Woods, M., Agarwal, S., Jones, D., Young, B., & Sutton, A. (2005). Synthesising qualitative and quantitative evidence: A review of possible methods. *Journal of Health Services Research & Policy*, *10*, 45–53.

Eaves, Y. D. (2001). A synthesis technique for grounded theory data analysis. *Journal of Advanced Nursing*, *35*, 654–663. doi:10.1046/j.1365-2648.2001.01897

Geeraert, L., Van den Noortgate, W., Grietens, H., & Onghena, P. (2004). The effect of early prevention programs for families with young children at risk for physical child abuse and neglect: A meta-analysis. *Child Maltreatment*, *9*, 277–291.

Glaser, B. G., & Strauss, A. L. (1967). *The discovery of grounded theory: Strategies for qualitative research*. New York, NY: Aldine.

Greenhalgh, T., Robert, G., Macfarlane, F., Bate, P., Kyriakidou, O., & Peacock, R. (2005). Storylines of research in diffusion of innovation: A meta-narrative approach to systematic review. *Social Science & Medicine*, *61*, 417–430. doi:10.1016/j.socscimed.2004.12.001

Hannes, K., & Lockwood, C. (2011). Pragmatism as the philosophical foundation for the Joanna Briggs meta-aggregative approach to qualitative evidence synthesis.

Journal of Advanced Nursing, 67, 1632–1642. doi:10.1111/j.1365-2648.2011
.05636

Hannes, K., & Lockwood, C. (Eds.). (2012). *Synthesizing qualitative research. Choosing the right approach.* Chichester, England: Wiley.

Hannes, K., & Macaitis, K. (2012). A move to more systematic and transparent approaches in qualitative evidence synthesis: Update on a review of published papers. *Qualitative Research, 12*, 402–442. doi:10.1177/1468794111432992

Hannes, K., & Pearson, A. (2012). Obstacles to the implementation of evidence-based practice in Belgium: A worked example of meta-aggregation. In K. Hannes & C. Lockwood (Eds.), *Synthesizing qualitative research. Choosing the right approach* (pp. 21–39). Chichester, England: Wiley.

Hannes, K., Von Arx, E., Christiaens, E., Heyvaert, M., & Petry, K. (2012). Don't pull me out!? Preliminary findings of a systematic review of qualitative evidence on experiences of pupils with special educational needs in inclusive education. *Procedia: Social and Behavioral Sciences, 69*, 1709–1713. doi:10.1016/j
.sbspro.2012.12.118

Kearney, M. H. (1998). Truthful self-nurturing: A grounded formal theory of women's addiction recovery. *Qualitative Health Research, 8*, 495–512. doi:10.1177/104973239800800405

Kearney, M. H. (2001). Enduring love: A grounded formal theory of women's experience of domestic violence. *Research in Nursing & Health, 24*, 270–282. doi:10.1002/nur.1029

Koricheva, J., & Gurevitch, J. (2013). Place of meta-analysis among other methods of research synthesis. In J. Koricheva, J. Gurevitch, & K. Mengersen (Eds.), *Handbook of meta-analysis in ecology and evolution* (pp. 3–13). Princeton, NJ: Princeton University Press.

McKenzie, J. (2014). *In lieu of meta-analysis: Methods for summary and synthesis.* Retrieved from http://methods.cochrane.org/sites/methods.cochrane.org/files/Mckenzie.pdf

Mohagheghi, P., & Conradi, R. (2006). Vote-counting for combining quantitative evidence from empirical studies—An example. In *Proceedings of the 5th ACM-IEEE International Symposium on Empirical Software Engineering (ISESE'06)* (pp. 24–26).

Munn, Z., Tufanaru, C., & Aromataris, E. (2013). Recognition of the health assistant as a delegated clinical role and their inclusion in models of care: A systematic review and meta-synthesis of qualitative evidence. *International Journal of Evidence-Based Healthcare, 11*, 3–19. doi:10.1111/j.1744-1609.2012.00304.x

Noblit, G. W., & Hare, R. D. (1988). *Meta-ethnography: Synthesising qualitative studies.* London, England: Sage.

Pearson, A. (2004). Balancing the evidence: Incorporating the synthesis of qualitative data into systematic reviews. *Joanna Briggs Institute Reports, 2*, 45–64. doi:10.1111/j.1479-6988.2004.00008.x

Pound, P., Britten, N., Morgan, M., Yardley, L., Pope, C., Daker-White, G., & Campbell, R. (2005). Resisting medicines: A synthesis of qualitative studies of medicine taking. *Social Science & Medicine, 61*, 133–155. doi:10.1016/j.socscimed .2004.11.063

Ring, N., Jepson, R., & Ritchie, K. (2011). Methods of synthesizing qualitative research studies for health technology assessment. *International Journal of Technology Assessment in Health Care, 27*, 384–390. doi:10.1017/S0266462311000389

Rosenthal, R. (1994). Parametric measures of effect size. In H. Cooper & L. V. Hedges (Eds.), *The handbook of research synthesis* (pp. 231–244). New York, NY: Russell Sage Foundation.

Ryan, R. (2013). *Cochrane Consumers and Communication Review Group: Meta-analysis.* Retrieved from http://cccrg.cochrane.org

Sandelowski, M., Voils, C. I., & Barroso, J. (2006). Defining and designing mixed research synthesis studies. *Research in the Schools, 13*(1), 29–40.

Thomas, J., & Harden, A. (2008). Methods for the thematic synthesis of qualitative research in systematic reviews. *BMC Medical Research Methodology, 8*, 45. doi:10.1186/1471-2288-8-45

Valentine, J. C., Pigott, T. D., & Rothstein, H. R. (2010). How many studies do you need? A primer on statistical power for meta-analysis. *Journal of Educational and Behavioral Statistics, 35*, 215–247. doi:10.3102/1076998609346961

Van den Noortgate, W., & Onghena, P. (2003). Multilevel meta-analysis: A comparison with traditional meta-analytical procedures. *Educational and Psychological Measurement, 63*, 765–790. doi:10.1177/0013164403251027

Van den Noortgate, W., & Onghena, P. (2008). A multilevel meta-analysis of single-subject experimental design studies. *Evidence-Based Communication Assessment and Intervention, 2*, 142–151. doi:10.1080/17489530802505362

Walker, D., & Myrick, F. (2006). Grounded theory: An exploration of process and procedure. *Qualitative Health Research, 16*, 547–559. doi:10.1177/ 1049732305285972

7

DATA SYNTHESIS FOR INTEGRATED MMRS LITERATURE REVIEWS

═══════════ ❧ ═══════════

Chapter Outline

In this chapter, we discuss various approaches that can be used to synthesize primary-level evidence within integrated MMRS literature reviews. First, we discuss techniques that can be used for "quantitizing" qualitative findings and techniques for qualitizing quantitative findings. These quantitizing and qualitizing techniques can be used in integrated MMRS literature reviews to enable joint synthesis of the empirical evidence from qualitative, quantitative, and mixed primary-level studies on the phenomenon of interest. Second, we discuss three mixed synthesis approaches that can be used for synthesizing qualitative, quantitative, and mixed primary-level studies in integrated MMRS literature reviews: narrative summary, critical interpretive synthesis, and realist synthesis.

═══════════ ❧ ═══════════

POSSIBLE DATA SYNTHESIS
APPROACHES FOR INTEGRATED MMRS

As we discussed in Chapter 2, the integrated MMRS design is based on the assumptions that (a) any differences between qualitative and quantitative studies that do exist do not warrant separate analyses and syntheses of their findings; (b) studies designated as qualitative or quantitative are not necessarily distinguishable from each other; (c) both qualitative and quantitative studies in a common research domain can address the same research purposes and questions; and (d) syntheses of both qualitative and quantitative findings can be produced from methods developed for qualitative and quantitative findings (Sandelowski, Voils, & Barroso, 2006, p. 35). In this chapter, we will first discuss techniques that can be used for *quantitizing* qualitative findings and techniques for *qualitizing* quantitative findings to enable joint synthesis of all the collected evidence in integrated MMRS literature reviews. Afterward, we will discuss mixed synthesis approaches that can be used for synthesizing qualitative, quantitative, and mixed primary-level evidence in integrated MMRS literature reviews. In Figure 7.1, we present an overview of the most often used data synthesis approaches for integrated MMRS literature reviews. These data synthesis approaches will be discussed in more detail in the remainder of this chapter. We want to stress that this list of synthesis approaches is not exhaustive.

QUANTITIZING APPROACHES

In integrated MMRS literature reviews, qualitative findings can be quantitized and/or quantitative findings can be qualitized to enable joint data synthesis of all the retrieved primary data. In this chapter, we will first discuss techniques that can be used for quantitizing data. *Quantitizing* refers to the process of converting qualitative data into quantitative data. Examples of quantitizing qualitative findings in integrated MMRS literature reviews are content analysis, vote counting, and calculating frequency effect sizes of qualitative findings.

Before zooming in on content analysis, vote counting, and calculating frequency effect sizes of qualitative findings, however, we want to discuss the general limitations of and issues with quantitizing approaches. In Chapter 1, we already stressed that the data included in an MMRS can be very divergent as the studies included in an MMRS can be qualitative, quantitative, and mixed primary-level studies on the phenomenon of interest. The goal of quantitizing approaches is to quantitize the qualitative findings reported in qualitative and mixed primary-level studies to enable joint data synthesis of all the retrieved primary data. In Chapter 1, we stressed the importance of trying to synthesize and integrate the various types of primary-level studies in an MMRS without ignoring their methodological identity and losing their

Figure 7.1 Data Synthesis for Integrated MMRS Literature Reviews

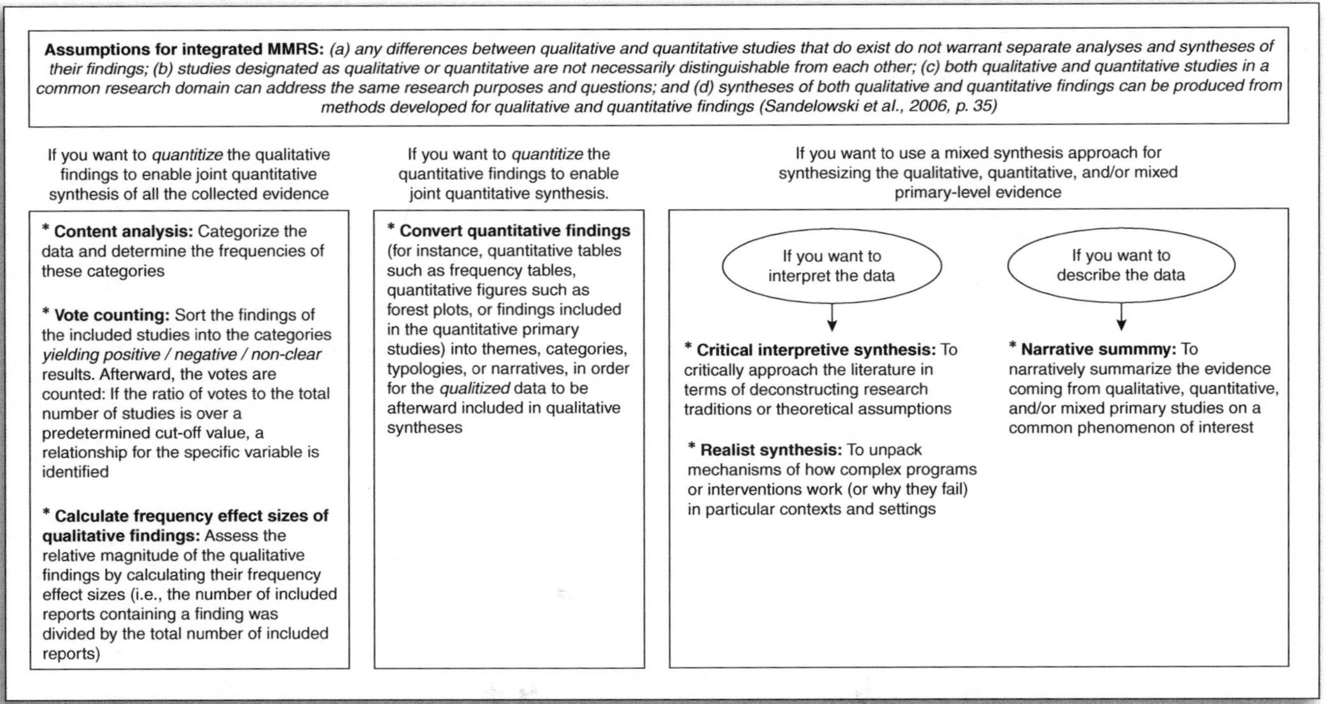

Assumptions for integrated MMRS: *(a) any differences between qualitative and quantitative studies that do exist do not warrant separate analyses and syntheses of their findings; (b) studies designated as qualitative or quantitative are not necessarily distinguishable from each other; (c) both qualitative and quantitative studies in a common research domain can address the same research purposes and questions; and (d) syntheses of both qualitative and quantitative findings can be produced from methods developed for qualitative and quantitative findings (Sandelowski et al., 2006, p. 35)*

If you want to *quantitize* the qualitative findings to enable joint quantitative synthesis of all the collected evidence

* **Content analysis:** Categorize the data and determine the frequencies of these categories

* **Vote counting:** Sort the findings of the included studies into the categories *yielding positive / negative / non-clear results*. Afterward, the votes are counted: If the ratio of votes to the total number of studies is over a predetermined cut-off value, a relationship for the specific variable is identified

* **Calculate frequency effect sizes of qualitative findings:** Assess the relative magnitude of the qualitative findings by calculating their frequency effect sizes (i.e., the number of included reports containing a finding was divided by the total number of included reports)

If you want to *quantitize* the quantitative findings to enable joint quantitative synthesis.

* **Convert quantitative findings** (for instance, quantitative tables such as frequency tables, quantitative figures such as forest plots, or findings included in the quantitative primary studies) into themes, categories, typologies, or narratives, in order for the *qualitized* data to be afterward included in qualitative syntheses

If you want to use a mixed synthesis approach for synthesizing the qualitative, quantitative, and/or mixed primary-level evidence

If you want to interpret the data

* **Critical interpretive synthesis:** To critically approach the literature in terms of deconstructing research traditions or theoretical assumptions

* **Realist synthesis:** To unpack mechanisms of how complex programs or interventions work (or why they fail) in particular contexts and settings

If you want to describe the data

* **Narrative summmy:** To narratively summarize the evidence coming from qualitative, quantitative, and/or mixed primary studies on a common phenomenon of interest

intrinsic nature. However, one might say that this is exactly what happens when you apply a quantitizing synthesis approach: You discard the qualitative nature of the data and the specific characteristics associated with it (e.g., thick descriptions), and you convert the data into something quantitative. Parallel to what we said in Chapter 1 about the appropriateness of using an MMRS approach for studying certain review topics and for answering certain review questions, we argue in this chapter that the use of quantitizing approaches is certainly not appropriate for studying every review topic and for answering every review question. Interpretive qualitative data cannot be reduced to quantitative codes and frequency effect sizes without using the intrinsic richness and value of the data. However, we agree with Corrine Voils, Margarete Sandelowski, Julie Barroso, and Victor Hasselblad (2008) that it might, for instance, be appropriate to use quantitizing approaches in the health sciences, where much so-called qualitative research is descriptive rather than interpretive and, therefore, fits better within a quantitatively oriented logic. Voils et al. argue that most qualitative research findings in the health sciences offer no concepts to synthesize, no metaphors to translate, and no coherent lines of argument to align or develop. They are basic descriptive accounts that are suited for quantitizing processes.

Content Analysis

Content analysis is an approach that can be used at the primary and at the synthesis levels. It involves the categorization of data and the determination of the frequencies of these categories (Dixon-Woods, Agarwal, Jones, Young, & Sutton, 2005). The advantages of content analysis are (a) that is a well-developed and widely used approach, with an established pedigree; (b) that it is fairly transparent in its processes and easily auditable; (c) that there are software packages for undertaking content analysis; and (d) that the synthesized evidence resulting from content analysis easily lends itself to tabulation (Dixon-Woods et al., 2005). However, important pitfalls of content analysis are (a) that the approach is inherently reductive and tends to diminish complexity and context; (b) that the approach is unlikely to preserve the interpretive properties that underlie the included qualitative evidence; (c) that content analysis may fail to reflect the structure or importance of the underlying phenomenon; (d) that the approach could treat the absence of evidence (i.e., nonreporting of evidence by primary-level authors) as evidence of absence (i.e., findings that are not important); and (e) that content analysis results may be oversimplified and review authors using content analysis may be tempted to count only what is easy to classify and count rather than what is truly important (Dixon-Woods et al., 2005).

An empirical example of a content analysis is the study of David Evans and Mary FitzGerald (2002). In Practical Tip 7.1, we describe how you can conduct a content analysis within an integrated MMRS.

Practical Tip 7.1: How to Conduct a Content Analysis

Aim: You read that the social stories intervention is a popular intervention for teaching social and behavioral skills to children with autism. You are interested in the reasons why professional caretakers use social stories for teaching social and behavioral skills to these children. Based on your initial reading on the topic, you suspect that there are different reasons for using this intervention based on the setting where this intervention was implemented. More specifically, you suspect there is a difference between residential settings and day schools. You want to use content analysis to synthesize the existing empirical evidence on this topic within your integrated MMRS. You aim to produce a descriptive summary of the reasons why professional caretakers use social stories for teaching social and behavioral skills to children with autism. Your hypothesis is that there will be different reasons depending on whether the intervention was implemented in residential settings or day schools.

Synthesis: As a preliminary step, you first read all of the included primary studies. Then when extracting the descriptive data (see Chapter 5), you probably also extracted information on the setting where the intervention was implemented (i.e., residential setting and day school) for each included primary study. Now it is time for you to conduct the following synthesis steps:

- First, while carefully reading the *Results/Findings* sections of the included primary studies, you note down the reasons why professional caretakers use social stories for teaching social and behavioral skills to children with autism according to

(Continued)

(Continued)

these studies. The result of this stage is a list of reasons for each included primary study.

- Second, you compile the separate list of reasons for each included primary study into one list. When doing that, you record for each reason in which primary study it was mentioned (e.g., by adding the study number between brackets to each reason).

- Third, you develop preliminary categories that group similar reasons.

- Fourth, you pilot test the preliminary categories by critically comparing them to the listed reasons, and you evaluate whether you need to revise the categories for them to fit the data better. For instance, you may decide to merge two of your preliminary categories together because they cover related reasons why professional caretakers use social stories. Or you may decide to split one preliminary category into two or three categories so that they more accurately group related reasons why professional caretakers use social stories. The result of this stage is your final list of categories.

- Fifth, you use this list to conduct the final categorization. You do that by going back to the reasons you noted down in the first step and by allocating each of these reasons to one of the categories in your final list. For each reason, you keep on recording in which primary study it was mentioned (e.g., by adding the study number between brackets to each reason).

- Sixth, you list for each of these final categories the reasons that were allocated to it. Again, the reasons are linked to the study numbers.

- Seventh, because the study numbers can be related to the setting that was coded for each study, you can calculate for each category in how many residential settings articles it was mentioned and in how many day schools articles it was mentioned. There are different options for presenting the results in your final report. A first option is to present the results of these calculations in percentages in the text.

A second option is to create a table that includes three columns: (1) the categories, (2) the percentage of residential settings articles that mentioned a reason belonging to this category, and (3) the percentage of day schools articles that mentioned a reason belonging to this category. Each row of this table refers to one category. A third option is to present the results in a graphical way, for instance, by generating one pie chart (or one bar chart) for each of the two settings. The first chart shows the distribution of the percentages for the residential settings articles, and the second chart shows the distribution of the percentages for the day schools articles.

Vote Counting

In Chapter 6, we already discussed a certain application of the vote counting approach when we were talking about the synthesis of the retrieved quantitative primary studies in the quantitative strand of a segregated MMRS. In case statistical meta-analysis was impossible or undesirable, an alternative option was to conduct a vote counting synthesis of the quantitative data instead.

Within an integrated MMRS, vote counting is a counting procedure that can be used to integrate quantitized qualitative findings with quantitative findings on a common phenomenon of interest. Vote counting can be an attractive procedure for review authors conducting an integrated MMRS for several reasons. First, the vote counting approach allows merging the findings of different types of studies. Qualitative, quantitative, and mixed primary-level studies can be combined into a single vote counting synthesis. Furthermore, it is no problem to combine different types of qualitative, quantitative, and mixed studies into a single vote counting synthesis. Second, the vote counting approach allows merging primary studies that report on different outcome measures as long as the outcome measures refer to the same underlying construct. Third, the vote counting approach requires a minimal amount of data from each primary study to be included in the synthesis. Fourth, the vote counting approach is relatively easy to conduct.

Conducting a vote counting synthesis involves two steps. First, the findings of the included studies are sorted into the categories *yielding clearly/significantly positive results, yielding clearly/significantly negative results,* and *yielding nonclear/nonsignificant results.* Second, after each study included in the MMRS has cast a vote relating to these three categories, the votes are counted. As discussed in Chapter 6, there are two common variants of the vote counting approach relating to this second step. The first variant is that you determine in which of the three categories most of the primary studies fall based on the counting results. You can declare this category to be the "winning category." This category is the largest and, thus, provides the most convincing evidence according to the vote counting approach. The second variant is that you decide only to formulate a definite conclusion if the ratio of votes to the total number of primary studies is over a predetermined cut-off value (Mohagheghi & Conradi, 2006).

In Chapter 6, we mentioned two critiques that have been raised against the vote counting approach. First, the approach gives *one* vote to *each* primary study that is included in the synthesis regardless of the sample size of the primary study (Koricheva & Gurevitch, 2013). Second, for the quantitative and mixed primary studies included in the synthesis, the vote counting approach treats *p* values that are larger than the significance level as evidence that an effect is absent, whereas in fact, small, moderate, or even large effect sizes may yield a large *p* value due to inadequate statistical power (Borenstein, Hedges, Higgins, & Rothstein, 2009). A third critique raised against the vote counting approach used within the context of an integrated MMRS is that there are no clear guidelines to decide whether the included qualitative and mixed primary studies should be sorted into the category *yielding clearly/significantly positive results,* the category *yielding clearly/significantly negative results,* or the category *yielding nonclear/nonsignificant results.* A fourth critique raised against the vote counting approach is that it only takes into account a very minimal amount of information from the primary studies: whether the primary authors found positive/no/negative results for the effectiveness of the intervention, treatment, or program under study. All other information provided in the primary studies is discarded. In Practical Tip 7.2, we describe how you can conduct a vote counting synthesis within an integrated MMRS.

Practical Tip 7.2: How to Conduct a Vote Counting Synthesis

Aim: Let's say you are interested in the effectiveness of noncontingent reinforcement interventions for reducing challenging behavior among persons with intellectual disabilities. You retrieved primary qualitative, quantitative, and mixed primary studies on this topic. You want to synthesize these studies altogether using a vote counting approach within your integrated MMRS.

Synthesis: First, you sort the findings of the primary studies that are included in your MMRS into the categories: (a) *yielding clearly/significantly positive results*, (b) *yielding clearly/significantly negative results*, and (c) *yielding nonclear/nonsignificant results*:

- The studies you assign to the first category show clear/significant evidence of the effectiveness of the noncontingent reinforcement interventions. For these studies, the noncontingent reinforcement interventions resulted in a clear/significant *decrease* of the challenging behavior.

- The studies you assign to the second category are studies in which the noncontingent reinforcement interventions resulted in a clear/significant *increase* of the challenging behavior.

- The studies you assign to the third category are studies that showed nonclear/nonsignificant results.

Second, you count the number of primary studies that you allocated to each of these three categories. In regard to the second step, there are two common variants of the vote counting approach. The first variant is that you determine in which of the three categories most of the primary studies fall based on your counting results. You can declare this category to be the "winning category." This category is the largest and, thus, provides the most convincing evidence about the effectiveness of noncontingent reinforcement interventions for reducing challenging behavior among persons with intellectual disabilities according to the vote counting approach.

The second variant is that you *a priori* decided only to formulate a definite conclusion if the ratio of votes to the total number of

(Continued)

(Continued)

studies is over a predetermined cut-off value (Mohagheghi & Conradi, 2006). For instance, you might have decided based on the results of your scoping review (see Chapter 2) that you would only conclude that noncontingent reinforcement interventions are effective for reducing challenging behavior among persons with intellectual disabilities when the ratio of *yielding clearly/significantly positive results* votes to the total number of studies would be greater than 75%.

Calculating Frequency Effect Sizes of Qualitative Findings

Calculating frequency effect sizes of qualitative findings is another example of how qualitative findings can be quantitized in integrated MMRS literature reviews. For instance, in their MMRS literature review on antiretroviral adherence in HIV-positive women, Voils et al. (2008) calculated the frequency effect sizes of the findings reported on in the included qualitative studies: They assessed the relative magnitude of the qualitative findings by calculating their frequency effect sizes (i.e., the number of included reports containing a finding was divided by the total number of included reports). As we discussed previously in this chapter, a first limitation is that this approach is not appropriate for synthesizing interpretive qualitative data. However, we agree with Voils et al. that it might be appropriate to use this approach for synthesizing descriptive qualitative data that fit a quantitatively oriented logic. A second limitation of this approach is that these frequency effect sizes calculated based on descriptive qualitative data are not directly comparable with the traditional quantitative effect sizes (see Chapter 6). Traditional quantitative effect sizes are based on the average effect across all participants included in a primary study and take into account the number of participants included in each study, whereas the frequency effect sizes calculated based on descriptive qualitative data are based on the presence of findings across reports even if present in only one report and based on only one participant (Voils et al., 2008). In Practical Tip 7.3, we describe how you can calculate the frequency effect sizes of descriptive qualitative research findings within an integrated MMRS.

Practical Tip 7.3: How to Calculate Frequency Effect Sizes of Qualitative Research Findings

Aim: Let's say you are interested in the responses of professional caretakers to the challenging behavior of clients with intellectual disabilities. Based on your scoping review (see Chapter 2), you know that several factors have been identified in empirical research that each may contribute to the responses of professional caretakers to this challenging behavior. With your synthesis, you aim to examine which factors are the most influential.

Synthesis:

- First, you determine which factors have been identified in the primary studies. You can do that by going through each of the included studies and noting down potential factors that are described in the studies. After doing this for each included study, you reread the list of potential factors and determine which of them are related and, thus, can be clustered into one factor. Afterward, you can check whether the factors you derived are mutually exclusive. This means that you have to avoid overlap between the factors.

- Second, you calculate the frequency effect size for each factor. You can do this by taking the primary study as the unit of analysis. For each factor, you calculate the frequency effect size by taking the number of primary studies containing this factor and dividing this number by the total number of primary studies included in the synthesis (Onwuegbuzie, 2003). This procedure results in one frequency effect size for each factor.

- Third, you sort the frequency effect sizes in descending order. The most influential factors appear at the top of your list.

QUALITIZING APPROACHES

When conducting an integrated MMRS literature review, you can quantitize qualitative findings to enable joint quantitative data synthesis of all the retrieved primary data, as discussed in the previous section. However, it is also possible to qualitize quantitative findings to facilitate the integration of the qualitative and quantitative data in an integrated MMRS. ***Qualitizing*** refers to the process of converting quantitative data into qualitative data. In this section, we will discuss how you can qualitize quantitative findings.

Converting Quantitative Findings

Examples of the qualitizing approach are to convert quantitative findings into themes, categories, typologies, or narratives for the qualitized data to be afterward included in qualitative syntheses. For instance, when several quantitative primary studies are retrieved that involve factor analysis, qualitative labels can be assigned to the factors found in the various studies, and these qualitative labels can be included in the qualitative synthesis. Other examples are quantitative tables (e.g., frequency tables), figures (e.g., forest plots), or findings included in the quantitative primary studies that are narratively described (e.g., what is happening in these frequency tables, what is happening in these forest plots, and what were statistically significant and nonsignificant findings). These narrative descriptions are afterward included in the qualitative synthesis.

A possible challenge when translating quantitative findings into qualitative statements is that it is not easy to try to maintain rigor. The Joanna Briggs Institute (2014) advises the following: (a) Try to *bracket* your personal influences in the qualitizing processes to minimize the impact of your own vested interests, personal experiences, and cultural beliefs on how you view and interpret data; and (b) try to take into account the specific context in which the quantitative data and findings were produced and report on the context in the MMRS report so that the reader can assess the usefulness of the MMRS findings for informing context-specific policy and practice decisions. Accordingly, in case you qualitize quantitative data, you should make explicit the context in which the primary-level interventions have taken place in the MMRS report. This can relate to the temporal, cultural, geographical, and/or socio-, political, or economical context of the primary studies in so far as these context characteristics are relevant to the MMRS. These context characteristics should be taken into account when you interpret and extrapolate the primary-level findings. Including these context characteristics in the synthesis allows you to import a more dynamic, socio-analytical, and critical lens into your MMRS. In Practical Tip 7.4, we show possible formats for qualitizing quantitative data.

Practical Tip 7.4: Possible Formats for Qualitizing Quantitative Data

Format for qualitizing quantitative pictorial data (e.g., forest plot data) for the quantitative data to be subsequently included in the qualitative synthesis:

Study	Synthesized finding								Textual description
Author(s) (Year)				Statistics for each study				Hedges g and 95% CI	Describe here what is shown in this forest plot

Model	Study name	Hedges's g	Standard error	Variance	Lower limit	Upper limit	Z-Value	p-Value
	Study A	0.499	0.141	0.020	0.221	0.776	3.525	0.000
	Study B	0.760	0.148	0.022	0.469	1.070	5.266	0.000
	Study C	0.297	0.098	0.010	0.105	0.489	3.036	0.002
	Study D	0.470	0.101	0.010	0.273	0.667	4.672	0.000
	Study E	0.832	0.101	0.010	0.635	1.030	8.270	0.000
	Study F	0.703	0.137	0.019	0.435	0.972	5.128	0.000
	Study G	0.252	0.069	0.005	0.116	0.388	3.637	0.000
	Study H	0.189	0.189	0.036	-0.182	0.559	0.999	0.318
	Study I	0.608	0.080	0.006	0.452	0.764	7.626	0.000
	Study J	0.418	0.189	0.036	0.048	0.787	2.215	0.027
Fixed		0.485	0.034	0.001	0.418	0.551	14.312	0.000

Hedges g and 95% CI: -1.00 -0.50 0.00 0.50 1.00

(Continued)

(Continued)

Format for qualitizing quantitative tabular data for the quantitative data to be subsequently included in the qualitative synthesis:

Study	Synthesized finding									Textual description
	Model	Overall effect size and 95% confidence interval						Test of the null hypothesis		Describe here what is shown in this table
Author(s) (Year)		Number of studies	Point estimate	Standard error	Variance	Lower limit	Upper limit	Z value	p value	
	Fixed	10	0.485	0.034	0.001	0.418	0.551	14.312	<.001	
	Random	10	0.508	0.074	0.005	0.363	0.653	6.875	<.001	

Format for qualitizing quantitative textual description data for the quantitative data to be subsequently included in the qualitative synthesis:

Study	Synthesized finding	Textual description
Author(s) (Year)	We compared the findings of empirical studies on 10-year-old children attending classes where program N was implemented with the findings of empirical studies on 10-year-old children attending classes where program O was still in use. By using the random effects model to meta-analysis, we rejected the null hypothesis that the mean of the true effects was zero, Z = 6.875, p < .001.	Describe here what is said in this excerpt

MIXED SYNTHESIS APPROACHES

Mixed approaches that are often used for synthesizing qualitative, quantitative, and mixed primary-level evidence in integrated MMRS literature reviews are narrative summary, critical interpretive synthesis, and realist synthesis (Barnett-Page & Thomas, 2009; Dixon-Woods et al., 2005; Hannes & Lockwood, 2012; Hannes & Macaitis, 2012; Ring, Jepson, & Ritchie, 2011). You have to select the synthesis approach that best matches your review objectives and that best fits the data included in your MMRS (see Figure 7.1). If you want to describe and summarize the empirical data reported in the primary studies, you can use the narrative summary approach. However, if you want to interpret the primary-level data, you can use the critical interpretive synthesis approach or the realist synthesis approach. Critical interpretive synthesis can be used to approach the literature on the phenomenon of interest critically with the aim of deconstructing research traditions or theoretical assumptions. Realist synthesis can be used to unpack mechanisms of how complex programs or interventions work (or why they fail) in particular contexts and settings. In the remainder of this chapter, we will discuss these three mixed synthesis approaches.

Narrative Summary

In Chapter 6, we already discussed a certain application of the narrative summary approach when we were talking about the synthesis of the retrieved quantitative primary studies in the quantitative strand of a segregated MMRS. In case statistical meta-analysis was impossible or undesirable, an alternative option was to develop a narrative summary of the quantitative data instead.

Within an integrated MMRS, the narrative summary approach can be used to summarize in words the evidence coming from qualitative, quantitative, and mixed primary studies on a common phenomenon of interest. As such, various forms of empirical evidence can be discussed side by side in a narrative summary. Narrative summaries vary from simple recounting and description of findings to more reflexive accounts that include commentary and higher levels of abstraction and that aim to account for complex dynamic processes (Dixon-Woods et al., 2005). In contrast with, for instance, the meta-ethnographical and formal grounded theory approaches that we discussed in the previous chapter, the narrative summary approach does not aim for theory-building

(Dixon-Woods, Bonas, et al., 2006). It simply aims for narrative description and summary. A critique raised against the narrative summary approach is that it is a largely informal approach that lacks transparency on the process of how to synthesize the included data (Dixon-Woods et al., 2005).

Empirical examples of narrative summaries are the studies of Andrew Abbott (1990) and L. Fairbank et al. (1999). In Practical Tip 7.5, we describe how you can conduct a narrative summary within an integrated MMRS.

Practical Tip 7.5: How to Conduct a Narrative Summary

Aim: Let's say you want to conduct an integrated MMRS on parents' needs, preferences, and factors associated with the management of the at-home challenging behavior of their children with intellectual disabilities. You retrieved several qualitative, quantitative, and mixed primary studies on this topic. You aim to describe and summarize narratively these studies in your integrated MMRS.

Synthesis: You can narratively summarize the empirical evidence described in the qualitative, quantitative, and mixed primary studies you retrieved by conducting the following steps:

- First, you carefully read all the primary-level papers you retrieved. You mark things that seem relevant to you in the papers and jot down some initial notes in the margins of the papers.

- Second, you group similar papers according to what is discussed in them. For instance, a first group of papers might focus on what the parents describe as their needs associated with the management of the at-home challenging behavior of their children. A second group of papers might focus on the parents' preferences relating to interventions for managing the at-home challenging behavior of their children. A third group of papers might focus on the factors described by parents that are associated with the management of the at-home challenging behavior of their children. Try out different groupings of the papers, and judge which grouping best fits the papers you included in your integrated MMRS.

- Third, for each of the three groups of papers you narratively summarize the empirical evidence that is described in the qualitative, quantitative, and mixed primary studies relating to this topic. When you decide to use the grouping presented earlier under the second bullet point, your *Findings* section will consist of three parts, with the headings *Parents' needs associated with the management of the at-home challenging behavior*, *Parents' preferences relating to interventions for managing the at-home challenging behavior*, and *Factors associated with the management of the at-home challenging behavior*. It is also possible that you may add subheadings. For instance, under the third heading, you might want to add two subheadings: *Facilitating factors* and *Impeding factors*. Alternative subheadings under this third heading are, for example, *Factors at the micro level*, *Factors at the meso level*, and *Factors at the macro level*. Try out different subheadings, and judge which subheadings best fit the data discussed in the papers you included in your integrated MMRS.

Critical Interpretive Synthesis

The **critical interpretive synthesis** approach developed by Mary Dixon-Woods (Dixon-Woods, Bonas, et al., 2006; Dixon-Woods, Cavers, et al., 2006) aims toward theory generation and a critically informed integration of evidence from qualitative, quantitative, and mixed primary studies. The synthesizing argument that is the outcome of the critical interpretive synthesis takes the form of a coherent theoretical framework comprising a network of constructs and the relationships between them, and links synthetic constructs (i.e., new constructs generated through synthesis) and existing constructs in the literature (Dixon-Woods, Cavers, et al., 2006, p. 10).

The critical interpretive synthesis approach shows some overlap with meta-ethnographical synthesis (see Practical Tip 6.2) and formal grounded theory (see Practical Tip 6.1), two qualitative synthesis approaches we discussed in the previous chapter. Parallel to meta-ethnography, critical interpretive synthesis involves line-of-argument syntheses. Parallel to formal grounded theory, critical interpretive synthesis involves theoretical sampling for selecting primary studies, uses the constant comparative method for analyzing the data, rejects a sequential *stage approach* to literature reviews, and implies an inductive approach to formulating the review question and to developing categories and concepts (Barnett-Page & Thomas, 2009).

The main feature that sets apart critical interpretive synthesis from meta-ethnographical synthesis and formal grounded theory is its **critical stance**. The critical stance of review authors conducting a critical interpretive synthesis refers to their explicit aim of being critical toward all data collected on the phenomenon of interest and all variables and processes involved in the phenomenon (e.g., the assumptions involved and the solutions proposed in the literature). Review authors conducting a critical interpretive synthesis critically question the assumptions and the premises of the primary-level authors with regard to the concepts used by these authors and with regard to the way in which these authors presented empirical problems and suggested empirical solutions for these problems. In other words, review authors conducting a critical interpretive synthesis critically question the entire "construction" of the "story" the primary-level authors told in their research reports. For instance, a primary-level author may argue that a certain solution is effective to solve a certain problem (e.g., a primary-level author may argue and demonstrate that using restraint interventions such as physical, mechanical, or environmental restraint is effective for decreasing the frequency of challenging behaviors of persons with intellectual disabilities). However, the review authors who include this primary-level study in their critical interpretive synthesis will be critical toward this solution and will, for instance, also question the desirability of this solution (e.g., restraint interventions conflict with certain values and ethical standards). A consequence is that the review authors have a very prominent role in the critical interpretive synthesis process. The review authors' voice will be central in an MMRS report on a critical interpretive synthesis process.

For analyzing and synthesizing the data within a critical interpretive synthesis, Dixon-Woods, Cavers, et al. (2006) proposed to start with closely inspecting the retrieved papers and then gradually identifying recurring themes and developing a critique. Next, themes could be generated that help to explain the phenomena being described in the literature by constantly comparing the theoretical structures being developed against the data in the papers and attempting to specify the categories of the analysis and the relationships between them (Dixon-Woods, Cavers, et al., 2006). Dixon-Woods et al. stated that the involvement of a large, multidisciplinary team in the critical interpretive synthesis is of utmost importance for introducing *checks and balances* and for allowing multiple perspectives on the phenomenon of interest. Foremost, Dixon-Woods et al. argued that the approach should involve a critical stance that is dynamic and reflexive: This critical stance is key to the critical interpretive synthesis process, it informs the sampling and data collection, and it plays a key role in interpretation and theory generation.

The advantages of the critical interpretive synthesis approach are (a) its critical stance toward the data collected and toward previous literature on the phenomenon of interest, and (b) that the approach allows for integrating qualitative, quantitative, and mixed evidence into a single review and for synthesizing a large number of primary studies. An issue with the critical interpretive synthesis approach is that it remains unclear how exactly the qualitative, quantitative, and mixed evidence is integrated. For instance, the Dixon-Woods, Bonas, et al. (2006) critical interpretive synthesis on access to health care by socioeconomically disadvantaged people in the United Kingdom included 119 papers. However, it is not clear what the proportion of qualitative, quantitative, and mixed primary studies included in the synthesis was; which types of studies or designs were included; what the contribution of the retrieved qualitative, quantitative, and mixed data to the end product of the critical interpretive synthesis was; and how exactly the qualitative, quantitative, and mixed evidence was integrated.

An empirical example of a critical interpretive synthesis is the study of Dixon-Woods, Bonas, et al. (2006). In Practical Tip 7.6, we describe how you can conduct a critical interpretive synthesis within an integrated MMRS.

Practical Tip 7.6: How to Conduct a Critical Interpretive Synthesis

Aim: Let's say you are interested in parents with intellectual disabilities. More specifically, you are interested in how these parents can be optimally supported. You aim to generate a theoretical framework on the optimal support for parents with intellectual disabilities. To do that, you want to integrate critically empirical evidence coming from quantitative, qualitative, and mixed primary studies on this topic within your integrated MMRS.

Synthesis: Your critical interpretive synthesis consists of the following steps:

- First, you carefully read the retrieved papers. During the reading and rereading process, you gradually identify recurring

(Continued)

(Continued)

themes, categories, patterns, and concepts within and across these papers. These themes are your initial themes, categories, patterns, and concepts.

- Second, based on your initial themes, categories, patterns, and concepts as well as on the raw data, you further think about which themes, categories, patterns, and concepts might optimally help to understand and map your phenomenon of interest. You can do this by constantly comparing the themes, categories, patterns, and concepts you developed against the data described in the papers. Think about which themes, categories, patterns, and concepts are essential to understand and map your phenomenon of interest, as well as how these themes, categories, patterns, and concepts are mutually related.

- Third, when more than one review author is involved in your integrated MMRS project (as would ideally be the case), let each of these review authors independently conduct steps 1 and 2. Afterward, compare the identified and developed themes, categories, patterns, and concepts and discuss which themes, categories, patterns, and concepts optimally help you to understand and map your phenomenon of interest. Involving several review authors in this process will allow multiple perspectives on your phenomenon of interest, and it will stimulate dynamic and reflexive processes. It will also encourage all the involved review authors to a more critical stance toward the data and toward the identified themes, categories, patterns, and concepts.

- Fourth, based on your discussions, you and the other involved review authors together think about which themes, categories, patterns, and concepts optimally help you to understand and map your phenomenon of interest. You can together describe and map which processes play a role in supporting parents with intellectual disabilities and what the dynamic interplays are between the processes involved, and you can together develop a theoretical framework about what constitutes the optimal support for parents with intellectual disabilities, and how it can be offered.

Realist Synthesis

A **realist synthesis** is a theory-driven synthesis aimed at unpacking mechanisms of how complex programs or interventions work (or why they fail) in particular contexts and settings (Pawson, Greenhalgh, Harvey, & Walshe, 2005, p. 21). Ray Pawson et al. (2005) developed the realist synthesis approach to answer to the complexity of social programs in health services and other public services that act on complex social systems. According to Pawson et al., these programs are not *magic bullets* that will always hit their targets, and their effects are crucially dependent on context and implementation. Pawson et al. found that other approaches for synthesizing primary evidence often resulted in statements such as *the evidence is mixed or conflicting* but that these approaches provided little insights into *why* the program or intervention worked or did not work when applied in different contexts or circumstances, deployed by different stakeholders, or used for different purposes. Pawson et al. outlined five stages for conducting a realist synthesis.

First, you should clarify the scope of the literature review. Pawson et al. (2005) described four possible purposes for conducting a realist synthesis: (1) theory integrity (*does the intervention work as predicted?*); (2) theory adjudication (*which theories fit best?*); (3) comparison (*how does the intervention work in different settings for different groups?*); and (4) reality testing (*how does the policy intent of the intervention translate into practice?*). The first stage also includes identifying the theories that (apparently) underlie the program or intervention of interest, grouping and categorizing these theories, and making explicit these theories' underlying assumptions about how the program or intervention is meant to work and what impacts it is expected to have (Pawson et al., 2005).

Second, you should search for various forms of evidence (e.g., qualitative, quantitative, and mixed study reports; case studies; and media reports) relating to the program or intervention of interest.

Third, you should appraise the retrieved primary studies based on their relevance and rigor, and extract relevant data from them.

The fourth stage relates to synthesizing the evidence and includes the following steps: (a) synthesizing the collected data to determine what works for whom, how, and under what circumstances; (b) allowing the purpose of the review (i.e., theory integrity, theory adjudication, comparison, or reality testing) to drive the synthesis process; (c) using *contradictory* evidence to generate insights about the influence of context; and (d) presenting conclusions as a series of contextualized decision points of the general format *If A, then B* or *In the case of C, D is unlikely to work* (Pawson et al., 2005).

The fifth stage concerns the dissemination, implementation, and evaluation of the findings of your synthesis. This stage truly sets apart the realist synthesis approach from other synthesis approaches by actively involving various stakeholders in the dissemination, implementation, and evaluation process. More precisely, this stage includes (a) drafting and testing out recommendations and conclusions with stakeholders relating to what works for whom, how, and under what circumstances; (b) working with stakeholders such as practitioners and policy makers to apply the recommendations in particular contexts; and (c) evaluating the extent to which programs were adjusted to take account of contextual influences revealed by the review; for instance, the *same* program might be expanded in one setting, modified in another, and abandoned in another (Pawson et al., 2005).

The advantages of the realist synthesis approach are that it combines theoretical understanding and empirical evidence and focuses on explaining the relationship between the context in which the program or intervention is applied, the mechanisms by which it works, and the outcomes that are produced (Pawson et al., 2005). As such, realist syntheses can deepen practitioners' and policy makers' understanding of the program or intervention and how it can be made to work most effectively for different target groups and under different circumstances at a national, regional, or local level (Pawson et al., 2005). Possible pitfalls for the realist synthesis approach are (a) the tendency to treat all forms of evidence as equally authoritative, (b) the contingency of the chains of evidence, (c) the vulnerability to the robustness of the theory being evaluated rather than the evidence being offered, and (d) the lack of explicit guidance on how to deal with contradictory evidence (Dixon-Woods et al., 2005).

An empirical example of a realist synthesis is the study of Geoff Wong, Trisha Greenhalgh, and Ray Pawson (2010). In Practical Tip 7.7, we describe how you can conduct a realist synthesis within an integrated MMRS.

Practical Tip 7.7: How to Conduct a Realist Synthesis

Aim: Let's say you are interested in multicomponent interventions for managing challenging behavior among persons with severe intellectual disabilities. You read about the nature, epidemiology, causes, and treatment outcomes of interventions for managing challenging behavior among persons with severe intellectual disabilities. What you read suggests that these multicomponent interventions work in a complex way for this population and that the outcomes of these interventions particularly depend on the contexts and settings in which they are implemented. With your integrated MMRS, you aim to study how these multicomponent interventions work (and why they fail) in particular contexts and settings for this population.

Synthesis: You follow the five stages outlined by Pawson et al. (2005) for conducting your realist synthesis:

- First, you clarify the scope of your integrated MMRS. You are interested in the question: *How do multicomponent interventions for managing challenging behavior among persons with severe intellectual disabilities work in different contexts and settings?* In this stage, you also search for theories that underlie these multicomponent interventions. Afterward, you group and categorize the theories you located based on their theoretical principles. You also note down these theories' underlying assumptions about how the multicomponent interventions for managing challenging behavior among persons with severe intellectual disabilities are meant to work and what impact they are expected to have.

- Second, you search for quantitative, qualitative, and mixed primary studies on multicomponent interventions for managing challenging behavior among persons with severe intellectual disabilities (see Chapter 3).

- Third, you critically appraise the retrieved primary studies (see Chapter 4), and you extract relevant descriptive data from them (see Chapter 5).

(Continued)

(Continued)

- Fourth, you synthesize the evidence you collected. This fourth stage consists of four substages:
  - In the first substage, you synthesize the collected empirical data to determine which multicomponent interventions work (a) for which persons with severe intellectual disabilities, (b) for managing which types of challenging behavior, (c) how, (d) under what circumstances, and (e) in which contexts and settings.
  - In the second substage, you allow the purpose of the review (i.e., *comparison* for your MMRS) to drive the synthesis process. This implies that you carefully examine all the collected empirical data focusing on the following question: *How do multicomponent interventions for managing challenging behavior among persons with severe intellectual disabilities work in different contexts and settings?* In other words, you focus on comparing different contexts and settings relating to your phenomenon of interest. For instance, you can generate hypotheses of the format *In context A, intervention I is likely to work for population P* and *In context B, intervention I is unlikely to work for managing challenging behavior of type T.* Afterward, you carefully test these hypotheses based on the empirical data you collected.
  - In the third substage, you search for *contradictory* evidence to generate insights about the influence of different contexts and settings on your phenomenon of interest. For instance, let's say that you generated a hypothesis in the format *In context A, intervention I is likely to work for population P* in the second substage. In this third substage, you critically search for evidence within the included quantitative, qualitative, and mixed primary studies that might contradict your hypothesis.
  - In the fourth substage, you gather all the conclusions you have drawn based on the first, second, and third substages. Based on them, you generate your final conclusions and formulate an answer to your review question. You present

your final conclusions as a series of contextualized decision points of the general format *If A, then B* or *In the case
of C, D is unlikely to work.*

- Fifth, you disseminate, implement, and evaluate the synthesis's findings with various stakeholders involved with multicomponent interventions for managing challenging
behavior among persons with severe intellectual disabilities. More precisely, (a) you draft and test out your synthesis's recommendations and conclusions with the
stakeholders, relating to what works for whom, how, and
under what circumstances; (b) you work with the stakeholders to apply your synthesis's recommendations in
particular contexts; and (c) you evaluate together with the
stakeholders the extent to which programs were adjusted to
take account of contextual influences revealed by your
realist synthesis; for instance, the same program might be
expanded in one setting, modified in another, and abandoned in another (Pawson et al., 2005). You write the
MMRS report in close collaboration with these stakeholders
(see Chapter 9). In the report, you describe the derived recommendations for policy and practice that relate to which
multicomponent interventions work for which persons with
severe intellectual disabilities, for managing which types of
challenging behavior, how, under what circumstances, and
in which contexts and settings.

Summary Points

- For integrated MMRS literature reviews, the qualitative findings can be
transformed into quantitative data (i.e., *quantitizing*) and/or the quantitative findings can be transformed into qualitative data (i.e., *qualitizing*) to
enable an overall quantitative and/or qualitative synthesis of the findings
of all the retrieved studies. However, it is also possible to use a mixed
synthesis approach for synthesizing qualitative, quantitative, and mixed
primary-level evidence in integrated MMRS literature reviews, which
does not involve the transformation of qualitative and/or quantitative data.

- Examples of quantitizing approaches that can be used within integrated MMRS literature reviews are content analysis, vote counting, and calculating frequency effect sizes of qualitative findings.
- Examples of qualitizing approaches that can be used within integrated MMRS literature reviews are converting quantitative findings into themes, categories, typologies, or narratives for the qualitized data to be included in qualitative syntheses.
- Mixed approaches for synthesizing qualitative, quantitative, and mixed primary-level evidence within integrated MMRS literature reviews are narrative summary, critical interpretive synthesis, and realist synthesis.

Questions for Thought

- If you are conducting an integrated MMRS, will you transform the qualitative findings into quantitative data to enable an overall quantitative synthesis of all the retrieved studies? Or will you transform the quantitative findings into qualitative data to enable an overall qualitative synthesis of all the retrieved studies? Or will you use a mixed approach for synthesizing the findings of all the retrieved studies, such as narrative summary, critical interpretive synthesis, or realist synthesis? Why?

Suggestion for Further Reading on Content Analysis

Evans, D., & FitzGerald, M. (2002). Reasons for physically restraining patients and residents: A systematic review and content analysis. *International Journal of Nursing Studies, 39*, 735–743.

Suggestion for Further Reading on Vote Counting

Hedges, L. V., & Olkin, I. (1980). Vote-counting methods in research synthesis. *Psychological Bulletin, 88*, 359–369.

Suggestion for Further Reading on Calculating Frequency Effect Sizes of Qualitative Findings

Voils, C. I., Sandelowski, M., Barroso, J., & Hasselblad, V. (2008). Making sense of qualitative and quantitative findings in mixed research synthesis studies. *Field Methods, 20,* 3–25. doi:10.1177/1525822X07307463

Suggestion for Further Reading on Qualitizing Quantitative Findings

Joanna Briggs Institute. (2014). *The Joanna Briggs Institute reviewers' manual 2014: Methodology for JBI mixed methods systematic reviews.* University of Adelaide, South Australia. Retrieved from http://joannabriggs.org/assets/docs/sumari/ ReviewersManual_Mixed-Methods-Review-Methods-2014-ch1.pdf

Suggestions for Further Reading on Narrative Summary

Abbott, A. (1990). Conceptions of time and events in social science methods: Causal and narrative approaches. *Historical Methods: A Journal of Quantitative and Interdisciplinary History, 23,* 140–150. doi:10.1080/01615440.1990.10594204

Fairbank, L., O'Meara, S., Renfrew, M. J., Woolridge, M., Sowden, A. J., & Lister-Sharp, D. (1999). A systematic review to evaluate the effectiveness of interventions to promote the initiation of breastfeeding. *Health Technology Assessment, 4,* 1–171.

Suggestions for Further Reading on Critical Interpretive Synthesis

Dixon-Woods, M., Bonas, S., Booth, A., Jones, D. R., Miller, T., Sutton, A., . . . Young, B. (2006). How can systematic reviews incorporate qualitative research? A critical perspective. *Qualitative Research, 6,* 27–44. doi:10.1177/1468794106058867

Dixon-Woods, M., Cavers, D., Agarwal, S., Annandale, E., Arthur, A., Harvey, J., . . . Sutton, A. J. (2006). Conducting a critical interpretive synthesis of the literature on access to healthcare by vulnerable groups. *BMC Medical Research Methodology, 6,* 35. doi:10.1186/1471-2288-6-35

Suggestions for Further Reading on Realist Synthesis

Pawson, R., Greenhalgh, T., Harvey, G., & Walshe, K. (2005). Realist review. A new method of systematic review designed for complex policy interventions. *Journal of Health Services Research & Policy*, *10*(Suppl. 1), 21–34. doi:10.1258/1355819054308530

Wong, G., Greenhalgh, T., Westhorp, G., Buckingham, J., & Pawson, R. (2013). RAMESES publication standards: Realist syntheses. *BMC Medicine*, *11*(1), 21.

References

Abbott, A. (1990). Conceptions of time and events in social science methods: Causal and narrative approaches. *Historical Methods: A Journal of Quantitative and Interdisciplinary History*, *23*, 140–150. doi:10.1080/01615440.1990.10594204

Barnett-Page, E., & Thomas, J. (2009). Methods for the synthesis of qualitative research: A critical review. *BMC Medical Research Methodology*, *9*, 59. doi:10.1186/1471-2288-9-59

Borenstein, M., Hedges, L. V., Higgins, J., & Rothstein, H. (2009). *Introduction to meta-analysis*. Chichester, England: Wiley.

Dixon-Woods, M., Agarwal, S., Jones, D., Young, B., & Sutton, A. (2005). Synthesising qualitative and quantitative evidence: A review of possible methods. *Journal of Health Services Research & Policy*, *10*, 45–53.

Dixon-Woods, M., Bonas, S., Booth, A., Jones, D. R., Miller, T., Sutton, A., . . . Young, B. (2006). How can systematic reviews incorporate qualitative research? A critical perspective. *Qualitative Research*, *6*, 27–44. doi:10.1177/1468794106058867

Dixon-Woods, M., Cavers, D., Agarwal, S., Annandale, E., Arthur, A., Harvey, J., . . . Sutton, A. J. (2006). Conducting a critical interpretive synthesis of the literature on access to healthcare by vulnerable groups. *BMC Medical Research Methodology*, *6*(35). doi:10.1186/1471-2288-6-35

Evans, D., & FitzGerald, M. (2002). Reasons for physically restraining patients and residents: A systematic review and content analysis. *International Journal of Nursing Studies*, *39*, 735–743.

Fairbank, L., O'Meara, S., Renfrew, M. J., Woolridge, M., Sowden, A. J., & Lister-Sharp, D. (1999). A systematic review to evaluate the effectiveness of interventions to promote the initiation of breastfeeding. *Health Technology Assessment*, *4*, 1–171.

Hannes, K., & Lockwood, C. (Eds.). (2012). *Synthesizing qualitative research. Choosing the right approach*. Chichester, England: Wiley.

Hannes, K., & Macaitis, K. (2012). A move to more systematic and transparent approaches in qualitative evidence synthesis: Update on a review of published papers. *Qualitative Research*, *12*, 402–442. doi:10.1177/1468794111432992

Joanna Briggs Institute. (2014). *The Joanna Briggs Institute reviewers' manual 2014: Methodology for JBI mixed methods systematic reviews.* University of Adelaide, South Australia. Retrieved from http://joannabriggs.org/assets/docs/sumari/ ReviewersManual_Mixed-Methods-Review-Methods-2014-ch1.pdf

Koricheva, J., & Gurevitch, J. (2013). Place of meta-analysis among other methods of research synthesis. In J. Koricheva, J. Gurevitch, & K. Mengersen (Eds.), *Handbook of meta-analysis in ecology and evolution* (pp. 3–13). Princeton, NJ: Princeton University Press.

Mohagheghi, P., & Conradi, R. (2006). Vote-counting for combining quantitative evidence from empirical studies—An example. *Proceedings of the 5th ACM-IEEE International Symposium on Empirical Software Engineering (ISESE'06),* pp. 24–26.

Onwuegbuzie, A. J. (2003). Effect sizes in qualitative research: A prolegomenon. *Quality & Quantity, 37,* 393–409.

Pawson, R., Greenhalgh, T., Harvey, G., & Walshe, K. (2005). Realist review. A new method of systematic review designed for complex policy interventions. *Journal of Health Services Research & Policy, 10*(Suppl. 1), 21–34. doi:10.1258/ 1355819054308530

Ring, N., Jepson, R., & Ritchie, K. (2011). Methods of synthesizing qualitative research studies for health technology assessment. *International Journal of Technology Assessment in Health Care, 27,* 384–390. doi:10.1017/S02664623 11000389

Sandelowski, M., Voils, C. I., & Barroso, J. (2006). Defining and designing mixed research synthesis studies. *Research in the Schools, 13*(1), 29–40.

Voils, C. I., Sandelowski, M., Barroso, J., & Hasselblad, V. (2008). Making sense of qualitative and quantitative findings in mixed research synthesis studies. *Field Methods, 20,* 3–25. doi:10.1177/1525822X07307463

Wong, G., Greenhalgh, T., & Pawson, R. (2010). Internet-based medical education: A realist review of what works, for whom and in what circumstances. *BMC Medical Education, 10*(1), 12. doi:10.1186/1472-6920-10-12

⚜ 8 ⚜

DATA SYNTHESIS FOR CONTINGENT MMRS LITERATURE REVIEWS

═══════════════════════ ಸಾ ═══════════════════════

Chapter Outline

In MMRS literature reviews following a contingent design, the results of synthesizing the findings of a first group of primary studies to answer one review question determine the next group of primary studies that will be retrieved and synthesized to answer a second review question, the results of which, in turn, may lead to the synthesis of a third group of primary studies retrieved to answer yet another review question, and so on, until a comprehensive MMRS can be presented that addresses all the review objectives. In this chapter, we discuss possible data synthesis approaches that can be used within contingent MMRS literature reviews.

═══════════════════════ ಸಾ ═══════════════════════

DATA SYNTHESIS FOR CONTINGENT MMRS

As we discussed in Chapter 2, in MMRS literature reviews following a contingent MMRS design, the results of synthesizing the findings of a first group of primary studies to answer one review question determine the next group of primary studies that will be retrieved and synthesized to answer a second review question, the results of which, in turn, may lead to the synthesis of a third group of primary studies retrieved to answer yet another review question, and so on, until a comprehensive MMRS can be presented that addresses all the review objectives (Sandelowski, Voils, & Barroso, 2006). Accordingly, the

248

Figure 8.1 Data Synthesis for Contingent MMRS Literature Reviews

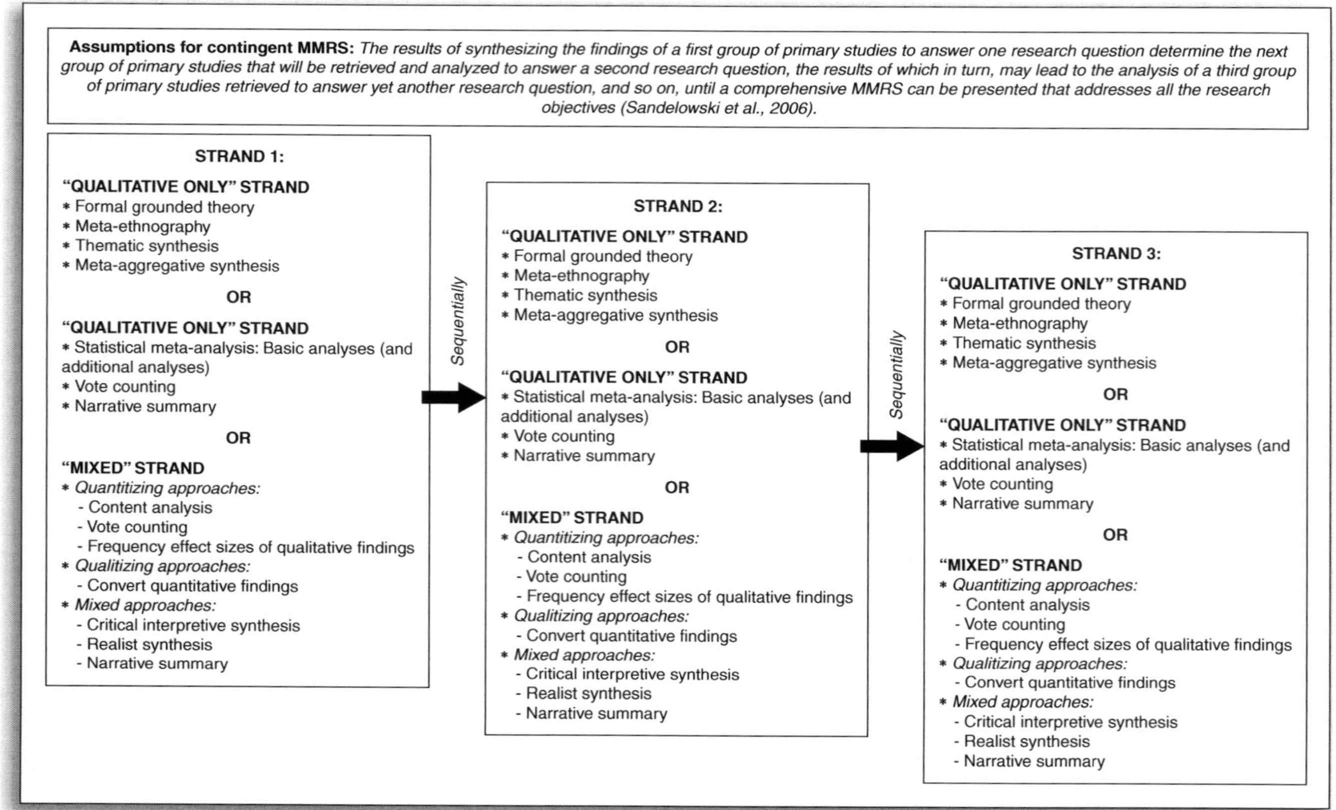

Assumptions for contingent MMRS: *The results of synthesizing the findings of a first group of primary studies to answer one research question determine the next group of primary studies that will be retrieved and analyzed to answer a second research question, the results of which in turn, may lead to the analysis of a third group of primary studies retrieved to answer yet another research question, and so on, until a comprehensive MMRS can be presented that addresses all the research objectives (Sandelowski et al., 2006).*

STRAND 1:

"QUALITATIVE ONLY" STRAND
* Formal grounded theory
* Meta-ethnography
* Thematic synthesis
* Meta-aggregative synthesis

OR

"QUALITATIVE ONLY" STRAND
* Statistical meta-analysis: Basic analyses (and additional analyses)
* Vote counting
* Narrative summary

OR

"MIXED" STRAND
* *Quantitizing approaches:*
  - Content analysis
  - Vote counting
  - Frequency effect sizes of qualitative findings
* *Qualitizing approaches:*
  - Convert quantitative findings
* *Mixed approaches:*
  - Critical interpretive synthesis
  - Realist synthesis
  - Narrative summary

Sequentially →

STRAND 2:

"QUALITATIVE ONLY" STRAND
* Formal grounded theory
* Meta-ethnography
* Thematic synthesis
* Meta-aggregative synthesis

OR

"QUALITATIVE ONLY" STRAND
* Statistical meta-analysis: Basic analyses (and additional analyses)
* Vote counting
* Narrative summary

OR

"MIXED" STRAND
* *Quantitizing approaches:*
  - Content analysis
  - Vote counting
  - Frequency effect sizes of qualitative findings
* *Qualitizing approaches:*
  - Convert quantitative findings
* *Mixed approaches:*
  - Critical interpretive synthesis
  - Realist synthesis
  - Narrative summary

Sequentially →

STRAND 3:

"QUALITATIVE ONLY" STRAND
* Formal grounded theory
* Meta-ethnography
* Thematic synthesis
* Meta-aggregative synthesis

OR

"QUALITATIVE ONLY" STRAND
* Statistical meta-analysis: Basic analyses (and additional analyses)
* Vote counting
* Narrative summary

OR

"MIXED" STRAND
* *Quantitizing approaches:*
  - Content analysis
  - Vote counting
  - Frequency effect sizes of qualitative findings
* *Qualitizing approaches:*
  - Convert quantitative findings
* *Mixed approaches:*
  - Critical interpretive synthesis
  - Realist synthesis
  - Narrative summary

defining feature of a contingent MMRS is the cycle of consecutive, emergent strands. Each strand is conducted to answer questions raised by a previous strand of the contingent MMRS.

A first implication of this design is that review authors who conduct a contingent MMRS may not start with a set of predefined review questions. Rather, the questions emerge *during* the contingent MMRS, based on the findings of the previous strands. That is why the contingent MMRS is said to follow an emergent or iterative logic, rather than an *a priori* logic.

A second implication of this design is that review authors who conduct a contingent MMRS do not know at the beginning of their journey which data synthesis approaches they will use for the consecutive strands as they at that time even do not know how many strands will be included in their contingent MMRS, nor what will be the questions to be answered by each strand, nor what will be the data included in each strand. Parallel to what we discussed for segregated and integrated MMRS in the two previous chapters, the selection of the data synthesis approaches has to fit the question posed within each strand of the contingent MMRS, the aims of that strand, and the data included in that strand. Thus, for the contingent MMRS, the selection of data synthesis approaches too is **emergent** rather than *a priori*. Figure 8.1 provides an overview of various data synthesis approaches that can be used within the consecutive strands of a contingent MMRS.

As illustrated in Figure 8.1, if you conduct a contingent MMRS, you may use the data synthesis approaches we discussed for segregated and integrated MMRS (see Chapters 6 and 7, respectively) for the subsequent strands. We want to stress that Figure 8.1 includes often used data synthesis approaches for contingent MMRS literature reviews and that we do not aim for this list of synthesis approaches to be exhaustive.

A CLOSER LOOK AT OFTEN USED DATA SYNTHESIS APPROACHES FOR CONTINGENT MMRS

Let us take a closer look at Figure 8.1. First, it is possible that the first strand of the contingent MMRS is a *qualitative only* strand. For this strand, a review question is posed that can be answered by synthesizing qualitative primary data by means of a qualitative data synthesis approach. In that case, a qualitative approach discussed in Chapter 6 could be applied for

Table 8.1   Overview of Possible Data Synthesis Approaches for a *Qualitative Only* Strand of a Contingent MMRS

Data synthesis approach	Possible motivations for selecting this approach	Practical Tip box
Formal grounded theory	If you want to generate theory and more specifically if you want to produce theories that are based on phenomena involving processes of contextualized understanding and action	Practical Tip 6.1
Meta-ethnographical synthesis	If you want to generate theory and more specifically if you want to bring together findings into an interpretative explanation that is greater than the sum of the parts	Practical Tip 6.2
Thematic synthesis	If you want to describe the themes in the empirical data	Practical Tip 6.3
Meta-aggregative synthesis	If you want to generate practical and usable *lines of action* (i.e., recommendations for policy and practice)	Practical Tip 6.4

synthesizing the data: formal grounded theory, meta-ethnography, thematic synthesis, or meta-aggregative synthesis. In Table 8.1, we present a brief overview of these data synthesis approaches and we mention in which Practical Tip box in Chapter 6 we discussed each data synthesis approach. For further details and guidance on these data synthesis approaches, we refer you back to Chapter 6.

Second, it is possible that the first strand of the contingent MMRS is a *quantitative only* strand. For this strand, a review question is posed that can be answered by synthesizing quantitative primary data. Within a *quantitative only* strand of a contingent MMRS, the included quantitative primary data are often synthesized by using statistical meta-analytical techniques. However, in Chapter 6, we discussed a number of conditions under which it is impossible or undesirable to synthesize quantitative primary data by using meta-analytical techniques. In case statistical meta-analysis is impossible or undesirable, you can synthesize the quantitative data by conducting a vote counting synthesis or by presenting a narrative summary of the data. In Table 8.2, we present a brief overview of these data synthesis approaches and we mention in which

Table 8.2   Overview of Possible Data Synthesis Approaches for a *Quantitative Only* Strand of a Contingent MMRS

Data synthesis approach	Possible motivations for selecting this approach	Practical Tip box
Statistical meta-analysis: Basic analyses (and additional analyses)	If the included primary studies are similar enough to be combined, you can conduct a basic meta-analysis, including (a) calculating or extracting an effect size and variance for each included study; and (b) calculating the summary effect size over all included studies and determining a confidence interval for, and statistical significance of, the overall effect. Additionally, when relevant to answer your review questions, you can assess homogeneity, conduct subgroup and/or meta-regression analyses, conduct a sensitivity analysis, a publication bias analysis, power analysis, or a cumulative meta-analysis.	Practical Tip 6.5
Vote counting synthesis	In case statistical meta-analysis is impossible or undesirable, you can conduct a vote counting synthesis of the quantitative data.	Practical Tip 6.6
Narrative summary	In case statistical meta-analysis is impossible or undesirable, you can develop a narrative summary of the quantitative data.	Practical Tip 6.7

Practical Tip box in Chapter 6 we discussed each data synthesis approach. For further details and guidance on these data synthesis approaches, we refer you back to Chapter 6.

Third, it is possible that the first strand of the contingent MMRS is a mixed synthesis strand. In that case, a data synthesis approach discussed in Chapter 7 could be applied. Based on your review objectives and on the included data, you could, for instance, decide to use one of the following approaches: (a) a *quantitizing* approach (such as content analysis, vote counting, or calculating frequency effect sizes of qualitative findings), (b) a *qualitizing* approach (i.e., converting quantitative findings into qualitative findings), or (c) a mixed approach (such as narrative summary, critical inter-pretive synthesis, or realist synthesis). In Table 8.3, we present a brief over-view of these data synthesis approaches and we mention in which Practical Tip box in Chapter 7 we discussed each data synthesis approach. For further details and guidance on these data synthesis approaches, we refer you back to Chapter 7.

The end result of the first strand of a contingent MMRS is an answer to the first posed review question. Based on the results of the first strand, a second review question might be posed. You can retrieve and synthesize a second group of primary studies to answer this second review question. Similar to the first strand, you can within this second strand decide to use qualitative synthesis approaches (see Table 8.1), quantitative synthesis approaches (see Table 8.2), or quantitizing, qualitizing, or mixed synthesis approaches (see Table 8.3) to answer this second review question.

Afterward, the answer to the second review question might prompt you to pose a third review question. A third group of primary studies can be retrieved

Table 8.3   Overview of Possible Data Synthesis Approaches for a Mixed Synthesis Strand of a Contingent MMRS

Data synthesis approach	Possible motivations for selecting this approach	Practical Tip box
Content analysis	If you want to quantitize the qualitative findings to enable joint quantitative synthesis of all the collected empirical evidence, you can categorize the data and afterward determine the frequencies of these categories.	Practical Tip 7.1
Vote counting synthesis	If you want to quantitize the qualitative findings to enable joint quantitative synthesis of all the collected empirical evidence, you can sort the findings of all the included studies into the categories *yielding positive/negative/nonclear results*, and afterward count the votes and determine whether there is a relationship between the variables of interest.	Practical Tip 7.2

Data synthesis approach	Possible motivations for selecting this approach	Practical Tip box
Calculate frequency effect sizes of qualitative findings	If you want to quantitize the qualitative findings to enable joint quantitative synthesis of all the collected empirical evidence, you can assess the relative magnitude of the qualitative findings by calculating their frequency effect sizes (i.e., dividing the number of included reports containing a finding by the total number of included reports).	Practical Tip 7.3
Converting quantitative into qualitative findings	If you want to qualitize the quantitative findings to enable joint qualitative synthesis of all the collected empirical evidence, you can convert the quantitative findings (e.g., quantitative tables such as frequency tables, quantitative figures such as forest plots, or findings included in the quantitative primary studies) into themes, categories, typologies, or narratives, for the qualitized data to be afterward included in qualitative syntheses.	Practical Tip 7.4
Narrative summary	If you want to synthesize the qualitative, quantitative, and mixed primary-level evidence, and if you want to describe the data, you can narratively summarize the evidence coming from the primary studies on a common phenomenon of interest.	Practical Tip 7.5
Critical interpretive synthesis	If you want to synthesize the qualitative, quantitative, and mixed primary-level evidence, and if you want to interpret the data, you can critically approach the literature in terms of deconstructing research traditions or theoretical assumptions.	Practical Tip 7.6
Realist synthesis	If you want to synthesize the qualitative, quantitative, and mixed primary-level evidence, and if you want to interpret the data, you can unpack mechanisms of how complex programs or interventions work (or why they fail) in particular contexts and settings.	Practical Tip 7.7

and synthesized to answer this third review question. Similar to the first and second strand, you can within this third strand decide to use qualitative synthesis approaches (see Table 8.1), quantitative synthesis approaches (see Table 8.2), or quantitizing, qualitizing, or mixed synthesis approaches (see Table 8.3) to answer this third review question.

It is possible that the answer to the third review question prompts you to pose a fourth review question and, thus, to include a fourth strand in your contingent MMRS. You can keep on adding consecutive strands until a comprehensive MMRS can be presented that addresses all your review objectives (Sandelowski et al., 2006).

ALTERNATIVE DATA SYNTHESIS APPROACHES FOR CONTINGENT MMRS: BAYESIAN SYNTHESES

In the beginning of this chapter, we said that a contingent MMRS consists of consecutive, emergent strands. However, Bayesian syntheses are contingent MMRS that form an exception to this general rule. These Bayesian contingent MMRS consist of consecutive strands, but the strands are not emergent. By conducting a (certain type of) Bayesian synthesis, you know from the beginning how many consecutive strands your contingent MMRS will include, which type of data you will collect for which strand, and which data synthesis approach you will use within which strand.

The **Bayesian synthesis** approach can be used to draw on both qualitative and quantitative evidence in a contingent MMRS. Generally, a Bayesian synthesis includes three strands: (1) developing a **prior distribution** that describes the probability of the values for the parameters that will be estimated, (2) constructing a function that describes the likelihood of the parameter values given the observed data (i.e., the **likelihood function**), and (3) creating a **posterior distribution** that describes the final probability of the parameter values based on the prior distribution and the likelihood function (Voils et al., 2009). We found three Bayesian synthesis approaches used within the context of MMRS literature reviews: the approaches of Karen Roberts, Mary Dixon-Woods, Ray Fitzpatrick, Keith Abrams, and David Jones (2002), of Corrine Voils et al. (2009), and of Jamie Crandell, Corrine Voils, YunKyung Chang, and Margarete Sandelowski (2011). In the remainder of this chapter, we will discuss these three Bayesian synthesis approaches.

The Bayesian Synthesis Approach of Roberts et al. (2002)

The Bayesian synthesis approach described by Roberts et al. (2002) uses data from empirical qualitative studies to create the prior distributions in the first strand of the contingent MMRS, whereas empirical quantitative studies are included in the next strands of the contingent MMRS. In Practical Tip 8.1, we describe how you can conduct a Bayesian synthesis following the approach described by Roberts et al.

Practical Tip 8.1: How to Conduct a Bayesian Synthesis Following the Approach of Roberts et al. (2002)

Aim: Let's say you are interested in behavioral interventions for reducing challenging behavior among persons with intellectual disabilities. More specifically, you want to study which factors affect the effectiveness of these interventions for reducing challenging behavior among this population. You searched for qualitative and quantitative primary studies reporting on such factors to be included in your contingent MMRS.

Synthesis: Your contingent MMRS consists of the following three strands:

- In the first strand, you generate prior distributions based on the qualitative studies that are included in your contingent MMRS. You extract the factors that are reported to affect the effectiveness of behavioral interventions for reducing challenging behavior from each primary study. Next, you rank the relative importance of these factors. You can do this by taking into account the number of qualitative studies that report each factor to affect the effectiveness of behavioral interventions for reducing challenging behavior. The prior distributions are based on these rankings. The prior distributions refer to the probability of each factor being important in affecting the effectiveness of behavioral interventions for reducing challenging behavior. Accordingly, within this first strand, the qualitative studies serve as a source of evidence that informs

(Continued)

(Continued)

the initial judgments (the *prior probabilities*) about the likely importance of the factors that affect the effectiveness of behavioral interventions for reducing challenging behavior among persons with intellectual disabilities (Dixon-Woods, Agarwal, Jones, Young, & Sutton, 2005).

- In the second strand, you extract data from the quantitative studies that are included in your contingent MMRS. You code the empirical data that you find in these quantitative studies by using the factors that you generated in the first strand when you were synthesizing the qualitative studies. If necessary, you can add new factors that were not used in the first strand of your contingent MMRS.

- In the third strand, you combine the prior probabilities (based on the qualitative evidence; see the first strand of your contingent MMRS) with evidence from the quantitative data (see the second strand of your contingent MMRS) to form posterior probabilities. This implies that the posterior probabilities are based on both the qualitative and quantitative studies that were included in your contingent MMRS. Following the guidelines of Roberts et al. (2002), you can use Bayes factor methods (Jones, Dixon-Woods, Abrams, & Fitzpatrick, 2005; Kass & Raftery, 1995) to compare two possible (fixed effect) meta-regression models for the log odds of uptake, for each possible factor. In the first model, the overall pooled level of uptake is estimated, ignoring the factor in question, and in the second model, a covariate is included for the factor in question (Roberts et al., 2002). It is possible that the posterior probabilities (based on the qualitative and quantitative evidence) considerably alter the estimates of the importance of the factors compared with the prior probabilities (based on the qualitative evidence only) (Dixon-Woods et al., 2005). In that case, you can conclude that using either the qualitative or the quantitative primary studies alone might not identify all relevant factors, or might result in inappropriate judgments about their importance, and could thus lead to the inappropriate formulation of policy and practice guidelines (Roberts et al., 2002).

The Bayesian Synthesis Approach of Voils et al. (2009)

The Bayesian synthesis approach described by Voils et al. (2009) involves the quantitizing of empirical qualitative data for both the quantitized qualitative data and the quantitative data to be used to calculate the relative likelihood. In Practical Tip 8.2, we describe how you can conduct a Bayesian synthesis following the approach described by Voils et al.

Practical Tip 8.2: How to Conduct a Bayesian Synthesis Following the Approach of Voils et al. (2009)

Aim: Let's say you are interested in behavioral interventions for reducing challenging behavior among persons with intellectual disabilities. Based on your scoping review (see Chapter 2), you know that some behavioral interventions are more complex than others, depending on the number of components included in these interventions and on the combination of the components included in these interventions. In the discussion section of one of the studies you read, a researcher formulated the hypotheses that more complex behavioral interventions are associated with lesser adherence, and that less complex behavioral interventions are associated with greater adherence. With your contingent MMRS, you want to test these two hypotheses empirically. First, you described how you will operationalize "more complex behavioral interventions" and "less complex behavioral interventions" for your MMRS. Second, you searched for qualitative and quantitative primary studies reporting on the adherence for various behavioral interventions used to reduce challenging behavior among persons with intellectual disabilities, including studies reporting on more complex and less complex behavioral interventions.

Synthesis:

- First, you formulate your prior distributions. In contrast with the Roberts et al. (2002) approach we described earlier, where "informative prior distributions" (i.e., the prior distributions are derived from a source, such as empirical data) were formulated

(Continued)

(Continued)

in the first strand that were based on the collected qualitative evidence, the Voils et al. (2009) approach prescribes to use "noninformative prior distributions." Noninformative prior distributions have no population basis and, thus, have a minimal effect on the posterior distribution, which is informed primarily by the empirical data used to construct the likelihood (Voils et al., 2009). Voils et al. proposed to use two approaches for generating the noninformative prior distributions in the first strand of your contingent MMRS: (a) the uniform prior, which gives every possible outcome the exact same prior probability, and (b) the prior by Harold Jeffreys (1961), whose mathematical properties make it fairly noninformative. For your contingent MMRS, you decided to focus on two findings: (1) More complex behavioral interventions are associated with lesser adherence, and (2) less complex behavioral interventions are associated with greater adherence.

- Second, you code for each participant described in each qualitative and quantitative study included in your contingent MMRS whether the data for this participant confirm finding (1) or (2). For the qualitative studies included in your contingent MMRS, you can do this by quantitizing the qualitative data. For each participant you code whether the data confirm finding (1) or (2). More concretely, you can do this for each finding by assigning a value of 0 or 1 to each participant described in the qualitative studies to indicate whether the finding was absent or present, respectively. Afterward, you calculate the proportion of participants associated with each finding over all the qualitative studies included in your contingent MMRS. For the quantitative studies included in your contingent MMRS too, you assign a value of 0 or 1 to each participant to indicate whether finding (1) or (2) was absent or present, respectively, and you afterward calculate the proportion of participants associated with each finding.

- Third, you use Bayesian methods to determine the probabilities of retrieving empirical evidence at the participant level that (a) a more complex behavioral intervention is associated with lesser adherence, and (b) a less complex behavioral intervention is associated with greater adherence. Following the approach described by Voils et al. (2009), you can analyze the data by using the two prior distributions (i.e., the uniform prior and the Jeffreys prior), calculate the likelihood for each primary study by using the observed data (using the Mathematica software; Wolfram, 1996), and finally combine the prior distribution and the likelihood to form a posterior distribution by using the modified Gauss-Newton method (Hartley, 1961) and by using the FAST*PRO Software (Eddy & Hasselblad, 1992).

The Bayesian Synthesis Approach of Crandell et al. (2011)

The Bayesian synthesis approach described by Crandell et al. (2011) involves the qualitizing of empirical quantitative data. The presence and absence of relationships between relevant factors and the dependent variable is coded for both the qualitative and quantitative studies included in the contingent MMRS, and these data are used to calculate the relative likelihood. In Practical Tip 8.3, we describe how you can conduct a Bayesian synthesis following the approach described by Crandell et al.

Practical Tip 8.3: How to Conduct a Bayesian Synthesis Following the Approach of Crandell et al. (2011)

Aim: Let's say you are interested in behavioral interventions for reducing challenging behavior among persons with intellectual disabilities. More specifically, you want to study which factors affect the effectiveness of these interventions for reducing challenging behavior among this population. You searched for qualitative and quantitative primary studies reporting on such factors and on the effectiveness of these behavioral interventions.

Synthesis:

- First, you carefully read all the qualitative and quantitative primary studies you included in your contingent MMRS.

(Continued)

(Continued)

During your reading of these studies, you note down which factors were reported to influence the effectiveness of behavioral interventions for reducing challenging behavior among persons with intellectual disabilities. Afterward, you code each primary study's findings about the relationship between each of the factors and the effectiveness of the behavioral interventions. For both the qualitative and quantitative primary studies, you can, for instance, assign code "1" if a factor was reported as promoting effectiveness of behavioral interventions, assign code ".50" if a factor was reported as having no effect on effectiveness, and assign code "0" if a factor was related to intervention noneffectiveness. More specifically, following the guidelines of Crandell et al. (2011), you can use Cohen's d for coding the quantitative studies and apply the following coding criteria: (a) Assign code "1" if $d \geq .20$ for a study, (b) assign code ".50" if $-.20 < d < .20$ for a study, and (c) assign code "0" if $d \leq - .20$ for a study. Following the guidelines of Crandell et al., you can apply the following specific coding criteria for the qualitative studies: (a) Assign code "1" if a factor was related to intervention effectiveness, (b) assign code ".50" if a factor was related to both intervention effectiveness and intervention noneffectiveness, or neither, and (c) assign code "0" if a factor was related to intervention noneffectiveness. You can keep record of all the codes you assigned by using a tabular format, with all the factors as column heads, and all the qualitative and quantitative studies included in your contingent MMRS as row heads. For both the qualitative and the quantitative reports, you can leave the cell in this table blank if a report did not address a certain factor.

- Second, you follow the approach described by Crandell et al. (2011) for conducting a first "naive analysis" that ignores the possible missing values in the data set (i.e., not every factor you listed might be described in every report included in your MMRS) by taking the average of the nonmissing values in each column to estimate the strength of the relationship between each factor and the effectiveness or noneffectiveness of the behavioral interventions.

- The naive analysis you conducted in the previous step ignored the empirical reports that did not address a certain factor, which implies that the number of reports on which an estimate was based might vary from factor to factor, and which might result in confidence intervals that are based on very small samples in case there is only a small number of "filled in" cells in the data set (Crandell et al., 2011). In case you are indeed confronted with such a missing data problem, you can use the Bayesian data augmentation procedure described by Crandell et al. (2011). This procedure implies that you use the available empirical data to impute the values of the missing data with Bayesian methods and that you afterward analyze the data set as if it were complete (Gelman, Carlin, Stern, & Rubin, 2004). The results of this analysis will enable you to summarize, rank, and compare the effects of each of the identified factors on the effectiveness of behavioral interventions for reducing challenging behavior among persons with intellectual disabilities.

Summary Points

- A contingent MMRS can simply involve consecutive *qualitative only strands* and *quantitative only strands* without *mixing* of qualitative and quantitative evidence and synthesis approaches within the strands. In that case, the qualitative and quantitative synthesis approaches discussed for segregated MMRS literature reviews can be applied for synthesizing the data.
- However, it is also possible that within one, some, or all of the strands of the contingent MMRS, a *qualitizing*, *quantitizing*, or *mixed* synthesis approach is used.
- Alternative data synthesis approaches that are sometimes used for contingent MMRS literature reviews are the Bayesian syntheses approaches. Bayesian synthesis approaches can be used to draw on both qualitative and quantitative evidence.

Questions for Thought

- If you are conducting a contingent MMRS, will your review simply involve consecutive *qualitative only strands* and *quantitative only strands* without *mixing* of qualitative and quantitative evidence and synthesis approaches? If so, which qualitative and quantitative synthesis approaches will you use? Why?
- Or will you use a *qualitizing, quantitizing,* or *mixed* synthesis approach for synthesizing the findings of the retrieved studies within one, some, or all of the strands of your contingent MMRS? If so, which qualitizing, quantitizing, or mixed synthesis approach will you use? Why?
- Or will you use a Bayesian synthesis approach to draw on both the qualitative and quantitative evidence you retrieved for your contingent MMRS? If so, which Bayesian synthesis approach will you use? Why?

Suggestions for Further Reading on Bayesian Syntheses

Crandell, J. L., Voils, C. I., Chang, Y., & Sandelowski, M. (2011). Bayesian data augmentation methods for the synthesis of qualitative and quantitative research findings. *Quality & Quantity, 45,* 653–669. doi:10.1007/s11135-010-9375-z

Roberts, K. A., Dixon-Woods, M., Fitzpatrick, R., Abrams, K. R., & Jones, D. R. (2002). Factors affecting uptake of childhood immunisation: A Bayesian synthesis of qualitative and quantitative evidence. *Lancet, 360,* 1596–1599. doi:10.1016/S0140-6736(02)11560-1

Voils, C. I., Hassselblad, V., Crandell, J., Chang, Y., Lee, E., & Sandelowski, M. (2009). A Bayesian method for the synthesis of evidence from qualitative and quantitative reports: The example of antiretroviral medication adherence. *Journal of Health Services Research & Policy, 14,* 226–233. doi:10.1258/jhsrp.2009.008186

References

Crandell, J. L., Voils, C. I., Chang, Y., & Sandelowski, M. (2011). Bayesian data augmentation methods for the synthesis of qualitative and quantitative research findings. *Quality & Quantity, 45,* 653–669. doi:10.1007/s11135-010-9375-z

Dixon-Woods, M., Agarwal, S., Jones, D., Young, B., & Sutton, A. (2005). Synthesising qualitative and quantitative evidence: A review of possible methods. *Journal of Health Services Research & Policy, 10,* 45–53.

Eddy, D., & Hasselblad, V. (1992). *Fast*Pro: Software for meta-analysis by the confidence profile method*. San Diego, CA: Academic Press.

Gelman, A., Carlin, J. B., Stern, H. S., & Rubin, D. B. (2004). *Bayesian data analysis* (2nd ed.). Boca Raton, FL: Chapman & Hall/CRC.

Hartley, H. (1961). The modified Gauss Newton method for the fitting of nonlinear regression functions by least squares. *Technometrics, 3*, 269–280.

Jeffreys, H. (1961). *Theory of probability*. New York, NY: Oxford University Press.

Jones, D. R., Dixon-Woods, M., Abrams, K., & Fitzpatrick, R. (2005). *Meta-analysis of qualitative and quantitative evidence: Full report of research activities and results* (ESRC ALCD 2 programme).

Kass, R. E., & Raftery, A. E. (1995). Bayes factors. *Journal of the American Statistical Association, 90*, 773–795.

Roberts, K. A., Dixon-Woods, M., Fitzpatrick, R., Abrams, K. R., & Jones, D. R. (2002). Factors affecting uptake of childhood immunisation: A Bayesian synthesis of qualitative and quantitative evidence. *Lancet, 360*, 1596–1599. doi:10.1016/S0140-6736(02)11560-1

Sandelowski, M., Voils, C. I., & Barroso, J. (2006). Defining and designing mixed research synthesis studies. *Research in the Schools, 13*(1), 29–40.

Voils, C. I., Hassselblad, V., Crandell, J., Chang, Y., Lee, E., & Sandelowski, M. (2009). A Bayesian method for the synthesis of evidence from qualitative and quantitative reports: The example of antiretroviral medication adherence. *Journal of Health Services Research & Policy, 14*, 226–233. doi:10.1258/jhsrp.2009.008186

Wolfram, S. (1996). *Mathematica*. Champaign, IL: Wolfram Research.

⚜ 9 ⚜

REPORTING MMRS LITERATURE REVIEWS

⭒⭒

Chapter Outline

In addition to conducting a high-quality literature review, it is of utmost importance to report clearly and critically on the MMRS, the findings and interpretations, as well as the implications and suggestions for future research, policy, and practice. In this chapter, we first discuss reporting templates for literature reviews and we provide practical tips for writing an MMRS literature review. Furthermore, we discuss how the intended audience has to be taken into account to make the MMRS report relevant and intelligible. In addition, we discuss ethics in the writing process as well as the sections to be included in the MMRS report. Next, we provide information on publication outlets for MMRS protocols and literature reviews. Finally, we discuss the challenges and pitfalls of reporting and publishing MMRS literature reviews.

⭒⭒

WRITING PROCESS

In Chapter 2, we encouraged you to write a review protocol (also called a "review proposal" or "review plan") before embarking on an MMRS journey. A review protocol enables you to document *a priori* the methodological and substantive choices for your MMRS. In the review protocol, you outline *what will be done*. In the **MMRS report**—which is the focus of this chapter—you describe the methods used and the findings of your MMRS literature review.

Throughout this book, we emphasized the importance of a transparent MMRS process. A transparent MMRS process implies that you describe as clearly as possible how each stage of the MMRS was conducted (see Figure 1.1 in Chapter 1 for an overview of the main stages of an MMRS), which methodological and substantive decisions were made throughout the MMRS process, and what the rationales were behind these decisions. In other words, it implies that you provide the reader with a clear audit trail.

In this section, we first discuss reporting templates for MMRS protocols and literature reviews. Second, we provide tips for writing an MMRS literature review. Third, we discuss the intended audience for MMRS literature reviews and how this audience influences the writing process. Fourth, we discuss ethical issues you should take into account when writing the MMRS report. We start with discussing reporting templates for MMRS protocols and literature reviews in Practical Tip 9.1.

Practical Tip 9.1: Reporting Templates

Several organizations promoting and disseminating literature reviews offer standard templates for literature review *protocols* and literature reviews, and they expect review authors to use these templates when they submit their protocol or literature review to this organization. Examples are:

- The Campbell Collaboration, for MMRS conducted in the field of crime and justice, education, international development, or social welfare (http://www.campbellcollaboration.org/systematic_reviews/index.php; http://www.campbellcollaboration.org/artman2/uploads/1/C2_Protocols_guidelines_v1.pdf)

- The Cochrane Collaboration, for MMRS conducted in the field of human health care or health policy (http://www.cochrane.org/handbook; http://www.cochrane.org/editorial-and-publishing-policy-resource/review-manager-revman)

In addition, other templates for reporting on literature review *protocols* have been developed, such as:

- The Preferred Reporting Items for Systematic Review and Meta-Analysis Protocols (PRISMA-P) 2015 statement (Shamseer et al., 2015)

Furthermore, templates for reporting on literature reviews have been developed by other organizations and authors, such as:

- The Centre for Reviews and Dissemination's (CRD) guidance for undertaking reviews in health care (http://www.york .ac.uk/inst/crd/SysRev/!SSL!/WebHelp/SysRev3.htm)
- Finding What Works in Health Care: Standards for Systematic Reviews (Morton, Levit, Berg, & Eden, 2011)

Additionally, templates have been developed for reporting on the specific data synthesis approaches we discussed in Chapters 6, 7, and 8, such as:

- Preferred Reporting Items for Systematic Reviews and Meta-Analyses: The PRISMA Statement (Moher, Liberati, Tetzlaff, & Altman, 2009)
- ENhancing Transparency in REporting the synthesis of Qualitative research (ENTREQ) (Tong, Flemming, McInnes, Oliver, & Craig, 2012)
- The RAMESES publication standards: Realist syntheses (Wong, Greenhalgh, Westhorp, Buckingham, & Pawson, 2013) (http:// www.ramesesproject.org/media/Realist_reviews_training_ materials.pdf)
- The Joanna Briggs Institute's (JBI) standards for reporting on a meta-aggregative synthesis (http://www.joannabriggs.org/ assets/docs/sumari/ReviewersManual-2014.pdf; http://www .joannabriggs.org/assets/docs/sumari/SUMARI-V5-User-guide.pdf)

Most of these reporting templates can be found on the EQUATOR (Enhancing the QUAlity and Transparency Of health Research) Network website (http://www.equator-network.org/).

For the time being, no reporting templates have been developed specifically for MMRS literature reviews. However, these templates may become available in the near future. Before writing out your MMRS literature review, we suggest that you first check on the availability of a reporting guideline for your type of MMRS.

In Practical Tip 9.2, we provide tips that can help you during the writing process. These tips may be perceived as common sense, but they are often overlooked by novice review authors.

Audience

A general advice for review authors is to keep in mind their *intended audience* when they are writing. Many MMRS literature reviews are mainly inspired by academic interests. In that case, the MMRS report is likely to be submitted to an academic journal, and the audience targeted is an academic

---

Practical Tip 9.2: The Writing Process

- Be aware that writing takes a lot of time. Start to write *while* you are conducting the MMRS, and save enough time in your schedule for writing.

- The notes you have been taking throughout the MMRS process (see *review diary* discussed in Practical Tip 1.1 in Chapter 1) will be very helpful for writing up your MMRS report.

- While writing, imagine that you are telling about your MMRS to a friend or colleague. Use clear, simple, efficient language to tell *what* you have been doing and *why*.

- Consider the style you are supposed to use (e.g., American Psychological Association style or Vancouver style). Style issues, for instance, relate to the references, within-text citations, headings, page numbering, spacing, and margins. In case you are writing up an MMRS for your master's thesis or doctoral dissertation, consult the guidelines provided by your institution. In case you want to submit your MMRS to an organization (e.g., the Campbell Collaboration, the Cochrane Collaboration, or the Joanna Briggs Institute), consult the guidelines provided by the organization (see Practical Tip 9.1). In case you want to send in your manuscript to a journal, the journal's *Guidelines for Authors* will often mention the style you have to use.

audience. Other MMRS literature reviews are commissioned by a practice or policy organization. In that case, the MMRS report can be written with the practitioners', stakeholders', or policy makers' interests in mind. It is also possible that the MMRS is not commissioned by a practice or policy organization but that you intend to influence and encourage change in policy and/or practice with your MMRS. In that case, the MMRS report will be written toward the targeted practitioners and/or government agencies.

The intended audience will influence the writing process in several ways. First, it will influence the language that is used and the format and content of the MMRS report. For instance, review authors who intend to address a broader audience better avoid using academic jargon in their MMRS report. An academic audience might be more drawn to theoretical discussions, an in-depth discussion of the methodological limitations of the MMRS, and suggestions about how others might cope with these limitations in their future literature review endeavors. Practitioners and stakeholders might be more interested in concrete and context-specific implications for practice. Policy makers might be more interested in concise answers to their questions and visually appealing presentations of the data and findings. If you write in the context of a specific call from a local government, you may need to consider a context-specific synthesis summarizing information generated on a national level only, in a particular region, or for a particular language group. The choice to move away from a multicontext or comprehensive type of review to a context-specific review has implications for various stages of the MMRS process. For example, context-specific syntheses may require a selective search strategy instead of an exhaustive one (see Chapter 3). For an overview of advantages and disadvantages of both approaches, we refer to Karin Hannes and Angela Harden (2012). Second, the alleged knowledge that the targeted audience has about the topic of interest will have an impact on the background information that needs to be provided in the MMRS report. Third, the audience might influence the synthesis method that is selected and the way the findings are presented. For instance, a meta-aggregative approach can be used in case you want to generate practical and usable *lines of action* as outcomes of the synthesis for the qualitative strand of your segregated or contingent MMRS, whereas a formal grounded theory approach can be used for this strand in case you want to generate a theory to explain the phenomenon of interest (see Chapters 6 and 8). Fourth, the audience will influence the *Implications for future research, policy, and practice* section, which will be discussed further in this chapter.

Ethics in the Writing Process

In Chapter 2, we already discussed some important ethical issues that you should take into account when conducting an MMRS, such as creating sensitivity toward aspects of vulnerability in the populations you target with your literature review and making explicit how people might benefit from the MMRS project. Review authors have the responsibility to think thoroughly about the necessity and the possible relevance of their MMRS project before they start conducting the literature review. In Chapter 2, we discussed how you can conduct a scoping review to make sure that the literature review you propose is original and that it is likely to fill a substantial need. While conducting the MMRS and writing the MMRS report, you should try to increase the MMRS's potential to move forward theory, research, policy, and/or practice. Additionally, you have the responsibility to disseminate the findings of your MMRS optimally, so that theory, research, policy, and/or practice can maximally benefit from it. Furthermore, you also have the responsibility to communicate the MMRS's methods and findings in a format and in language that is understandable and appropriate for your targeted audience.

Sometimes representatives from the target group (also called "end users," "consumers," or "stakeholders") are actively involved in the MMRS process. End users can be involved from the onset of the MMRS project (e.g., for determining the relevance of the review objectives and review questions, see Chapter 2) until the reporting and dissemination stage. Potential advantages of involving end users during the reporting stage are that you can evaluate the accessibility and appropriateness of the language, format, and content of the preliminary MMRS report to your targeted audience. Involving end users during the reporting stage can help you to enhance the readability of the MMRS report as well as the relevancy of the report to the targeted audience. For instance, end users can comment based on the preliminary MMRS report that it might be relevant to include more details in the final MMRS report on the content of the interventions that are reviewed as well as context-specific details about the factors that influence whether an intervention is successfully implemented (Rees & Oliver, 2012). When end users are actively involved in the MMRS process, their contribution should be acknowledged in the final report.

Furthermore, throughout the entire MMRS process, you have the responsibility to work as methodologically sound and accurate as possible. When the

MMRS has methodological shortcomings, you have the responsibility to describe and discuss these shortcomings in the MMRS report.

During the writing stage, you have the responsibility to report on the conducted MMRS and the findings as transparently as possible, and to discuss the strengths and limitations of the MMRS as thoroughly as possible, so that they can be taken into account by the readers. The findings and conclusions of most MMRS are context bound. You should in sufficient detail report on your MMRS's contextual details and delineate the boundaries of the generalizations you make.

Furthermore, there are some general ethical issues related to the reporting and publishing of research that have to be taken into account by authors of literature reviews. A first issue is the order of the authors. Different disciplines have different conventions for author ordering. Often, the review author who did the majority of the work is listed as the first author, and the other members of the MMRS team are listed as authors in order of decreasing contribution (Wager & Wiffen, 2011). The project leader is typically listed as the last author. All the review authors who contributed to the MMRS should be listed as authors of the MMRS report. To enhance transparency, the specific contribution of each review author to the MMRS can explicitly be mentioned in the MMRS report. Furthermore, review authors should in their MMRS report also be transparent about the funding they received for their work and about their competing interests (Wager & Wiffen, 2011).

Another ethical issue is plagiarism. In your MMRS report, you should not use the words, images, data, ideas, or any other original creations from another person or from another publication without acknowledgment or without asking formal permission (Wager & Wiffen, 2011). Finally, when you uncover a case of plagiarism of primary-level studies (e.g., data sets and findings on which a first group of researchers reported in a first publication are republished by a different group of authors in a second publication without a reference to the first publication) during the data collection or data extraction stage of your MMRS, you should alert the publishers of both publications to point out the similarity (Wager & Wiffen, 2011).

THE MMRS REPORT

In this section, we will discuss the outline and content of an MMRS report. An MMRS report starts with a title and an abstract. Most MMRS reports include four major sections: (1) *Introduction*, including the background of the MMRS, the theoretical or conceptual model that was used (if any), the review objectives, and the posed review question(s); (2) *Methods*, including information on the MMRS design, the eligibility criteria, the sampling strategy, the search strategy, the critical appraisal (in case the retrieved articles were critically appraised), the descriptive data extraction, and the data synthesis; (3) *Findings*, including the MMRS's findings; and (4) *Discussion*, including interpretations and discussion of the findings, and the MMRS's implications for future research, policy, and practice. Sometimes a separate *Conclusion* section is added. Furthermore, an MMRS report often includes an acknowledgments section, a bibliography, and appendices.

In Chapter 2, we provided suggestions for the outline and the content of the review protocol. These suggestions will also be relevant for writing the *Introduction* and the *Methods* sections of the MMRS report. Compared with Chapter 2, we will discuss the outline and the content of the various sections of the MMRS report in closer detail in the present chapter.

Sometimes review authors deviate from what they have written in their review protocol during the MMRS process. When this happens, you have to make explicit in the MMRS report when and where you deviated from what was written in the review protocol, and why these deviations were made. This can, for instance, be done in a *Preface*.

Title and Abstract

The MMRS report starts with a title and an abstract. The title should summarize the content of the review report as concisely and clearly as possible. Often, the title includes the methodological nature of the study, as well as the content of the study. Examples of published MMRS titles are the following: *Community-Based Dietary and Physical Activity Interventions in Low Socioeconomic Groups in the UK: A Mixed Methods Systematic Review* (Everson-Hock et al., 2013), *A Review of Mixed Methods Research on Bullying and Peer Victimization in School* (Hong & Espelage, 2012), *Impact of Clinical Information-Retrieval Technology on Physicians: A Literature Review of Quantitative, Qualitative and Mixed Methods Studies* (Pluye, Grad, Dunikowski, & Stephenson, 2005), and *Factors Affecting the Clinical Use of Non-invasive Prenatal Testing: A Mixed Methods Systematic Review* (Skirton & Patch, 2013). The abstract briefly summarizes the main aspects and findings of the literature review (see Practical Tip 9.3).

Practical Tip 9.3: The MMRS Abstract

Elaine Beller et al. (2013) developed reporting guidelines for writing abstracts of systematic reviews and meta-analyses. We advise you to evaluate critically whether your MMRS abstract meets the following standards and includes the following information:

- Title: Identify the report as an MMRS literature review
- Background:

  Objectives: Describe your review question (including information on the phenomenon of interest, the population or target group of interest, and the types of outcomes, perceptions, or experiences you are interested in)

- Methods:

  Eligibility criteria: Describe which criteria you used to include and exclude primary studies
  Information sources: Describe which resources you searched

- Results:

  Included studies: Describe the number of included primary studies and their most relevant characteristics
  Synthesis of findings: Describe the main findings of your MMRS literature review

- Discussion:

  Strengths and limitations: Briefly summarize the strengths and limitations of your MMRS literature review
  Interpretation: Provide an overall interpretation of your findings and the most important implications of your MMRS literature review

- Other:

  Funding: Acknowledge any source of funding that supported the MMRS literature review
  Registration: Registration of literature reviews provides a record of literature reviews that have been initiated, even if they

(Continued)

(Continued)

have not been published. Registration alerts review authors to literature reviews that are in progress and serves as a public record of the proposed literature review. If you registered your MMRS protocol, mention the registration number and registry name

Source: Beller, E. M., Glasziou, P. P., Altman, D. G., Hopewell, S., Bastian, H., Chalmers, I., . . . PRISMA for Abstracts Group. (2013). PRISMA for abstracts: Reporting systematic reviews in journal and conference abstracts. *PLoS Medicine, 10*(4), e1001419.

Introduction

Most MMRS reports start with a description of the topic of the literature review or the problem that is addressed by the literature review. Furthermore, the *Introduction* includes the background of the MMRS (often encompassing a justification for conducting the MMRS and a description of the significance of the literature review) and key literature that is relevant to the MMRS (summarizing the state of the art with respect to the topic or problem of interest, and its implications for the current review). If existing theoretical and/or conceptual frameworks are used during the MMRS, they can be introduced and described to the reader in this first section. The main elements of the framework(s) can be discussed, and a visual representation of the framework(s) can be provided. We advise you to be clear about the role the framework(s) will play during the MMRS (e.g., Will it be used to guide the sampling? Will it be used in the data synthesis and interpretation stage?) and to provide a rationale for applying the framework(s). When relevant, you can also describe contextual considerations that are important for your MMRS in this first section. Two important components of the *Introduction* section that are often explicitly mentioned near the end of this section are the review objectives and the posed review question(s) (as discussed in Chapter 2).

Methods

The *Methods* section includes detailed information on how the MMRS was conducted, including a description and rationale for the MMRS design, the eligibility criteria, the sampling strategy, the search strategy, the critical appraisal (in case the retrieved articles were critically appraised), the descriptive data extraction, and the data synthesis.

MMRS design. When describing the design used for the MMRS and the stages included in the MMRS process, it can be beneficial to visualize this for the reader by including a flowchart. Figures 9.1, 9.2, and 9.3 represent example flowcharts for a segregated, an integrated, and a contingent MMRS, respectively. We provided more information on MMRS designs in Chapter 2.

Eligibility criteria. Describe in your MMRS report which eligibility criteria you applied to include and exclude retrieved primary studies from the MMRS. Eligibility criteria can refer to the phenomenon or intervention under study, the population of interest, the outcome or evaluation measures of

Figure 9.1   Example Flowchart for a Segregated MMRS Literature Review

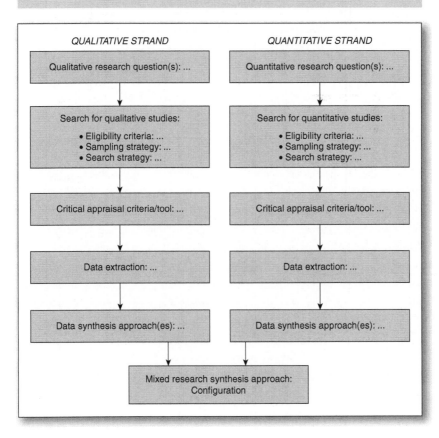

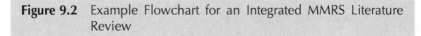

Figure 9.2   Example Flowchart for an Integrated MMRS Literature Review

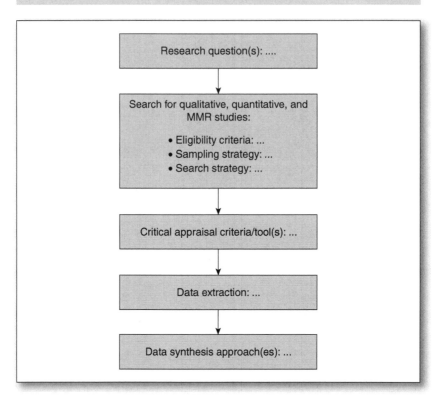

interest, the geographical location, the setting, the time span, the language, the research methodology, and any other criterion relevant to the MMRS. We provided more information on eligibility criteria for MMRS in Chapter 3.

Sampling strategy. Next, describe the applied sampling strategy in the MMRS report. You can describe whether you used an exhaustive, selective, or purposeful sampling strategy (Booth, 2006), and what the rationale was for selecting this strategy. If you used a purposeful sampling strategy, you have to be explicit about the type of purposeful sampling strategy that was applied and your rationale for selecting this type (see Table 3.1 in Chapter 3). We provided more information on sampling strategies for MMRS in Chapter 3.

Search strategy. Furthermore, the search strategy should be described in sufficient detail in the MMRS report. A detailed description of the search strategy allows other review authors to repeat the process in case there are

Figure 9.3 Example Flowchart for a Contingent MMRS Literature Review

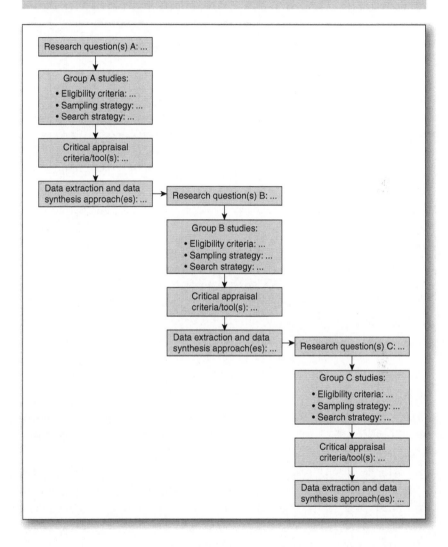

potential doubts on whether a search was technically correct or in case an update of the literature review needs to be done. Regarding the search process, you should describe in the MMRS report which resources were searched, as well as all the details of the conducted searches (see Chapter 3). Regarding the search results, you should describe (a) the number of retrieved publications for each resource; (b) the number of duplicate publications excluded (by review management software and manually); (c) the number of duplicate studies excluded (see Box 3.1 in Chapter 3 on multiple publication bias); (d) the number of publications and studies that were included and excluded (along with the reasons for exclusion) in every screening stage; and (e) how several (independent) review authors were involved in the search and selection process. In regard to this last point, the MMRS report can include more information on (a) whether more than one review author examined each title and abstract to exclude obviously irrelevant reports in the initial screening stage; (b) whether the review authors who examined each full-text report to determine eligibility did that independently in the final screening stage; (c) whether the review authors involved in screening primary studies are content area experts, methodologists, or both; (d) whether the review authors assessing the relevance of the studies knew the names of the authors, institutions, journal of publication, and results when they applied the eligibility criteria; and (e) how disagreements were handled (Higgins & Deeks, 2011).

We advise you to use a flowchart or study retrieval diagram to report on the MMRS search process and the search results. Figures 3.1, 3.2, and 3.3 in Chapter 3 included examples of how you can document on the search process and search results when using an exhaustive, a selective, and a purposeful sampling strategy, respectively. Regarding the search process, it might be useful to include a sample search strategy (e.g., for one bibliographic database searched, see Coemans, Wang, Leysen, & Hannes, 2015) as an appendix to the MMRS report. Also the formal screening form that was used in the final screening stage (i.e., the screening of full texts) can be added as an appendix to the MMRS report. We provided more information on the search strategy and the screening of the retrieved primary studies in Chapter 3.

Quality assessment. If you assessed the methodological quality of the retrieved primary-level studies, this critical appraisal process should be described in the MMRS report. Describe how you evaluated the methodological quality of the retrieved qualitative, quantitative, and MMR primary studies. If you used existing critical appraisal frameworks or tools for evaluating the qualitative, quantitative, and/or MMR primary studies, you should make explicit which frameworks or tools were used (and provide a rationale for selecting these frameworks or tools) and how exactly the frameworks or tools were used, or how you adapted the goals of the MMRS. If you developed a critical appraisal framework or tool for evaluating the qualitative, quantitative, and/or MMR primary studies, you should describe how the framework or tool was developed, and whether and how it was pilot tested and applied for the MMRS. We advise you to add newly developed frameworks or tools used for the critical appraisal as an appendix to the MMRS report, preferably along with a user's guide, so that review authors who want to update the MMRS will be able to use these frameworks or tools appropriately. For an MMRS using an already existing critical appraisal framework or tool as well as for an MMRS using a newly developed critical appraisal framework or tool, it might be useful to add an overview of the critical appraisal scores or judgments given by the review authors involved in the critical appraisal stage. We provided more information on critical appraisal in Chapter 4.

Descriptive data extraction. Next, we advise you to report which descriptive data were extracted, and how the data were extracted. You can add the data extraction form and the coding guide used for the descriptive data extraction in an appendix to the MMRS report. We provided more information on descriptive data extraction in Chapter 5.

Data synthesis. Finally, you should clearly describe how the included data were synthesized. Describe which synthesis approaches you used (Figures 6.1, 7.1, and 8.1 included a selection of data synthesis approaches that are used within segregated, integrated, and contingent MMRS literature reviews, respectively), provide a rationale for selecting the synthesis approaches, and describe whether and how certain software programs were used for the data synthesis. We provided more information on data synthesis in Chapters 6, 7, and 8.

Findings

The *Findings* section often starts with an overview of the extracted descriptive characteristics for the primary studies included in the MMRS. When the number of studies included in the MMRS is relatively small (e.g., up to 40 included studies), the extracted descriptive data for each primary study is often presented in tabular format in the review report (an example was shown in Table 5.1 in Chapter 5). When a larger amount of studies is included in the MMRS, the descriptive data table can be presented as an appendix or online annex to the MMRS report.

When writing down the findings of the data synthesis, it is often interesting to use a combination of textual, tabular, and visual representations. In the

Practical Tip boxes we presented in Chapters 6, 7, and 8, we provided examples of how textual, tabular, and visual representations could be used for reporting the findings of often used synthesis approaches within segregated, integrated, and contingent MMRS literature reviews, respectively.

Discussion

In the *Discussion* section, you can interpret and discuss the findings, and state the MMRS's implications for future research, policy, and practice.

Interpreting and discussing the findings. The *Discussion* is the section in which the circle of the story you want to tell closes. The relevant background literature and theoretical and/or conceptual frameworks that were presented in the introduction, together with the MMRS's objectives and review questions, are revisited in the *Discussion* section. In the *Discussion* section, you go *beyond* the analyses and interpret the MMRS's findings in relation to the posed review questions: *What do the findings mean?*

A first approach for structuring the *Discussion* section and interpreting the MMRS's findings is to answer consecutively the review questions posed and discuss the findings regarding each review question. A second approach for structuring the *Discussion* section and interpreting the findings is to use theoretical frameworks. A theoretical framework can inform or guide review authors' interpretations. The MMRS's findings can be viewed and discussed in light of the framework. The theoretical framework can be the lens through which review authors look at the findings and make sense out of them. A third approach for structuring the *Discussion* section and interpreting the findings is to confront the MMRS's findings with results from previously conducted studies and literature reviews. This can be done by critically contextualizing the findings, considering the contribution of the MMRS to this field, and discussing similarities, connections, and/or contradictions between the published literature and the MMRS's findings. It is also possible to use a combination of these three approaches when writing up the *Discussion*.

The *Discussion* is also the section in which the findings of the MMRS can be discussed in light of the literature review's strengths and limitations. You can discuss how the MMRS approach you applied *worked* for answering your review questions, and what the methodological and substantive strengths of your MMRS were. Furthermore, it is the place for critical reflections on the methodological shortcomings of the MMRS and how these shortcomings may have affected the MMRS's findings. These shortcomings can relate to all stages of the MMRS process, for instance, the sampling strategy, the search strategy, the critical appraisal, the data extraction, or the data synthesis.

Another issue that can be addressed in the *Discussion* section is the added value of the MMR approach and the specific MMRS design type that you opted for. It is possible that it is from the onset of a literature review project clear that an MMRS is not suitable for answering the review questions, review objectives, and/or the data you envisioned. In that case, a *mono-method* quantitative or qualitative literature review can be conducted (see Chapter 1). However, when you decided to conduct an MMRS, because this seemed appropriate for reaching your review objectives and for answering your review questions, you should account for the added value of the MMR approach in the MMRS report, and discuss how the selection of a segregated, integrated, or contingent MMRS design was beneficial for your literature review.

Implications and suggestions for future research, policy, and practice. In addition to interpreting the MMRS's findings, the *Discussion* is also the section in which you can discuss the literature review's implications for the scientific field (e.g., with respect to theory or empirical research), policy, and practice. For instance, you can discuss whether, and how, policy and/or practice could be changed based on the MMRS's findings.

Suggestions for future research can be formulated based on interesting new questions or hypotheses that emerged during or as a result of the MMRS, but also on the identified methodological shortcomings of the MMRS. The formulated suggestions for future research can relate to the question of how the theoretical and/or empirical research can be expanded, deepened, or improved in this field. Another valid finding of a literature review can be that there is already enough cumulative knowledge on the studied topic to yield convincing evidence, and that future research should no longer focus on this review question or review topic. For instance, Sofie Kuppens, Mieke Heyvaert, Wim Van den Noortgate, and Patrick Onghena (2011) conducted a systematic review that involved sequential meta-analytical techniques (see Chapter 6) to determine the sufficiency of cumulative knowledge on the effectiveness of contingency management interventions (e.g., reward, praise, and attention for positive behaviors) for decreasing challenging behavior among persons with intellectual disabilities. They found sufficient evidence for at least a small beneficial effect of contingency management for decreasing challenging behavior among persons with intellectual disabilities, and concluded that future research should focus on potential moderators of this effect. When an MMRS is written for a specific audience (e.g., the organization that commissioned the MMRS), the suggestions for future research, policy, and practice should be tailored toward this audience.

Conclusion

MMRS reports may include a *Summary* or *Conclusion* as the final section. The most important findings of the MMRS can be briefly summarized (the *take home message*), and the importance and implications of the MMRS can be briefly discussed. It is advised not to introduce new concepts or ideas in this final section. However, it *is* advised to *come full circle* with the MMRS's story by referring back to the MMRS's main objectives and review questions, and to provide clear and concise answers to these review questions.

Acknowledgments, Bibliography, and Appendices

An *Acknowledgments* section can be used to acknowledge the help of individuals—apart from the MMRS authors—for providing assistance, materials, or advice. Some examples include information retrieval specialists that have not been listed as an author, lay persons involved in producing the review protocol, and statisticians that may have assisted in analyzing complex data. The *Acknowledgments* section can also be used to acknowledge any source of funding that supported the MMRS.

Each MMRS report should include a *Bibliography* or *Reference list*. This list contains all the references that were referred to in the MMRS report. Furthermore, you should document in the MMRS report which primary-level studies were included in the MMRS. There are several ways to do this. First, when the number of primary-level studies included in the MMRS is relatively small, the references to the primary-level studies can be included in the report's *Reference list*. Often, the references to the primary-level studies are marked in this *Reference list*; for instance, they can be preceded by an asterisk. An example of this approach can be found in Mieke Heyvaert, Karin Hannes, Bea Maes, and Patrick Onghena (2013). Second, you can list the references to the included primary-level studies separately from the other references. You can, for instance, do this in a separate appendix, in an online annex, or in a box included in the MMRS report. An example of the latter approach can be found in Karin Hannes, Elisabeth Raes, Katrien Vangenechten, Mieke Heyvaert, and Filip Dochy (2013).

Most MMRS reports include *Appendices*. In these *Appendices*, you can, for instance, provide detailed outlines of the search strategy (see Chapter 3), the screening form (see Chapter 3), newly developed frameworks or tools that were used for the critical appraisal (see Chapter 4), and the descriptive data table when a larger amount of studies is included in the MMRS (see Chapter 5).

PUBLICATION OUTLETS FOR MMRS PROTOCOLS AND LITERATURE REVIEWS

In Chapter 2, we discussed protocols for MMRS literature reviews. Sometimes, protocols are published separately from the literature review (see Coemans et al., 2015, for an example). Other times, review authors mention in their MMRS report that a protocol was developed prior to conducting their literature review, and that this protocol is available on request from the first author (see Emmers, Bekkering, & Hannes, 2015, for an example). If you intend to submit your MMRS to an organization such as the Campbell or the Cochrane Collaboration, you are obligated to develop in advance a protocol for your literature review, which has to undergo peer review (see Practical Tip 9.1).

Several publication outlets for MMRS protocols and literature reviews exist. First, MMRS protocols and literature reviews can be submitted to organizations promoting and disseminating literature reviews, such as the Campbell Collaboration, the Cochrane Collaboration, or the Joanna Briggs Institute. In Practical Tip 9.1, we referred to the standard templates for protocols and literature reviews that were offered by these organizations. These organizations expect review authors to use these templates when they submit their protocol or literature review to them (see Practical Tip 9.1). An important consequence of submitting an MMRS to an organization such as the Campbell or the Cochrane Collaboration is that the review authors engage themselves to update their literature review regularly. Alternatively, the original review authors can pass on this task to another review team. For instance, Cochrane literature reviews should either be updated within two years of the first published version or the previous update or have a commentary added to the *Published notes* section of the literature review to explain why this is done less

> ### Practical Tip 9.4: Deciding to Which Journal You Will Send Your MMRS Report
>
> It is important to think carefully about the journal you will be sending your MMRS report to. Most review authors submit their MMRS report to a substantive journal. If you used a rather *novel* MMRS design, or if you focused on the *novel* methodological features of your MMRS in your manuscript, it is also possible to submit the manuscript to a methodological journal specializing in MMR or research synthesis methods. We strongly advise you always to check the scope of the journal (available on the journal's website) to see whether your manuscript will fit into the journal. In addition, it can be useful to go through this journal's previously published issues and to read some manuscripts that were previously published in this journal to check whether your manuscript will fit into this journal.

frequently (see http://www.cochrane.org/editorial-and-publishing-policy-resource/cochrane-review-updates). Each update of a Cochrane literature review must involve a search for new studies, and any new studies that are found must be added to the literature review.

Second, an MMRS literature review or protocol can be submitted to an academic journal or an academic book publisher. In Practical Tip 9.4, we provide tips for review authors who are deciding to which journal they will send their MMRS report.

Third, you may have conducted an MMRS commissioned by a practice or policy organization. In that case, the MMRS report can be published and distributed by this practice or policy organization. However, it is also possible that the MMRS report is only for private use within the specific practice or policy organization.

CHALLENGES OF REPORTING AND PUBLISHING MMRS LITERATURE REVIEWS

When you conduct an MMRS literature review, it is of utmost importance that you clearly and critically report on the included MMRS stages, your findings and interpretations, as well as the suggestions for future research, policy, and practice. In this section, we will discuss common pitfalls and challenges of the reporting process.

A first pitfall in writing up an MMRS literature review is when review authors do not report on the rationales for the decisions they made throughout the MMRS process. Ideally, each methodological and substantive decision made throughout the MMRS process should be made explicit in the review report and should explicitly be accounted for. For instance, when you use search limits (such as limiting the search for primary studies on publication language, publication type, or publication period) based on theoretical or pragmatic reasons, you should provide a rationale for these limits especially because various types of bias might be introduced to the MMRS by setting search limitations (see Chapter 3).

A second pitfall in writing up an MMRS literature review is when review authors do not report their findings in a way that corresponds to the data synthesis approaches they applied. In Chapters 6, 7, and 8, we described various data synthesis approaches that can be used to synthesize the collected data within segregated, integrated, and contingent MMRS literature reviews, respectively. We strongly advise you to consult the handbooks, articles, and (reporting) guidelines on the data synthesis approaches you applied, and to report your findings in accordance with these guidelines (see Chapters 6, 7, and 8 and Practical Tip 9.1). For instance, a meta-aggregative synthesis should result in practical and usable *lines of action* as outcomes of the synthesis for the qualitative strand of a segregated or contingent MMRS; a meta-ethnography should report on reciprocal, refutational, or line-of-argument relationships; and a formal grounded theory should result in a theory that explains the phenomenon of interest (see Chapters 6 and 8).

A third challenge MMRS review authors can be confronted with is to end up with an empty literature review. The term *empty literature review* is used to describe a literature review for which the review authors find no primary-level studies that answer to the eligibility criteria (see Chapter 3). Possible reasons for ending up with an empty literature review include (a) the literature review relates to an area of study that is very new, (b) the posed review question is highly specific and the substantive inclusion criteria are accordingly very stringent (e.g., there may be restrictions on the population by age, context, diagnostic criteria, or intervention criteria), and (c) the review authors use very stringent methodological inclusion criteria because they only want to include high-quality primary-level studies (e.g., there may be restrictions on the study design, outcome measures, or comparison conditions that may not be available in existing primary studies) (Yaffe, Montgomery, Hopewell, & Shepard, 2012). Review authors who end up with an empty literature review must not refrain from trying to publish their findings because the conclusion that there, for the time being, are no primary-level studies of a particular type on a particular topic can be a very powerful message, and it is potentially useful information for policy makers, practitioners, and researchers (Lang, Edwards, & Fleiszer, 2007; Schlosser & Sigafoos, 2009). For instance, an empty literature review can provide a clear direction for future primary-level research.

A fourth challenge of writing up an MMRS literature review relates to space limitations. Especially when you intend to submit your MMRS to an academic journal, you have to deal with word and page limitations. Most MMRS reports include *Appendices*, in which you can, for instance, provide detailed outlines of the search strategy, the screening form, frameworks or tools that were used for the critical appraisal, and the descriptive data table. However, for some journals, the *Appendices* are included for the word or page count. A solution can be to work with *Online annexes* or to make this information available on the review group's or first author's website.

A fifth challenge related to publishing an MMRS literature review is that some review authors who submitted their full MMRS report to an organization (e.g., the Campbell Collaboration, the Cochrane Collaboration, or the Joanna Briggs Institute) might additionally want to submit a concise report on their MMRS to an academic journal, to more broadly disseminate their MMRS's findings. If you plan to do this, we advise you first to check the copyright rules stipulated by the organization and the academic journal at hand: *Under which circumstances is it allowed to submit such a concise report on your MMRS to an academic journal?* However, Elizabeth Wager and Philip Wiffen (2011) advocate against the duplicate publication of a literature review, for instance, as a Campbell or Cochrane literature review and as a journal article. They argue that journal space, peer reviewers' time, and readers' time is limited, and that the repeated publication of one literature review may prevent other literature reviews from being published (Wager & Wiffen, 2011).

Summary Points

- Several templates for reporting literature review protocols and literature reviews have been developed.

- The intended audience influences the writing process and the MMRS report.
- Review authors have the ethical responsibility to report on the conducted MMRS and the findings as transparently as possible, and to discuss the strengths and limitations of the MMRS as thoroughly as possible.
- Other ethical issues in the MMRS writing process concern involving end users, the order of the authors, and plagiarism.
- Most MMRS reports include four major sections: (1) *Introduction*, including the background of the MMRS, the theoretical or conceptual model that was used (if any), the review objectives, and the posed review question(s); (2) *Methods*, including information on the MMRS design, the eligibility criteria, the sampling strategy, the search strategy, the critical appraisal (in case the retrieved articles were critically appraised), the descriptive data extraction, and the data synthesis; (3) *Findings*, including the MMRS's findings; and (4) *Discussion*, including interpretations and discussion of the findings, and the MMRS's implications for future research, policy, and practice.
- Review authors have the responsibility to disseminate the findings of their MMRS optimally, so that theory, research, policy, and/or practice can maximally benefit from it.
- Publication outlets for MMRS protocols and literature reviews are international nonprofit organizations producing and disseminating literature reviews (e.g., the Campbell Collaboration, the Cochrane Collaboration, the Joanna Briggs Institute), academic journals, and academic book publishers. Furthermore, an MMRS commissioned by a practice or policy organization might be published and distributed by this organization.

Questions for Thought

- Who is the intended audience for your MMRS report? How will you tailor your MMRS report toward your audience?
- What are the strengths and limitations of your MMRS? What are the methodological shortcomings of your MMRS? How may these shortcomings have affected your MMRS's findings?
- What was the added value of the MMRS approach for your review?

- What are the implications of your MMRS for future research, policy, and practice? Formulate suggestions for future research, policy, and practice based on your MMRS's findings.
- What sort of dissemination channels do you see in your topical area to publish your MMRS findings, and what are the options to trim the full MMRS report down to a format that is digestible to readers?
- How can you potentially anticipate the risk of ending up with an "empty review" or nothing to write about?

Exercises

- Write down a number of possible titles for your MMRS. Afterward, check the clarity and accuracy of these possible titles and try to improve them by posing to yourself the following questions: Could I guess what this study would be about by simply reading this title? Could I make this title catchier, more appealing to the reader, without losing its substantive richness? Could I shorten this title to make it more powerful? Decide which title optimally fits your MMRS.
- Locate an MMRS report in your area of interest. Evaluate the following components of the report:
  - Were the review authors explicit about their intended audience?
  - Did the review authors actively involve representatives from the target group (also called "end users," "consumers," or "stakeholders") in the MMRS process? How were they involved?
  - Did the review authors sufficiently report on the rationales for the methodological and substantive decisions they made throughout the MMRS process?
  - Did the review authors report their findings in a way that corresponds to the data synthesis approaches they applied? For instance, a meta-aggregative synthesis should result in practical and usable *lines of action* as outcomes of the synthesis for the qualitative strand of a segregated or contingent MMRS; a meta-ethnography should report on reciprocal, refutational, or line-of-argument relationships; and a formal grounded theory should result in a theory that explains the phenomenon of interest (see Chapters 6 and 8).

    o Did the review authors report on their MMRS's contextual details, and did they delineate the boundaries of the generalizations they made?

    o Were the review authors in their report transparent about the specific contribution of each team member to the MMRS?

Suggestions for Further Reading

Moher, D., Liberati, A., Tetzlaff, J., & Altman, D. G. (2009). Preferred reporting items for systematic reviews and meta-analyses: The PRISMA statement. *Annals of Internal Medicine, 151,* 264–269. doi:10.7326/0003-4819-151-4-200908180-00135

Morton, S., Levit, L., Berg, A., & Eden, J. (Eds.). (2011). *Finding what works in health care: Standards for systematic reviews.* Washington, DC: National Academies Press.

Shamseer, L., Moher, D., Clarke, M., Ghersi, D., Liberati, A., Petticrew, M., . . . Stewart, L. A. (2015). Preferred reporting items for systematic review and meta-analysis protocols (PRISMA-P) 2015: Elaboration and explanation. *BMJ, 349,* g7647. doi:10.1136/bmj.g7647

Tong, A., Flemming, K., McInnes, E., Oliver, S., & Craig, J. (2012). Enhancing transparency in reporting the synthesis of qualitative research: ENTREQ. *BMC Medical Research Methodology, 12,* 181. doi:10.1186/1471-2288-12-181

Wager, E., & Wiffen, P. J. (2011). Ethical issues in preparing and publishing systematic reviews. *Journal of Evidence-Based Medicine, 4,* 130–134. doi:10.1111/j.1756-5391.2011.01122.x

References

Beller, E. M., Glasziou, P. P., Altman, D. G., Hopewell, S., Bastian, H., Chalmers, I., . . . PRISMA for Abstracts Group. (2013). PRISMA for abstracts: Reporting systematic reviews in journal and conference abstracts. *PLoS Medicine, 10*(4), e1001419.

Booth, A. (2006). "Brimful of STARLITE": Toward standards for reporting literature searches. *Journal of the Medical Library Association, 94,* 421–429.

Coemans, S., Wang, Q., Leysen, J., & Hannes, K. (2015). The use of arts-based methods in community-based research with vulnerable populations: Protocol for a scoping review. *International Journal of Educational Research.* doi:10.1016/j.ijer.2015.02.008

Emmers, E., Bekkering, T., & Hannes, K. (2015). Prevention of alcohol and drug misuse in adolescents: An overview of systematic reviews. *Nordic Studies on Alcohol and Drugs.* doi: 10.1515/nsad-2015-0019

Everson-Hock, E. S., Johnson, M., Jones, R., Woods, H. B., Goyder, E., Payne, N., & Chilcott, J. (2013). Community-based dietary and physical activity interventions in low socioeconomic groups in the UK: A mixed methods systematic review. *Preventive Medicine, 56*, 265–272. doi:10.1016/j.ypmed.2013.02.023

Hannes, K., & Harden, A. (2012). Multi-context versus context-specific qualitative evidence syntheses: Discussing their value for practice and policy decision making processes. *Research Synthesis Methods, 2*, 271–278. doi:10.1002/jrsm.55

Hannes, K., Raes, E., Vangenechten, K., Heyvaert, M., & Dochy, F. (2013). Experiences from employees with team learning in a vocational learning or work setting: A systematic review of qualitative evidence. *Educational Research Review, 10*, 116–132. doi:10.1016/j.edurev.2013.10.002

Heyvaert, M., Hannes, K., Maes, B., & Onghena, P. (2013). Critical appraisal of mixed methods studies. *Journal of Mixed Methods Research, 7*, 302–327. doi:10 .1177/1558689813479449

Higgins, J. P. T., & Deeks, J. J. (2011). Chapter 7: Selecting studies and collecting data. In J. P. T. Higgins & S. Green (Eds.), *Cochrane handbook for systematic reviews of interventions Version 5.1.0* (updated March 2011). Retrieved from http://www .cochrane-handbook.org

Hong, J. S., & Espelage, D. L. (2012). A review of mixed methods research on bullying and peer victimization in school. *Educational Review, 64*, 115–126. doi:10.1080/ 00131911.2011.598917

Kuppens, S., Heyvaert, M., Van den Noortgate, W., & Onghena, P. (2011). Sequential meta-analysis of single-case experimental data. *Behavior Research Methods, 43*, 720–729. doi:10.3758/s13428-011-0080-1

Lang, A., Edwards, N., & Fleiszer, A. (2007). Empty systematic reviews: Hidden perils and lessons learned. *Journal of Clinical Epidemiology, 60*, 595–597. doi:10.1016/ j.jclinepi.2007.01.005

Moher, D., Liberati, A., Tetzlaff, J., & Altman, D. G. (2009). Preferred reporting items for systematic reviews and meta-analyses: The PRISMA statement. *Annals of Internal Medicine, 151*, 264–269. doi:10.7326/0003-4819-151-4- 200908180-00135

Morton, S., Levit, L., Berg, A., & Eden, J. (Eds.). (2011). *Finding what works in health care: Standards for systematic reviews.* Washington, DC: National Academies Press.

Pluye, P., Grad, R. M., Dunikowski, L. G., & Stephenson, R. (2005). Impact of clinical information-retrieval technology on physicians: A literature review of quantitative, qualitative and mixed methods studies. *International Journal of Medical Informatics, 74*, 745–768. doi:10.1016/j.ijmedinf.2005.05.004

Rees, R., & Oliver, S. (2012). Stakeholder perspectives and participation in reviews. In D. Gough, S. Oliver, & J. Thomas (Eds.), *An introduction to systematic reviews.* London, England: Sage.

Schlosser, R. W., & Sigafoos, J. (2009). "Empty" reviews and evidence-based practice. *Evidence-Based Communication Assessment and Intervention, 3*, 1–3. doi:10.1080/17489530902801067

Shamseer, L., Moher, D., Clarke, M., Ghersi, D., Liberati, A., Petticrew, M., . . . Stewart, L. A. (2015). Preferred reporting items for systematic review and meta-analysis protocols (PRISMA-P) 2015: Elaboration and explanation. *BMJ*, *349*, g7647. doi:10.1136/bmj.g7647

Skirton, H., & Patch, C. (2013). Factors affecting the clinical use of non-invasive prenatal testing: A mixed methods systematic review. *Prenatal Diagnosis*, *33*, 532–541. doi:10.1002/pd.4094

Tong, A., Flemming, K., McInnes, E., Oliver, S., & Craig, J. (2012). Enhancing transparency in reporting the synthesis of qualitative research: ENTREQ. *BMC Medical Research Methodology*, *12*, 181. doi:10.1186/1471-2288-12-181

Wager, E., & Wiffen, P. J. (2011). Ethical issues in preparing and publishing systematic reviews. *Journal of Evidence-Based Medicine*, *4*, 130–134. doi:10.1111/j.1756-5391.2011.01122.x

Wong, G., Greenhalgh, T., Westhorp, G., Buckingham, J., & Pawson, R. (2013). RAMESES publication standards: Realist syntheses. *BMC Medicine*, *11*, 21. doi:10.1186/1741-7015-11-21

Yaffe, J., Montgomery, P., Hopewell, S., & Shepard, L. D. (2012). Empty reviews: A description and consideration of Cochrane systematic reviews with no included studies. *PloS One*, *7*(5), e36626. doi:10.1371/journal.pone.0036626

EPILOGUE

The aim of this book was twofold. We wanted to provide you with an accessible and step-by-step guide to conduct literature reviews, and we wanted to show you how both qualitative and quantitative evidence can be aggregated, combined, and integrated into one overall MMRS literature review. We have tried to achieve this double aim by using a didactical chapter-by-chapter presentation of the several steps to conduct literature reviews and by writing the book from a consistent mixed methods perspective, starting with the conceptual framework in the introductory chapter until the last chapter on reporting and communicating the findings of the MMRS literature review.

However, as an author team, we were also confronted with some specific issues in taking this didactical stance and in applying the mixed methods perspective at the review level. In this epilogue, we want to present some of those remaining issues. Furthermore, we want to propose some future directions for MMRS literature reviews and give a personal reflection on writing this book. For the more specific challenges in each of the steps in the MMRS literature review, we refer to the corresponding chapters.

LOOSE ENDS

A first issue is related to the breadth, depth, and complexity of the MMRS literature reviews. Although we consider these features to be assets for the MMRS literature reviews, there are also potential drawbacks. It is a matter of judgment how much complexity a review can take. Sometimes an MMRS literature review runs the risk of collapsing by its own weight, and a literature review might be better off and benefit more from a high-quality, well-focused mono-method review than from a large-scale badly integrated MMRS literature review dealing with ill-focused review questions.

A second issue is of a more general kind and refers both to our step-by-step approach for conducting a literature review and to the use of literature reviews by researchers, policy makers, and practitioners. Our step-by-step approach serves a didactical purpose, but it might give the impression that a literature review is a mechanical process and that there is a guaranteed outcome if the separate steps are followed meticulously and conscientiously. However, more often a literature review is an iterative nonlinear process, including extensive discussion among the review authors before finding

293

closure. In the same vein, there is a risk that researchers, policy makers, and practitioners only superficially scan the outcomes of literature reviews, and that literature reviews become the *Reader's Digest* of research, the fast food of science. "Don't think, don't judge, just follow procedures, guidelines, and checklists." This message would be antithetical to the goals of academic research; it would deny the fact that science is a dynamic, human enterprise, and that the most interesting parts of science are about debates and controversies.

A final issue is the possible lack of attention by reviewers and users of literature reviews to theory testing and theory building. Although literature reviews can make a substantial contribution to theory testing and theory building, superficial literature reviews might nurture the impression that scientific evidence is about the accumulation of incontestable empirical facts. Superficial literature reviews ignore the fact that scientific evidence usually borrows its strength and meaning from a cultural and historical context in a specific scientific community, and that the elucidation of this strength and meaning in a broader scientific theory might be beneficial for the advancement of both science and its applications. MMRS literature reviews might be ideally suited to counter this issue because of their combined focus on both aggregation and configuration (Gough, Oliver, & Thomas, 2012; Sandelowski, Voils, Leeman, & Crandell, 2012; Voils, Sandelowski, Barroso, & Hasselblad, 2008).

WHERE DO WE GO FROM HERE?

The methodology of MMRS literature reviews and the discussion of alternative review methodologies are far from finished. We see several possibilities for new methodological developments.

A first direction is related to the kind of documents that are included in a literature review. Although our approach was broad in terms of the kind of studies that may be included, we restricted the MMRS literature review to primary-level studies that contain new empirical data. In some areas and for some applications, this might be too restrictive, and a broader perspective might be worthwhile, for example, by including legal documents, cost-efficiency studies, historical texts, opinions, art, or even theoretical elaborations.

A second direction is related to the mixing of levels in a literature review. Consider three levels: the single-case study level, the group study level, and the study review level. How can you combine and integrate these different levels of information? How do you combine a single-case study and a group study (Van den Noortgate & Onghena, 2008)? Does the single-case study merely add an independent observation to the group study (already consisting of multiple cases), are there differences in weighting the evidence, or is a more qualitative integration more appropriate? These questions are remarkably similar to questions about the integration of new group studies in so-called cumulative reviews or sequential meta-analyses: How do you combine a new study and the review (already consisting of multiple studies) (Kuppens, Heyvaert, Van den Noortgate, & Onghena, 2011; Kuppens & Onghena, 2012)?

A third direction is to study the effects of literature reviews on the way primary-level studies are designed and conducted, and on the way research agendas are set. In this way, an interesting feedback loop is created. By their focus on the state of the art and on quality appraisal, literature reviews may provide a strong impetus to enhance the quality of primary-level studies. Literature reviews may inform researchers about the primary research that is required, the kind of research questions that are relevant, the methods and approaches that are most appropriate, and the gaps in current knowledge that are ready to be filled. By taking a helicopter view, literature reviews may discover patterns that were impossible to perceive in each of the primary-level studies separately, construct configurations that lead to new theory development, and generate new hypotheses and predictions to be tested in independent primary-level studies. In cumulative reviews and sequential meta-analyses, the focus is explicitly on the convergence of the evidence, on the sufficiency and stability of the evidence, and ultimately on stopping rules regarding new studies to examine identical phenomena (Muellerleile & Mullen, 2006). Literature reviews may guard us from reinventing the wheel and, at the same time, show us which research about wheels is still valuable (e.g., about their applications, sizes, materials, and contexts).

As a fourth and final direction, literature studies have become an interesting focus of scientific inquiry themselves. Published literature reviews on a specific topic have their own strengths and weaknesses, and they should be scrutinized, for example, by using a quality appraisal instrument at the review level such as the AMSTAR (Shea et al., 2007) or PRISMA-P (Moher et al., 2015). This is especially interesting for reviews of systematic reviews (Mehta, Claydon, Hendrick, Winser, & Baxter, 2015), for systematic reviews of meta-analyses (López, Uribe, & Martinez, 2015), and for so-called mega-reviews and umbrella reviews (Whittemore, Chao, Jang, Minges, & Park, 2014). Furthermore, literature reviews bring about new ethical considerations: the inclusion of unpublished studies that did not pass an ethical committee, the detection of duplicate publications, plagiarism or questionable research practices, possible conflicts of interest, and the validity at the review level of informed consent given for the primary-level studies (Vergnes, Marchal-Sixou, Nabet, Maret, & Hamel, 2010; Wager & Wiffen, 2011). Finally, literature reviews have become the research object of thought-provoking case studies. For example, Mark Bolland and Andrew Grey (2014) performed a case study of overlapping meta-analyses regarding the effect of vitamin D supplements on fractures. They analyzed seven meta-analyses on this topic, published in the highest ranking general medicine journals. The conclusions of these meta-analyses were disturbingly discordant, ranging from strong statements that vitamin D prevents fractures to equally strong statements that vitamin D without calcium does not prevent fractures. Apparently, results from literature reviews of high-level evidence on a certain topic should not automatically be accepted as the accumulation of scientific evidence to the highest level (Sackett, Rosenberg, Gray, Haynes, & Richardson, 1996). Literature reviews should be critically evaluated, taking into account their specific review questions, their inclusion and exclusion criteria, and general methodology. Although literature reviews can provide convincing evidence and rich information, we should not pretend that they give the final answer in all circumstances. In many cases, they add a voice to an ongoing broader scientific debate.

THROUGH THE LOOKING GLASS, AND WHAT THE AUTHORS FOUND THERE

An exciting and challenging aspect in the process of writing this book was that many of the recommendations for review authors we came up with were also applicable to our own work as an author team. Also, for this book, we developed an argument for the mixed methods perspective and we built an author team with a diverse methodological and topical background: mixed, qualitative, and quantitative; educational sciences and disability studies; andragogy and medical-social sciences; and psychology (Chapter 2). We searched for relevant publications on the topic (Chapter 3), and we critically evaluated all material we discovered (Chapter 4). We analyzed, synthesized, and organized the material (Chapters 5 to 8), and finally we reported our results, interpretations, and recommendations in this book (Chapter 9).

A lot of questions emerged during our writing and during team discussions. Were we as transparent as we planned to be? Were we biased in our methodological approach to the literature review? Did we succeed in presenting valuable options for synthesis? Did we connect to our intended audience? We leave it to the reader to be the final judge on these questions.

And what about our own ontological orientation and epistemological stance? As authors of a textbook, we took a didactical orientation toward this issue, and as an author team, we mainly worked from a pragmatic orientation, answering questions like "Does this kind of presentation work?" "What are the alternatives?" "Is this figure functional for understanding the text?" This resulted in a user-focused step-by-step guide for conducting MMRS literature reviews. "Pragmatism points to the importance of joining beliefs and actions in a process of inquiry that underlies any search for knowledge, including the specialized activity that we refer to as research" (Morgan, 2014, p. 1051). This description also fits for doing a literature review. Furthermore, there is a close link between the mixed methods approach and pragmatism as an ontological orientation and epistemological stance (Johnson & Onwuegbuzie, 2004; Morgan, 2007).

One tenet of this book, and one implication of our pragmatic perspective, is that the purpose of the study and the kind of questions that we ask drive the methodological choices we make. The choice for an MMRS instead of another approach (e.g., meta-synthesis or meta-analysis) is primarily related to the purpose of the review and the review questions we want to be answered alongside the practicalities such as the available time, budget, and expertise (Chapter 2). Also, after choosing an MMRS, purposeful choices have to be made and justified, for example, with respect to the selection of an appropriate MMRS design (Chapter 2), the strategy for searching primary-level studies (Chapter 3), and the kind of critical appraisal that will be used (Chapter 4).

Notwithstanding this purpose- and question-driven approach, another interesting feedback loop might be created. Studying methods and techniques, and knowing about the availability of, for example, MMRS, in its turn might have an effect on the kind of review questions that will be considered valuable, for example, with respect to breadth, depth, and complexity of the literature review. It is not only the case that review questions drive the methodological choices we make, but it is also true that knowledge and insight into methods and techniques shape the kind of review questions we pose and the kind of review questions that we consider answerable by scientific research. "If all you have is a hammer, everything looks like a nail" (Maslow, 1966, p. 15).

CONCLUSION

Literature reviews constitute a powerful tool for researchers, policy makers, and practitioners. In many research domains, literature reviews are needed to cope with the vast amount of scientific information. In many policy domains and practical settings, they are needed to learn about the best available evidence and to consider this evidence in busy day-to-day decision-making processes. The MMRS approach to literature reviews is a promising new approach for gaining depth and breadth in reviewing the literature and in integrating both quantitative and qualitative strands of evidence. This approach enables researchers, policy makers, and practitioners to take the complexity of the scientific literature into account and to more fully understand complex phenomena that contain both quantitative and qualitative characteristics and perspectives.

Because the proof of the pudding is in the eating, we hope that this book will encourage many new and innovative applications of MMRS literature reviews. Good exemplars of truly integrated MMRS literature reviews would be welcomed in many domains. Ultimately, we hope that such examples will foster further developments in the methodology of conducting literature reviews, and that science, policy, and practice will benefit.

References

Bolland, M. J., & Grey, A. (2014). A case study of discordant overlapping meta-analyses: Vitamin D supplements and fracture. *PLoS ONE, 9*(12), e115934. doi:10.1371/journal.pone.0115934

Gough, D., Oliver, S., & Thomas, J. (2012). *Introduction to systematic reviews.* London, England: Sage.

Johnson, B., & Onwuegbuzie, A. (2004). Mixed methods research: A research paradigm whose time has come. *Educational Researcher, 33*, 14–26. doi:10.3102/0013189X033007014

Kuppens, S., Heyvaert, M., Van den Noortgate, W., & Onghena, P. (2011). Sequential meta-analysis of single-case experimental data. *Behavior Research Methods, 43*, 720–729. doi:10.3758/s13428-011-0080-1

Kuppens, S., & Onghena, P. (2012). Sequential meta-analysis to determine the sufficiency of cumulative knowledge: The case of early intensive behavioral intervention for children with autism spectrum disorders. *Research in Autism Spectrum Disorders, 6*, 168–176. doi:10.1016/j.rasd.2011.04.002

López, N. J., Uribe, S., & Martinez, B. (2015). Effect of periodontal treatment on preterm birth rate: A systematic review of meta-analyses. *Periodontology 2000, 67*, 87–130. doi:10.1111/prd.12073

Maslow, A. H. (1966). *The psychology of science: A reconnaissance.* Chapel Hill, NC: Maurice Bassett.

Mehta, P., Claydon, L., Hendrick, P., Winser, S., & Baxter, G. D. (2015). Outcome measures in randomized-controlled trials of neuropathic pain conditions: A systematic review of systematic reviews and recommendations for practice. *Clinical Journal of Pain, 31*, 169–176. doi:10.1097/AJP.0000000000000088

Moher, D., Shamseer, L., Clarke, M., Ghersi, D., Liberati, A., Petticrew, M., ... PRISMA-P Group. (2015). Preferred reporting items for systematic review and meta-analysis protocols (PRISMA-P) 2015 statement. *Systematic Reviews, 4*, 1. doi:10.1186/2046-4053-4-1

Morgan, D. L. (2007). Paradigms lost and pragmatism regained: Methodological implications of combining qualitative and quantitative methods. *Journal of Mixed Methods Research, 1*, 48–76. doi:10.1177/2345678906292462

Morgan, D. L. (2014). Pragmatism as a paradigm for social research. *Qualitative Inquiry, 20*, 1045–1053. doi:10.1177/1077800413513733

Muellerleile, P., & Mullen, B. (2006). Sufficiency and stability of evidence for public health interventions using cumulative meta-analysis. *American Journal of Public Health, 96*, 515–522. doi:10.2105/AJPH.2003.036343

Sackett, D. L., Rosenberg, W. M., Gray, J. A., Haynes, R. B., & Richardson, W. S. (1996). Evidence based medicine: What it is and what it isn't. *British Medical Journal, 312*, 71–72.

Sandelowski, M., Voils, C. I., Leeman, J., & Crandell, J. L. (2012). Mapping the mixed methods-mixed research synthesis terrain. *Journal of Mixed Methods Research, 6*, 317–331. doi:10.1177/1558689811427913

Shea, B. J., Grimshaw, J. M., Wells, G. A., Boers, M., Andersson, N., Hamel, C., . . . Bouter, L. M. (2007). Development of AMSTAR: A measurement tool to assess the methodological quality of systematic reviews. *BMC Medical Research Methodology, 7*, 10. doi:10.1186/1471-2288-7-10

Van den Noortgate, W., & Onghena, P. (2008). A multilevel meta-analysis of single-subject experimental design studies. *Evidence-Based Communication Assessment and Intervention, 2*, 142–151. doi:10.1080/17489530802505362

Vergnes, J.-N., Marchal-Sixou, C., Nabet, C., Maret, D., & Hamel, O. (2010). Ethics in systematic reviews. *Journal of Medical Ethics, 36*, 771–774. doi:10.1136/jme.2010.039941

Voils, C. I., Sandelowski, M., Barroso, J, & Hasselblad, V. (2008). Making sense of qualitative and quantitative findings in mixed research synthesis studies. *Field Methods, 20*, 3–25. doi:10.1177/1525822X07307463

Wager, E., & Wiffen, P. J. (2011). Ethical issues in preparing and publishing systematic. *Journal of Evidence-Based Medicine, 4*, 130–134. doi:10.1111/j.1756-5391.2011.01122.x

Whittemore, R., Chao, A., Jang, M., Minges, K. E., & Park, C. (2014). Methods for knowledge synthesis: An overview. *Heart & Lung, 43*, 453–461. doi:10.1016/j.hrtlng.2014.05.014

GLOSSARY

Agreement percentage: Measure to indicate agreement between assessors, calculated as the number of agreements divided by the number of agreements plus disagreements (times 100, expressed as a percentage).

Applicability (in the context of program or intervention evaluation): The extent to which a particular program or intervention is appropriate and feasible.

Appropriateness (in the context of program or intervention evaluation): The extent to which a particular program or intervention fits with, or is apt to fit in, a situation from the perspective of both the target group and the providers.

Assessment of methodological quality: Assessment of the extent to which study authors conduct their research to the highest possible standards.

Audit trail: Part of the content of the review diary and/or the review report that explicitly lists the review choices, the reasons why you have turned down certain choices, and the reasons why you have considered and put into practice certain choices.

Backward tracking (in searching for relevant studies): Strategy in searching for relevant studies in which all the reference lists of the included publications from previous search steps are screened.

Bayesian synthesis: Type of contingent mixed method research synthesis in which Bayesian statistical analysis techniques, assumptions, and approaches are used.

Bias: Extent to which the description of reality differs from reality itself. In literature reviews, bias refers to the potential negative impact of the subjective lens of personal beliefs and values of the review author in judging studies on critical appraisal outcomes or synthesized statements, on systematic differences between groups compared in a study, or on the difference between reported and unreported findings.

Boolean operators: Simple words ("operators") that are used in Boolean algebra (i.e., an algebraic system of logic formulated by the 19th century English mathematician George Boole) and that can be used in searching bibliographic databases to combine keywords and, in that way, to narrow or broaden the search. The two most popular Boolean operators used in literature reviews are AND and OR.

Citation tracking (in searching for relevant studies): Strategy in searching for relevant studies in which all citations to the included publications from previous search steps are screened. *Synonym:* Forward tracking.

Coding guide: Collection of coding instructions that accompanies the data extraction form. The coding instructions include guidelines on how the data extraction form has to be completed. The coding instructions make explicit which decision rules have to be applied for coding each descriptive characteristic of a primary-level study included in the literature review. *Synonym:* Coding manual.

Cohen's kappa statistic: Measure of agreement for categorical items between two raters, proposed by the psychologist Jacob Cohen in 1960. It is defined as:

$$\kappa = \frac{P_o - P_E}{1 - P_E}$$

in which P_O is the observed proportion of agreement and P_E is the expected proportion of agreement based on chance.

Complementarity (in a segregated mixed methods research synthesis): Extent to which the qualitative and quantitative research findings in a segregated mixed methods research synthesis relate to and complement each other.

Complex interventions discourse: Line of argument that inspired the development and use of meta-syntheses, in addition to meta-analyses, and eventually the development and use of mixed methods research synthesis literature reviews. Essentially this line of argument says that because most social, educational, behavioral, and biomedical interventions contain multiple components and multiple layers, a literature review has to take this complexity into account and include these multiple components and layers, how these components and layers are related, and how these components and layers interact.

Comprehensive sampling strategy: Sampling strategy aimed at identifying all relevant studies on the topic or phenomenon of interest. *Synonym:* Exhaustive sampling strategy.

Comprehensiveness: Stopping rule for an exhaustive sampling strategy; the data collection stops when all possible resources are searched.

Configuration (in a segregated mixed methods research synthesis): Arrangement of the qualitative and quantitative research findings in a segregated mixed methods research synthesis in line of argument, into a theory that posits relationships among concepts, or in narrative that posits a temporal ordering of events.

Confirmability: Extent to which findings are qualitatively confirmable through the analysis being grounded in the data and through examination of the audit trail.

Congruence (of the choices made during the literature review process): Goodness-of-fit between the choices made in the different stages of the literature review process, as written down in the *review diary*.

Constant comparison of data: Inductive analysis technique used in grounded theory in which new data are continuously compared with previously collected data, findings, and interpretations.

Content analysis: Analytical technique for making replicable and valid inferences from texts (or other meaningful matter) to the contexts of their use.

Contingent MMRS design: Type of mixed methods research synthesis design that consists of a cycle of research synthesis studies conducted to answer questions raised by previous phases in a mixed methods research synthesis or stand-alone mono-method syntheses. A contingent design contains an iterative cycle of reviewing evidence until a comprehensive research synthesis can be presented that addresses the review authors' objectives rather than a set of predefined review questions.

Credibility: Extent to which the representation of data fits the views of the participants studied, whether the findings hold true.

Critical interpretive synthesis: Type of integrated mixed methods research synthesis that consists of a critically informed integration of evidence from qualitative, quantitative, and mixed primary studies. The outcome of a critical interpretive synthesis takes the form of a coherent theoretical framework comprising a network of constructs and the relationships between them, and links synthetic constructs and existing constructs in the literature. The defining feature of a critical interpretive synthesis is the critical stance adopted by the review authors.

Critical stance: Defining feature of a critical interpretive synthesis that refers to the review authors' attitude of being critical toward all data collected on the phenomenon of interest and all variables and processes involved in the phenomenon (e.g., the assumptions involved and the solutions proposed in the literature).

Data saturation logic: Possible stopping rule for a purposeful sampling strategy; the data collection stops when a saturation point is reached. This means that if the search process would continue, the inclusion of more studies will not lead to additional insights related to the topic of interest, and will not lead to a more accurate answer to the review question(s).

Data sufficiency logic: Possible stopping rule for a purposeful sampling strategy; the data collection stops when sufficient evidence for achieving the purpose of the literature review is collected. Review authors have to decide and justify what constitutes sufficient evidence.

Data synthesis: Stage in a mixed methods research synthesis in which the primary studies are summarized, aggregated, or configurated.

Data type: Type of data that are generated by the outcome measures of the included studies (e.g., binary data or continuous data).

Dependability: Extent to which the process of research is logical, traceable, and clearly documented, particularly on the methods chosen and the decisions made by the researchers.

Descriptive data (in literature reviews): Characteristics of the primary studies. Examples of descriptive data include characteristics relating to the phenomenon or intervention under study, sample and participant characteristics, outcome or evaluation measures, geographical location and setting characteristics, characteristics relating to the design and methods used in the primary studies, and process and implementation characteristics.

Double quotes ("") (in bibliographic searches): Option in bibliographic searches to search for a specific string of keywords. For example, "social stories" refers to this specific string of two keywords; articles containing the words "social" and "stories" not directly following each other will not be retrieved by the search.

Effect size: Calculated magnitude of an effect in a quantitative primary-level study, according to some predefined effect size measure.

Effect size measure: Measure that indicates the magnitude of an effect in a quantitative primary-level study.

Effectiveness (in the context of program or intervention evaluation): The extent to which a particular program or intervention, when used appropriately, achieves an intended effect.

Eligibility criteria: Term that refers to both the inclusion and the exclusion criteria, which are specified in the review protocol. Only studies that meet all inclusion criteria and do not meet any of the listed exclusion criteria are considered eligible for inclusion in the literature review.

Emergent procedures (in scientific research): Procedures that develop and change over the course of a research project in response to new information and insights gained in previous stages of the study.

Epistemology: The philosophical study of the nature and scope of knowledge and justified beliefs in particular areas of inquiry.

Evidence-based practice (EBP) movement: Scientific movement that has shifted the basis of decision making about which interventions or programs to offer, from authority, intuition, tradition, and anecdote to a rational, transparent, systematic process based on evidence from scientific research. The evidence-based practice movement aims to identify treatments and practices that are evidence based and those that are not, and it privileges the former over the latter.

Exhaustive sampling strategy: Sampling strategy aimed at identifying all relevant studies on the topic or phenomenon of interest. *Synonym:* Comprehensive sampling strategy.

Explanatory variable: Variable that is supposed to be statistically related to the outcome variable. Depending on the design or the statistical model, this variable can offer a causal explanation or a prediction of the variability in the outcome variable. *Synonym:* Predictor.

External validity: Extent to which the conclusions in a study would hold for other persons, settings, situations, or timeframes. *Synonym:* Generalizability.

Feasibility (in the context of program or intervention evaluation): The extent to which a particular program or intervention is practical and can work in the way it was intended, taking into account the conditions or circumstances that need to be fulfilled.

First-order constructs: Key concepts identified in a meta-ethnographical synthesis.

Fixed effect meta-analysis: Type of meta-analysis that is built on the assumption that there is one true effect size that underlies all the included studies.

Flowchart (in reporting about the search for relevant studies): Diagram to document and report the process and results of the literature search process. *Synonym:* Study retrieval diagram.

Formal grounded theory: Qualitative method at the synthesis level that uses theoretical sampling, is aimed at theory building, uses the inductive constant comparative method for synthesizing the included studies, and involves continuation of study collection and study analysis until theoretical saturation is reached. Formal grounded theory starts from a core variable generated from previously published research. By using constant comparison, the review authors expand the general implications by generating grounded conceptual categories about it from many different areas reported on and by expanding abstract conceptual generalizations. Unlike the substantive grounded theory approach, formal grounded theory arrives at conceptualizations about a predefined core category, abstracted from the particulars of time, place, and persons' experiences reported on by others. The synthesis is not intended to change the core variables of the theory but to modify and refine them.

Forward tracking (in searching for relevant studies): Strategy in searching for relevant studies in which all citations to the included publications from previous search steps are screened. *Synonym:* Citation tracking.

Gray literature: Literature produced on all levels of government, academics, business, and industry in electronic and print formats not controlled by commercial publishers. *Synonym:* Fugitive literature.

Grounded theory: Approach used for analyzing qualitative data within a primary study. The purpose of the grounded theory approach is to generate a new theory from empirical data to explain a phenomenon of interest by using an inductive analysis called constant comparison of data. The essentials of the grounded theory approach are theoretical sampling, concurrent data collection, and data analysis phases; an inductive approach to analysis; the use of constant comparative analysis; the premise that theory can emerge from the data; and the continuation of the processes of data collection and data analysis until theoretical saturation is reached.

Idealist orientations (toward research synthesis): Orientations that go beyond what is described and reflected in the primary-level studies. Review authors that have this orientation often seek to reveal patterns or relationships between concepts and structures that remained hidden before. These review authors often intend to challenge reigning knowledge claims and dominant discourses, including the strategies put forward by proponents of the evidence-based practice movement. *See also: Ontology.*

Index terms: Terms in bibliographic databases that are assigned to publications by authors and compilers of databases, and that refer to topics central to the publication. *Synonyms:* Controlled vocabulary; Thesaurus terms; Subject headings.

Integrated MMRS design: Type of mixed methods research synthesis design that treats qualitative and quantitative studies in a similar and integrated way, analyzes them together, and uses the same methods for synthesizing both qualitative and quantitative findings. For example, qualitative findings retrieved from primary-level studies can be transformed into quantitative data ("quantitizing") or the quantitative findings can be transformed into qualitative data ("qualitizing") in order for the data to be synthesized together.

Internal validity: Extent to which a causal statement is true.

Keywords: Words that describe the most important elements of the topic of interest and the question(s) of the literature review. For example, keywords may refer to the phenomenon or intervention under investigation, the population of interest, and the primary outcome measure. *Synonym:* Key search terms.

Likelihood function: Function used in Bayesian synthesis that describes the likelihood of the parameter values given the observed data.

Line-of-argument meta-ethnographical synthesis: Type of meta-ethnographical synthesis in which the included primary studies represent different arguments or different parts of the puzzle that can be lined up, with the goal of creating a picture of the whole phenomenon of interest from studies of its parts.

Literature review: Overview of a body of research literature with the goal of synthesizing the content of primary-level studies and other primary-level data sources on a certain topic, problem, intervention, program, or phenomenon of interest. Conducted by *review authors*.

Location bias: Bias in a literature review that occurs because certain studies are published in journals that are not indexed in bibliographic databases and therefore may not be identified by the search.

Meaningfulness (in the context of program or intervention evaluation): The extent to which a particular program or intervention is positively experienced by the target group. Meaningfulness refers to the personal opinions, values, thoughts, beliefs, and interpretations of the members of the target group.

Meta-aggregative approach: Qualitative approach for synthesizing evidence from qualitative primary-level studies that involves three stages: (1) extracting qualitative research findings from the primary studies and rating these findings according to their credibility based on supporting illustrations for each finding (called level 1 findings); (2) categorizing the level 1 findings on the basis of similarity in meaning (called level 2 categories); and (3) conducting a meta-synthesis on the level 2 categories, aiming to produce "lines of action" that can be used as a basis for evidence-based practice or informing policy decisions.

Meta-analysis: Overall statistical analysis of several statistical analyses reported in quantitative primary-level studies with the goal of estimating an overall parameter, testing an overall effect, or investigating moderating variables for the overall parameter or effect.

Meta-ethnographical approach: Qualitative approach for synthesizing evidence from qualitative primary-level studies with the goal of creating a whole that adds something new to these primary studies. The meta-ethnographical approach enables a systematic and detailed understanding of how studies are related through the comparison of findings within and across studies. In the meta-ethnographical approach, these studies are coded and condensed into themes that ultimately provide a holistic interpretation of the body of research.

Meta-inference: Extent to which the inferences made in the findings or conclusion sections of a mixed methods research study incorporate and are grounded in the inferences made in the separate strands of evidence.

Meta-synthesis: Qualitative synthesis of several qualitative primary-level studies with the goal of generating new insights and understanding from inter-related qualitative research findings.

Meta-transfer: Extent to which the complexity level featured in a mixed method research study and addressed by the different strands of evidence is of a similar nature to other persons, settings, situations, or timeframes.

Meta-validity: Extent to which the overarching arguments or inferences made in a mixed method research study remain sensitive to the original ideas as expressed in both the quantitative and the qualitative strands of evidence.

Methodological filters (in bibliographic searches): Search limits or set of keywords that are used to select the studies with certain designs or the studies with certain methodologies.

Methodological triangulation: Methodological strategy involving the use of divergent methods and techniques to study the same phenomenon. The goal of methodological triangulation is to evaluate whether similar results are being found and, in this way, to corroborate or test the validity of the findings.

Mixed methods research synthesis (MMRS): Literature review that combines qualitative, quantitative, and mixed primary-level studies by applying a mixed methods approach for synthesizing and integrating those studies, with the goal of enhancing the breadth and depth of understanding complex phenomena, problems, and topics.

Mixed methods research synthesis (MMRS) report: Report that describes the mixed methods research synthesis, its background, the research question(s), the methodological implementations, its findings, and the implications for practice, policy, and research.

Mixing rationale: Extent to which the mixing of the results and findings in a mixed methods study is clearly illustrated, motivated, and documented in terms of additional value of the mixed component.

Multiple publication bias: Bias in a literature review that occurs because several articles and reports may refer to the same study and the same data. Including the articles and reports as independent sources of information (confirming each other) may result in giving an inappropriately large weight to this study and its findings.

Narrative summary: Technique commonly used for synthesizing data from quantitative primary-level studies by summarizing the evidence in words. Within an integrated mixed methods research synthesis, a narrative summary can be used to synthesize the evidence coming from qualitative, quantitative, and mixed primary studies on a common phenomenon of interest.

Objectivity: Extent to which a person has the quality of being true or bias-free, outside of individual biases, interpretations, feelings, and imaginings.

Ontology: The philosophical study of "what is"; the study of reality. In science, the ontological orientation toward research is related to the kind of research questions being asked, the kind of methods and techniques being applied, and the kind of conclusions and interpretations considered valid or worthwhile. Ontological orientations toward research are often positioned on a continuum with on the one end the realist orientations and on the other end the idealist orientations. Researchers following realist orientations consider reality to be an external, concrete structure, whereas researchers following idealist orientations consider reality to be constructed, to be a projection of human imagination.

Peer review: Method to evaluate and improve the quality of scientific work in progress by submitting it to a critical assessment, which is usually done by peers or colleagues working in a similar domain.

Posterior distribution: Statistical distribution used in Bayesian synthesis that describes the probability of the parameter values based on the prior distribution and the likelihood function.

Predictor: Variable that is supposed to be statistically related to the outcome variable. Depending on the design or the statistical model, this variable can offer a causal explanation or a prediction of the variability in the outcome variable. *Synonym:* Explanatory variable.

Primary-level study: Typical empirical study in which qualitative and/or quantitative data are collected directly from the research participants, for example, through interviews, observations, and/or questionnaires. *Synonym:* Original study. Conducted by *researchers.*

Primary outcomes: Outcome measures that are directly relevant to the target group and the research questions.

Prior distribution: Statistical distribution used in Bayesian synthesis that describes the probability of the values for the parameters that will be estimated.

Protocol: Document prepared before conducting a literature review that contains all methodological and substantive choices that will be made throughout the review process. The protocol usually contains information regarding the review objectives and review questions, the review design, the sampling and search strategy, the inclusion and exclusion criteria, and the synthesis approaches and techniques.

Publication bias: Bias in a literature review that occurs because of publication procedures, publication behavior of authors, and publication traditions of journals. It usually refers to the tendency for authors to submit, and for journals to accept, manuscripts for publication based on the specific direction, magnitude, or significance of the study findings.

Purposeful sampling strategy: Sampling strategy aimed at finding information-rich studies that will provide an answer to the posed review question(s).

Qualitizing: Converting quantitative data into qualitative data.

Quality assessment: Process of systematically examining research evidence to assess its validity and its relevance before including it into the literature review. *Synonyms:* Quality appraisal; critical appraisal.

Quantitizing: Converting qualitative data into quantitative data.

Random effects meta-analysis: Type of meta-analysis that is built on the assumption that the true effect could vary across the included studies.

Rapid reviews: Literature reviews in which only a limited number of resources is searched due to time management reasons or because of the urgency of a project.

Rationale (for the choices made during the literature review process): Reasons, arguments, and justifications for the methodological and substantive choices made throughout the literature review process, as written in the review diary or review report.

Realist orientations (toward research synthesis): Orientations that treat the primary reports included in the literature review as more or less faithfully reflecting the primary-level studies that were conducted, and the findings described in those primary reports as more or less faithfully reflecting the phenomenon under study, regardless of how those primary-level studies were themselves ontologically located. *See also: Ontology.*

Realist synthesis: Type of integrated mixed methods research synthesis that is theory driven and aims at unpacking mechanisms of how complex programs or interventions work (or why they fail) in particular contexts and settings.

Reciprocal meta-ethnographical synthesis: Type of meta-ethnographical synthesis in which the key metaphors, themes, and concepts from the individual primary studies are directly comparable with one another. Key metaphors, themes, and concepts can be translated into one another and can evolve into overarching concepts or metaphors.

Reference management software: Software that helps to organize, save, edit, and report references, titles, and abstracts from publications. Examples of free reference management software include EndNote Basic, Zotero, and Mendeley. Examples of commercial reference management software are EndNote, Reference Manager, RefWorks, and Review Manager.

Refutational meta-ethnographical synthesis: Type of meta-ethnographical synthesis in which there are important contradictions among the included primary studies. In a refutational meta-ethnographical synthesis, these contradictions are explored and explained.

Reliability: Extent to which the results or findings are consistent and repeatable.

Researchers: Persons who conduct original research, leading to the publication of primary-level studies.

Review authors: Persons who conduct and report on a literature review.

Review diary: Digital or written record of everything that was done, considered, and reflected upon during the literature review process.

Risk of bias: Potential over/underestimation of an effect in a literature review.

Scoping reviews: Preliminary literature reviews that explore the literature available on a topic, identifying the key concepts, theories, sources of evidence, and gaps in the research. Scoping reviews are often undertaken when the feasibility of a full literature review is a concern of the review authors.

Scoping searches: Preliminary searches of bibliographic databases to test several variations of the search string. A scoping search can be useful when designing the strategy for searching bibliographic databases, for example, to try out different keywords, Boolean operators, truncation, double quotes, and search limits.

Search limits (in bibliographic searches): Limits set to specify the bibliographic search. For example, limits might be set on the publication language, publication type, or publication period.

Secondary outcomes: Outcome measures that are not directly relevant to the target group and the research questions but nevertheless worthwhile to register and report.

Second-order interpretations: Interpretations derived from the chosen papers in a meta-ethnographical synthesis based on the concepts identified to build first-order constructs.

Segregated MMRS design: Type of mixed methods research synthesis design that initially treats the retrieved qualitative and quantitative studies separately. The findings of the qualitative and quantitative studies are separately synthesized: Qualitative methods are used for synthesizing the retrieved qualitative primary-level studies, and quantitative methods are used for synthesizing the retrieved quantitative primary-level studies. Both strands of evidence are only combined or confronted with each other in the last stage of the literature review (i.e., discussion section and conclusion).

Selective sampling strategy: Sampling strategy in which only a limited number of resources or only relevant studies within very specific limits are consulted.

Sensitivity analysis: Analytical technique to investigate whether findings remain robust after including or excluding certain observations or after changing conditions. A sensitivity analysis in a statistical meta-analysis is meant to examine how the results and conclusions might be affected depending on the kind of studies that are included or excluded. For example, a sensitivity analysis might investigate whether similar summary statistics are obtained if studies with low methodological quality are excluded. In qualitative evidence syntheses, sensitivity analysis is used to evaluate whether the synthesized statements, theories, or lines of arguments remain stable after excluding certain insights (usually those derived from lower quality papers).

Study retrieval diagram: Diagram to document and report the process and results of the literature search process. *Synonym:* Flowchart.

Summary effect size: Calculated magnitude of an effect, summarized over all quantitative primary-level studies included in a statistical meta-analysis, according to some predefined effect size measure.

Systematic reviews: Literature reviews that attempt to identify, appraise, and synthesize all the empirical evidence that meets prespecified eligibility criteria to answer given review questions.

Team leader: Leader of a review team who is ideally knowledgeable on both the content of the review as well as the different methodological traditions that are brought together in a mixed methods research synthesis project.

Thematic analysis: Qualitative analytical method for a qualitative primary-level study in which themes are identified and qualitative empirical data are analyzed using thematic headings. Thematic analysis usually includes the following phases: familiarization with the data, generating the initial codes, searching for themes among the codes, reviewing themes, defining and naming themes, and producing the final report.

Thematic synthesis: Qualitative method to bring together and integrate the findings of several qualitative primary-level studies. Thematic synthesis involves identifying prominent or recurrent themes and summarizing the findings of the included primary-level studies under thematic headings. Thematic synthesis is conducted in three stages: (1) coding of text line by line, (2) development of descriptive themes, and (3) generation of analytical themes. The synthesis remains close to the data reported in the retrieved primary studies in stages 1 and 2, and it aims to go beyond the retrieved primary studies to generate new constructs, explanations, or hypotheses in stage 3.

Third-order interpretations: Interpretations made at the third level of a meta-ethnographical synthesis based on the first-order constructs and second-order interpretations.

Transferability: Extent to which research findings are transferable to other specific persons, settings, situations, or timeframes.

Transparency (of a literature review): One characteristic of a high-quality literature review. It entails the explicit reporting of the sampling strategy, of all the details of the conducted searches for primary-level studies, of the number of publications retrieved by each search step, of the inclusion and exclusion criteria, and of the number of studies included and excluded, along with the reasons for exclusion. Transparency is needed to make the search process and other stages of the literature review replicable.

Truncation (in bibliographic searches): Option in bibliographic searches in which some letters in keywords are replaced by symbols (as wildcards). For example, if * can be used as a truncation symbol, then the keyword "disabilit*" refers to all the words that start with the letters "disabilit," such as "disability," "disabilities," and so on.

Validity: Extent to which the results or findings correspond to the true state of affairs. *See also: Internal validity; external validity.*

Vote counting: Technique for synthesizing data from quantitative primary-level studies by counting the number of findings that are statistically significantly positive, significantly negative, and nonsignificant.

INDEX

Made in the USA
Columbia, SC
09 March 2021